ROUTLEDGE LIBRARY EDITIONS:
INTERNATIONAL TRADE POLICY

I0028041

Volume 4

BRITISH ECONOMIC
FOREIGN POLICY

BRITISH ECONOMIC FOREIGN POLICY

J. HENRY RICHARDSON

Routledge
Taylor & Francis Group

LONDON AND NEW YORK

First published in 1936 by George Allen & Unwin Ltd

This edition first published in 2018
by Routledge
2 Park Square, Milton Park, Abingdon, Oxon OX14 4RN

and by Routledge
711 Third Avenue, New York, NY 10017

Routledge is an imprint of the Taylor & Francis Group, an informa business

British Library Cataloguing in Publication Data
A catalogue record for this book is available from the British Library

ISBN: 978-1-138-06323-5 (Set)
ISBN: 978-1-315-14339-2 (Set) (ebk)
ISBN: 978-1-138-10597-3 (Volume 4) (hbk)
ISBN: 978-1-138-29722-7 (Volume 4) (pbk)
ISBN: 978-1-315-09944-6 (Volume 4) (ebk)

Publisher's Note
The publisher has gone to great lengths to ensure the quality of this reprint but points out that some imperfections in the original copies may be apparent.

Disclaimer
The publisher has made every effort to trace copyright holders and would welcome correspondence from those they have been unable to trace.

BRITISH ECONOMIC FOREIGN POLICY

by

J. HENRY RICHARDSON

LONDON
GEORGE ALLEN & UNWIN LTD
MUSEUM STREET

FIRST PUBLISHED IN 1936

PREFACE

UNTIL recently the economic foreign policy of Great Britain has called for so little positive action by the Government that it has not commanded public attention. The changes made during the depression, however, represent a departure from traditional policy comparable in magnitude with, though much less discussed than, the "New Deal" of the United States. In consequence, measures taken by the Government now directly involve economic relations with foreign and Empire countries, and also affect the prosperity of British industries.

It is yet too early to reach final conclusions upon the new policy, but there is value at the present stage in making a preliminary survey of the trends of policy and the measures applied. The policy is still too new to have taken definite shape, and much constructive thinking is necessary if a system suited to present day political and economic conditions is to be evolved. Important decisions must be made in the near future. Many trade agreements with foreign countries are due for reconsideration during the next two or three years. In 1937 the Ottawa Agreements will be revised. Monetary policy is still unsettled. Also, after adequate experience has been gained, the electorate, which in the elections of 1931 and 1935 gave little thought to the problems of protection and Imperial Preference, will require to consider whether it desires to maintain permanently the policies which were applied primarily to deal with crisis conditions.

In this volume chief attention is directed to monetary policy, financial policy—particularly the regulation of international lending—protection, reciprocity, retaliation and most-favoured-nation treatment, Imperial Preference and the principle of the open door, agricultural policy, and labour policy as expressed by the British Government's participation in the work of the International Labour

Organisation. Reference is made to other features of policy, such as control of essential raw materials, and defence of the economic interests of British nationals who have been injured by measures contrary to international law taken by a foreign Government.

Certain questions of policy are not treated. The problem of war debts and reparations is omitted because it is only of short-term interest and the lines of solution are already drawn. Migration policy is not discussed as this is now more a question of Empire settlement than of relations with foreign countries. Nor is an account given of measures lately taken to protect British fishing interests; these methods are still tentative and they also closely resemble, though on a more modest scale, some of the methods reviewed in the chapter on agricultural policy.

In writing on this subject I have had the advantage which membership of the International Labour Office Staff for a number of years afforded of considering the effects of British economic and labour policy both upon British conditions and upon conditions in foreign countries. During the last few years I have had special opportunities of discussing these questions with representatives of British employers' organisations and trade unions.

I wish to express my thanks to Sir Alfred Zimmern and to Professor J. H. Jones for reading the manuscript and for many useful suggestions, to Mr. Harold Butler for constructive criticism of the chapter on Labour Policy, and to Mr. Henry Clay for his valuable advice on the chapters dealing with monetary and financial policy.

J. HENRY RICHARDSON

THE UNIVERSITY, LEEDS
February 1936

CONTENTS

BRITISH ECONOMIC FOREIGN POLICY

CHAPTER I

INTRODUCTION

The financial crisis of 1931 marked a turning-point in British economic foreign policy. Within a few months *laissez-faire* principles which had been applied for seventy years were abandoned and an active interventionist policy was introduced. Though previously the electorate had consistently rejected interventionist proposals, and though the Government in 1931 was accorded "a doctor's mandate" to deal only with an emergency, the new orientation was accepted almost as a matter of course. It may be doubted, however, whether the country yet fully appreciates the significance and implications of the fundamental changes so recently made.

Throughout the period from 1860 to 1931 business men were given maximum liberty to pursue their own policies in international economic relations, the Government remaining passive. Business affairs were conducted independently of the Government and were regarded as falling outside the field of Government action. Non-intervention was so complete and consistent that it was hardly considered to be an element of foreign policy at all. So long as the Government maintained a *laissez-faire* policy it was not able to reinforce its political foreign policy by economic means, and indeed it might find that business men in the exercise of their economic freedom were acting in ways which conflicted with its political aims.

The transformation of British economic policy from a passive to an active one permits of its coordination with political foreign policy, the one being used to support the other. Up to the present, however, the need for and the

possibilities and limitations of such coordination have only
been discerned in part. Inconsistencies between the two
policies are frequent, and harmony is often accidental
rather than a consequence of conscious policy, the economic
and the political being still treated as largely independent.

Coordination of Political and Economic Policy

It should not be assumed that the Government can extensively use the country's economic resources in peace time
to support politically friendly States or to injure potential
enemies. Apart from the difficulty of knowing for more than
short periods which States fall into these categories such
discriminations could not fail to intensify international
animosities, and thus increase the risk of war. This danger
prevents the establishment of complete coordination between
political and economic foreign policy. Thus the expressed
political disapproval by Great Britain and other countries
of Japan's disregard of treaty obligations in her treatment
of China and in her intervention in Manchuria in 1931 and
1932 might logically have been supplemented by economic
pressure. Such action taken independently by one country
alone would undoubtedly involve serious risk of conflict.
Where several countries unite in the exercise of economic
pressure the risk is reduced, though, in circumstances of
intense national feeling in the country against which the
boycott is directed, the danger of war might not altogether
disappear. Still smaller is the risk from collective economic
action taken by a large number of countries, as by the
League of Nations in the dispute between Italy and Abyssinia, against aggression committed in disregard of international obligations. Such sanctions would, however, be
more effective against some countries than against others,
and the system might even encourage a movement towards
greater national self-sufficiency by potential aggressors so
as to reduce their vulnerability to economic pressure.

In principle, little objection is raised against a policy of discrimination in favour of the nationals of a country, provided it is directed uniformly against the nationals of all other countries. Even this policy may, however, arouse resentment abroad if the discrimination is so drastic that foreign traders are virtually excluded from the home market. Also irritation is caused by sudden changes which dislocate production and trade abroad. This may be avoided, in part at least, if the countries most likely to be affected are given the right to be heard and if arrangements to minimise the dislocations are jointly discussed.

It is widely admitted, too, that special arrangements favouring the trade of the mother country in colonial areas, thus discriminating against foreign traders, are not offensive if all foreign countries are treated alike. An "open door" policy is more satisfactory from the point of view of international relations, but during recent years its application has steadily diminished. Nor are preferences between the self-governing Dominions of the British Commonwealth of Nations regarded by foreign countries as violating the principles of international economic relations. Quite different is the attitude towards discriminations which place one foreign country in a relatively more favourable position than another, these being treated as matters of grievance and complaint. Indeed, the long vogue of the unconditional most-favoured-nation clause was due to its value in avoiding this difficulty. Now that the unconditional clause has become almost a dead letter attempts to find acceptable interpretations of conditional most-favoured-nation treatment are made for this same purpose.

The basis of these understandings is that a country may reasonably organise its economic system and make arrangements with its colonies and dominions so as to ensure its maximum strength, security and welfare in relation to the international political and economic conditions prevailing at the time. It may not, however, openly discriminate in peace time in its economic relations with foreign Powers. To do so would be considered unfriendly by those adversely affected, and would evoke protest. The distinction is between "internal" and "external." Apart from prohibitive measures of wide range or sudden dislocating changes, the view is generally accepted that a country may do what it wishes internally; and "internally" is interpreted, as already indicated, to cover so extensive an area as Great Britain, the Colonies, and the self-governing Dominions of the British Commonwealth. Externally, discriminations are considered to be acts of economic war and to justify retaliations. So long as external discriminations are avoided a State may bring its economic and political foreign policies into harmony. There is, however, no parallel in economic diplomacy to the political policy of balance of power. Though countries may be grouped politically by secret agreements or open alliances and understandings, their official economic relations are not brought into conformity with this pattern. Indirectly, however, the nationals of a country may be encouraged to trade with and travel in certain countries to the disadvantage of others. This method has been frequently used during recent years.

Risk of war and deterioration of political relations are not the only difficulties preventing the adoption of a unified political and economic foreign policy. Business interests within the country may at times demand an economic policy at variance with the Government's political policy. Thus the political opposition of certain British Governments to Communism and to Soviet foreign propaganda has conflicted with the economic desire of business men for more trade. On the other hand, the safeguarding of economic interests not infrequently involves economic conflicts which inflict injury upon political friends. For example, acute monetary and financial struggles between Great Britain and France have been frequent since the war, while sharp disputes over tariffs and quotas extending from 1932 until the summer of 1934 disturbed the economic but not the political relations between these countries. Still more striking were the bitter economic controversies at the

Ottawa Conference between Great Britain and some of the self-governing Dominions, and the disputes arising in the operation of the agreements concluded there, culminating in a boycott of Australian goods by Lancashire towns; this was in protest against higher Australian tariffs on certain cotton goods in opposition, as it was thought, to the spirit of the agreements. Yet political relations remained entirely cordial. Evidently economic warfare may be waged for a time between political friends, or even between members of the same political "family," though a protracted struggle would undermine the strength of the association.

Amid the rapid changes in international political and economic relations it would, indeed, be impracticable to maintain continuous agreement between the two policies, and from time to time the short-period economic and political interests of a country inevitably diverge. But in their long-range trends these policies must be consistent with one another.

The main object of a country's joint policies depends largely upon its estimate of the possibilities of war or of peace. A country will organise for war either because it is itself warlike and aggressive, or because, though peace-loving, it feels that it may be forced into war by the aggression of another power. Speaking during a period of insecurity and uncertainty in international relations, Signor Mussolini emphasised that for Italy, "the whole life of the nation, political, economic, and spiritual, must be systematically directed towards our military requirements."[1] In such a period the first consideration will be to secure adequate self-sufficiency and maximum fighting strength, while material standards of comfort must be sacrificed in so far as they result from an organisation of production and trade which would increase the country's vulnerability in time of war. Wars in the modern world are no longer affairs of mercenaries or even of regular armies; they draw upon the whole of a country's human and material resources, and the

[1] From a speech delivered on August 24, 1934.

present wave of economic nationalism is largely a consequence of intense political nationalism and fear of war. Cobden was right in linking peace with freedom of trade; unless there is reasonable expectation of peace international trade will inevitably be diverted from its natural channels.

There is often a close relationship between wealth and fighting strength, and a country which exaggerated the adaptation of its industry and trade to the purposes of war might impoverish itself, thus weakening instead of increasing its power. Under the conditions of world trade prevailing before the war Great Britain so much increased her wealth by free-trade policy that her fighting strength was greater than if a more restrictive policy had been pursued.

Though diminution or removal of the risk of war is chiefly desired on moral and humanitarian grounds, this would open the way to an international organisation of production and trade which would ensure the best utilisation of the world's resources and the highest standards of comfort. Also, political foreign policy would become less prominent, and increasing attention could be given to economic, social, and cultural relations—a desirable change, as these represent the chief interests of the great mass of mankind. Because of her peculiar advantages for world trade Britain has a special interest in the pacification of international relations.

GENERAL TRENDS OF BRITISH ECONOMIC DEVELOPMENT AND POLICY

For many years the main features of British economic development and policy were influenced by the fact that Great Britain was the first nation to apply extensively the technique of modern industrial production, and the products of the factory system readily found markets abroad. Being first in the field, British foreign trade was complementary rather than competitive. British manufactures were exchanged with mutual advantage for raw materials produced abroad. The balance of trade was favourable and this permitted the use of British capital to open up undeveloped areas. London became the monetary centre of the world, thus permitting a unified control over a large part of the world's monetary system. The British navy, which was almost unchallenged, patrolled the seas, ensuring security for trade and facilitating the progress of economic internationalism.

The expansion and direction of British commercial relations were subject to little conscious control. Free trade was accepted almost as a natural law and the policy of the "open door" was applied throughout the Empire. Britain "attained its great position not by the pursuit of any preconceived plan, but by a process of almost haphazard evolution based on trial and error and aided by the practical aptitudes and instincts of our race, as well as by certain fortunate accidents in the way of natural resources and geographical position. There has been little conscious direction of the national activities to definite ends."[1]

Britain's commercial supremacy did not long remain unchallenged. In the years immediately preceding the war she experienced growing competition from Germany and the United States, while other countries were also developing their industries and displacing British products. This competition was felt not only in foreign markets but even within Great Britain. To some extent British imports of manufactured articles were on a complementary basis, Britain buying from abroad certain specialities instead of organising their production within the country, but part of the trade was competitive. It was, therefore, for economic as well as for political reasons, that Mr. Joseph Chamberlain began in 1903 to advocate a policy of protection and Imperial preference.

The challenge to Britain's industrial, commercial, and financial supremacy was accelerated by the war. Being deprived during the war of adequate supplies of British

---

[1] Macmillan Committee on Finance and Industry.

manufactures, many countries began to meet their own needs, while others, particularly the United States and Japan, organised their industry and commerce to supply markets hitherto almost exclusively British. By the end of the war the United States had been transformed from a debtor to a creditor nation, with ambition to play a larger part in the world's monetary and financial system. France, largely for political reasons, was determined to exert great monetary and financial influence, particularly in Europe. Being the chief continental victor she sought supremacy in the economic affairs of Europe in time of peace. In place of pre-war internationalism the world became sectionalised into economic groups, within which a complicated system of barriers to trade and economic relations were established. It may indeed be said that the war killed Cobdenism.

The war itself had involved in Great Britain, as in other countries, a high degree of economic organisation and control; also inability to obtain supplies from abroad had resulted in a movement towards greater self-sufficiency. At the end of the war Britain was faced with the alternatives of retaining and developing the war-time system of control and of establishing greater self-sufficiency, or of returning to the pre-war policy of *laissez-faire*. The first of these alternatives received some support. For example, in May 1918 Sir Albert Stanley, then President of the Board of Trade, referring in the House of Commons to our greater self-sufficiency, attained, as he said, with so little apparent discomfort, urged that "it would be a great pity if we failed to bear in mind this lesson, and allowed ourselves again to drift into a condition of dependence upon foreign sources for so large a part of our actual needs." Such appeals were unheeded. War-time restrictions and privations had made pre-war conditions seem by contrast to be the Golden Age. The Defence of the Realm Act, under which many of the restrictions had been imposed, was regarded as anathema and public opinion was insistent in demanding restoration of the pre-war system, though in doing so there was failure to recognise that conditions had changed.

The opinion was widely supported that Great Britain could recover her position in world trade and finance only by removing trade barriers and abandoning restrictions upon the investment of capital abroad.[1] Free trade and freedom of capital investment were, therefore, rapidly restored, with, however, a few significant exceptions, particularly the protection of "key" industries. Though Britain joined with her allies in imposing heavy reparation burdens upon Germany she did not favour a policy of isolating Germany and other ex-enemy countries economically after the war. Whatever might be the political attitude adopted toward defeated powers, Britain desired rapidly to re-establish trade relations with them. This policy is indicated by the following quotation from a Board of Trade White Paper issued in 1919: "It may be expected that there will be a considerable demand in late enemy countries for all kinds of goods; as this market is now open to all the world, it is no part of the policy of His Majesty's Government to discourage British traders from competing therein and it is desirable that British traders should make every effort to secure a proper footing in Central Europe." So active was British policy for the resumption of trading relations with ex-enemy countries that France became irritated by our apparent eagerness to help Germany and to assist in the economic recovery of Central Europe. France also resented the opening of British trade negotiations with Russia in 1920, contending that any goods which Russia could export should be the property of France and other creditors.

An important section of British opinion, however, considered that the policy of resuming free trade was unsound, and in the Conservative Party's programme for the 1923

---

[1] This opinion is indicated by the following quotation from the *Economist*, June 29, 1918: "If we are to get back our old position as centre of the world's trade and finance we shall only do so by opening our doors wide to all the goods and services that all other nations like to sell us."

General Election protection of British industry occupied a prominent place. Nevertheless public opinion was not yet ready for a change in fiscal policy. The protectionist policy was rejected at the polls. A substantial majority of the electorate still believed free trade to be in the national interests and to be a sound principle of international morality.[1]

The next big step towards the restoration of pre-war economic conditions was Britain's return to the gold standard in 1925. Although voices were raised against the expediency of this policy, it was generally approved by the business community, an influential argument being that an international monetary system was necessary for the proper development of international trading and financial relations, and that, in view of the importance of international trade and finance to Great Britain, this country should give a lead. The initiative seemed justified when during the next two or three years country after country stabilised its money in terms of gold.

This was also a period of appeasement in Europe during which the Locarno Treaties were concluded, Germany was admitted to the League of Nations, and the Briand–Kellogg Pact signed by almost the whole world. These seemed to provide the political basis for a post-war economic system similar to that which the war had disturbed, and the World Economic Conference, Geneva, 1927, was called to plan its reconstruction. The prospect was viewed by many with optimism; some were so enthusiastic as to say "Cobdenism has at last come true. Our trumpets sounded and the Protectionist Jericho tottered."

---

[1] See article by J. M. Keynes in the *Manchester Guardian*, Reconstruction in Europe Series. Mr. Keynes expressed the opinion that "we must hold to Free Trade in its widest interpretation as an inflexible dogma to which no exception is admitted. We must hold to it even where we receive no reciprocity of treatment and even in those rare cases where by infringing it we could obtain a direct economic advantage." Yet Mr. Keynes saw the writing on the wall, and shortly afterwards published his pamphlet *The End of Laissez-Faire*, and seven or eight years later, during the great depression, he advocated tariff measures as a remedy for difficulties which could scarcely have been forecasted some years earlier.

But the walls did not fall, and the strength of their foundations was soon to be revealed. Every attempt to translate the Conference's liberal recommendations on international relations into effective agreements ended in failure. Even the modest proposal for a Tariff Truce, for which Mr. William Graham, President of the Board of Trade, worked so strenuously, was virtually rejected. This was an economic parallel of the breakdown of the World Disarmament Conference.

Faced with increasingly severe foreign competition and with trade hampered by the barriers of economic nationalism, Britain was no longer in the favoured pre-war position. From 1921 onwards she rarely had less than a million workpeople unemployed, or about 10 per cent of the insured population, this being two or three times higher than before the war, while almost all the exporting industries remained depressed. Yet for nearly a decade the opinion was widely held among industrialists that Britain's troubles were caused mainly by the impoverishment of Europe and by unfair competition arising from currency depreciation. With restoration of currency stability and greater purchasing power as countries became wealthy again it was thought that prosperity would return to Britain's foreign trade. Writing in 1924, Professor André Siegfried said "Lancashire is perfectly sanguine of success, once normal conditions have been restored. She asks for no assistance from the State so long as she is buoyed up by the prosperity of the world." This unfounded optimism stands in sharp contrast with Lancashire's present desire for State intervention.

Yet other countries were making progress; the trade of the world was increasing, but Britain's share was diminishing.[1] Economic nationalism abroad forced her to consider whether a substantial readjustment of her productive organisation might not be necessary. The ground was prepared for a change of policy. The increased strain of the world depression upon the British economic system completed the change in

[1] See A. Loveday, *Britain and World Trade.*

outlook. Within a year or two unemployment doubled, then almost trebled. Britain, long the leader among exporting countries, fell to the third place. The volume and value of exports were greatly reduced while imports were maintained at high levels. Britain, being the only remaining important free trade market, became a dumping ground for foreign producers selling at sacrifice prices.

By the year 1931, the adverse balance of British "visible" trade was so great that all the "invisible" items in her international balance-sheet were insufficient to pay for the surplus of imports. Not only had the net revenue from British shipping services fallen heavily but the income from British investments in the Dominions, colonies, and foreign countries had been greatly reduced, the decline being specially heavy in the dividends on industrial investments. The failure of the Credit Anstalt and the freezing of assets in Germany added substantially to Britain's difficulties. This imposed such a heavy strain upon sterling that, when the situation was aggravated by political and social difficulties, a breaking-point was reached, and in September 1931 the gold standard was suspended.

The six months which followed the suspension of the gold standard mark the real end of *laissez-faire*, which had been the key to British economic foreign policy for seventy years. Legislation providing the basis for a new policy of intervention, regulation, and control, was rapidly passed through Parliament. The Bill providing for the suspension of the gold standard was passed through all its stages in one day. Three days only were required for passing the Abnormal Imports Bill in November 1931, while the Import Duties Bill to place the new British tariff system on a more permanent basis took only six days of Parliamentary time in February 1932. The speed with which these measures transforming British policy were passed through Parliament serves as an answer to those who complain that a democratic system works much too slowly to meet the needs of present-day government.

The new policy was further developed by the Ottawa Agreements extending the principle of Empire preferences and by measures for improving the economic position of British agriculture. These changes were strongly supported by the Conservatives, but were opposed by a section of the Liberal Party, which left the National Government as a protest against the Agreements. Indeed, the inauguration of the new policy seemed to complete the break up of the Liberal Party, which philosophically, though not in practice, was founded upon non-interventionist principles incompatible with present trends. There now remains only "the bloodless ghost of the old fiscal issue."

The view is now widely held that Britain's economic system was too vulnerable in post-war conditions of world competition. This vulnerability implied disorganisation of British production during peace time, especially in periods of world depression, while excessive dependence upon foreign supplies involved risk in time of war. Some adjustment in face of almost universal economic nationalism abroad was also necessary. As already indicated, the moment for changing policy was determined by the severity of the world depression and the resulting heavy adverse balance of payments of more than £100 million in 1931. Fundamentally too the world's economic system is distorted by insecurity and fear of war. It is recognised that the maintenance of world peace is uncertain, and countries therefore try to safeguard their position by increasing their self-sufficiency. The world has grave doubts about the effectiveness of the collective system in enabling the nations to live at peace, and adapts its economic house to this uncertainty. States are pursuing the process of identifying and coordinating economic with political sovereignty, and Governments are undertaking increasingly the conscious direction of economic affairs. In this world Britain is rapidly making up the leeway which resulted from the tenacity with which until 1931 she clung to *laissez-faire*.

MACHINERY OF ECONOMIC DIPLOMACY

The machinery of economic diplomacy is much less concentrated than that of political diplomacy. Whereas the latter is dealt with mainly by the Foreign Office, international economic relations are spread over a number of departments. There is also less tradition in economic than in political relations, partly because the country is only now beginning to realise that there is such a thing as an economic foreign policy.

Until recently economic affairs have been treated as somewhat of a Cinderella. The political diplomatic services, dealing with questions of national honour, prestige, official representation, Court formalities, and diplomatic courtesies, tended in the past to regard the business man and his economic problems as being on a lower level of importance. Commerce and money were the affairs of shopkeepers and tradesmen and were treated as quite secondary to the problems of politics and government, diplomacy, military and naval service, and even professional work. They were often little understood by the diplomatic services and attempts to remedy this defect were unsuccessful. This was no doubt partly because, under free trade, international commercial and financial relations were controlled by private business men, and rarely called for Government intervention. The main help required was information and facilities abroad provided by the consular services and trade commissioners.

Nevertheless attitudes had been changing. The Balfour Committee on Industry and Trade was able to state in its Final Report in 1929 that there had been "a decline in the feeling which formerly prevailed among the business men that commerce and economic considerations were regarded by His Majesty's Government as essentially inferior in importance to political interests, and that where the two clashed the former always had to give way." This change of attitude, with a growing recognition of the interconnexion between political and economic policies, is also illustrated by the composition of the British delegation at the World Economic Conference, 1933. In addition to the Prime Minister, who presided, the Treasury, Foreign Office, Board of Trade, Dominions Office, Colonial Office, and the Ministry of Agriculture were each represented by their political chiefs, these forming a large proportion of the Cabinet, and they were assisted by junior ministers, and also by many experts from their departments.

The Board of Trade is the Department chiefly responsible for economic foreign policy. On most questions it is the official mouthpiece on policy and it also advises other Departments upon the commercial bearings of negotiations. Upon the Foreign Office devolves the responsibility for insuring coordination between economic and political foreign policy. The role of the Colonial and Dominion Offices is self-evident; they deal with economic questions affecting the Empire and the Commonwealth, and are of interest in the present study because any preferences within these areas imply discriminations against foreign countries. The Ministry of Agriculture is involved, as the agricultural policy applied within Great Britain may have important effects upon foreign trade; the Ministry of Agriculture also represents the Government in the international discussion of agricultural questions, for example, at the World Economic Conference and in the work of the International Institute of Agriculture at Rome. On questions of monetary and financial policy the Treasury takes the lead, working in close association with the Bank of England, while the Ministry of Labour represents the Government in its efforts to improve labour conditions by international conventions and other agreements either through the International Labour Organisation or occasionally in direct negotiations with particular countries.

Evidently the distribution of responsibility for economic questions over so many departments demands methods of coordination to avoid conflicting policies. During negotiations

involving both political and economic questions the British
Embassy or Legation concerned may have the help of an
officer sent abroad by the Board of Trade in agreement
with the Foreign Office. Where economic questions predominate, the negotiations may be conducted by the
Board of Trade, with a representative of the Foreign Office
for purposes of liaison. Commercial information is compiled
by the Department of Overseas Trade, which is jointly
responsible to the Foreign Office and the Board of Trade;
it collects data for both Departments under authority
delegated from both, and it supplies information to exporters about trade openings abroad. Reports on economic
and trade conditions and also commercial opportunities are
prepared by the commercial attachés at Embassies and
Legations and also by the consular services.

The Balfour Committee on Industry and Trade emphasised
that the vital significance of British overseas trade to the
national economy should be throughly realised by all the
responsible officers of the diplomatic service, as well as by
those of the home departments concerned, and they recommended that every member of the diplomatic service should
early gain contact with the trade situation by working for
a time on the commercial staff of the service. In this way
it was hoped that British trade would be assisted and that
greater harmony would be established between economic and
political policy. The Committee also advised that close
relations should be maintained between business men and
the Board of Trade not only for information but because,
by systematic consultation, business men would learn to
make allowance for possible difficulties of an international
or political character which could not always be disclosed
but which might seriously limit the success of the best
equipped commercial diplomat.

The relationship of unofficial organisations with the
Government departments dealing with economic foreign
policy is more intimate and the influence of these organisations upon policy is greater than in political foreign policy.

In international political relations the Government enjoys more freedom from the pressure of private bodies. The broad lines of political foreign policy are included in the programmes of the various parties, and, on important issues, the influence of public opinion is brought to bear upon the Government through mass meetings, resolutions, and representations by political and other organisations. But, except in times of crisis or when some moral issue is involved, the Government's policy is determined with little consultation or direct influence from outside. Indeed, on many questions, the public are not in possession of the facts upon which to form a sound judgment, being told by the Government that "it is not in the public interest" to disclose all the relevant circumstances.

In economic relations, the Government is largely dependent upon organisations of business men for information, advice, and guidance on questions of policy. Unofficial influences upon economic foreign policy are more powerful and more directly interested than upon political foreign policy. Formal and informal consultations and representations are almost continuous to ensure that business interests are fully considered in new developments of policy. Not infrequently the Government's policy is based upon proposals submitted to it by business organisations, including the Association of British Chambers of Commerce, the Federation of British Industries, the National Confederation of Employers' Organisations, the General Council of the Trades Union Congress, and organisations representing the interests of particular industries.

These relationships between business interests and Government Departments have greatly increased in post-war years, especially since 1931 when the scope of the Government's policy was extended. They represent a new development in British politics. Now that the Government is equipped with economic weapons of defence and offence it is able to grant favours to particular industries and other sectional interests. Where these are in conflict with the

general welfare, the Government's responsibility is to act
in the best interests of the country as a whole, and it is
to be hoped that the active economic foreign policy recently
adopted will not lead to log-rolling and corruption, which
have been so extensive in certain countries.

Unofficial organisations influence policy not only by direct
representations to the Government, but by their relationship
with business interests abroad. Especially interesting are
unofficial trade missions of business men who visit foreign
countries with a view to improvement of commercial
relations. These missions must sometimes be viewed with
concern by the Government, as they may make arrangements
inconsistent with official policy. On the other hand, unofficial missions often proceed abroad with Government
encouragement and may support and supplement the
official policy.

A recent example of an unofficial trade mission is
that sent to Manchukuo by the Federation of British
Industries in the autumn of 1934 with the declared
object of ascertaining what openings there might be for
British trade. The sending of this mission raised delicate
questions as to where the borderline should be drawn
between official and unofficial relations, as the British
Government was a party to the League of Nations' agreement
of non-recognition of Manchukuo. Formally the mission was
unofficial, the Government adopting the traditional pre-war
laissez-faire policy of sharply separating the political from
the economic and of assuming no responsibility for the
activities of the business community. It seems unlikely
that such a mission would be organised against the wishes
of the Government, and this raises the question of the
significance of *de jure* non-recognition with the maintenance
of *de facto* relations.[1] Also although it was reiterated that
the mission was in no sense political, the Japanese seemed

[1] There are, of course, many illustrations of this situation, for example,
the trading relations of American business men with Soviet Russia for
many years before the United States recognised the Soviet Government.

to consider it as having political significance, and as being a step towards recognition of the Manchukuo *régime*, and the Japanese Foreign Minister in a speech of welcome expressed the hope that the mission would "promote diplomatic as well as economic relations with Manchukuo." With the British Government now taking a more active part in economic foreign policy, the sharp separation of pre-war years between official and private relations is difficult to maintain, and unofficial trade missions may be used as instruments of official policy and may on occasion form part of the machinery of diplomacy.

Scope of the Survey

The expression "foreign policy" as applied to economic affairs requires explanation. Its significance differs from that in political affairs where relationships are maintained between separate States acting as units. Also, so long as war is avoided, changes in political policy may not immediately and directly affect the internal affairs of each country and the economic activities of its members. Political foreign policy affects people mainly through the risk of war, and strained political relations, though increasing the feeling of insecurity, may have little effect upon economic relations, except in the field of international finance. Thus, during the period of political strain in 1914 economic life was singularly little affected until a few days before war was declared. It is true that changes in political policy may lead to increase or reduction in armaments during peace time, thus involving alterations in the burden of taxation and affecting production and trade within the various countries. Also political policy often influences economic policy. Apart, however, from these indirect effects, changes in political foreign policy may have little immediate repercussion upon internal conditions.

On the other hand, changes in economic foreign policy, whether due to political or economic causes, directly and immediately affect business interests both within the country and abroad, with repercussions upon prosperity, employment, and standards of living. The inter-relation between external policy and home affairs is thus more continuous and intimate in the economic than in the political field. Further, in most States the maintenance of economic relations between private business interests in the different countries prevents that concentration of control in economic affairs which is so marked a feature of political foreign relations. A high degree of control is, however, established in "totalitarian" States, while control is complete under the system of State trading in the Soviet Union.

Along these lines, economic foreign policy is concerned with matters which directly affect internal as well as external economic conditions. At first sight the recent schemes for the re-organisation and development of agriculture in Great Britain might seem to come within the scope of domestic policy, but their application involves interference with international trade. They must, therefore, be included in a study of economic foreign policy. Again, from some points of view the economic relations between the component parts of the British Commonwealth of Nations are considered, as already indicated, to be internal or domestic questions, but arrangements such as the Ottawa Agreements, 1932, affect other countries. The policy of Great Britain in the economic affairs of the Commonwealth must therefore be included. It may be emphasised here that in the present volume "British policy" is interpreted to mean the policy of Great Britain; except incidentally, the policies of the other self-governing members of the British Commonwealth are not discussed.

Attention is directed mainly to those aspects of policy in which, in the regular course of international relations, economic purposes predominate or in which economic and political motives are jointly involved. Only brief references are made to exceptional circumstances where economic instruments are used for political purposes, for example, an economic boycott against an aggressor State. For this reason and also because they are internal affairs of the British Commonwealth, such questions are excluded, as the Indian boycott directed some years ago against British goods with the object of enforcing consitutional reforms, and the economic conflict between Great Britain and the Irish Free State over the refusal of the latter, on political grounds, to continue payment of the land annuities.

As already indicated, the subjects successively reviewed are: monetary policy, including the abandonment of gold and the establishment of British leadership in the sterling group of countries; financial policy, with special reference to the regulation of international loans; commercial policy, particularly tariffs, quotas, and the most-favoured-nation system; Imperial policy, including preferential arrangements, the Ottawa Conference, and the policy of the "open door"; agricultural policy, particularly the international consequences of the recent marketing and other schemes for the development of British agriculture; labour policy, represented by attempts through the International Labour Organisation to reduce competition resulting from unduly low conditions of work abroad.

It is evident that with this wide range of problems only the broad issues of policy can be discussed in a relatively short volume. The post-war period is chiefly considered, with particular reference to the new orientation of policy since 1931.

CHAPTER II

MONETARY POLICY

Few economic questions have received so much attention during recent years as monetary policy. Before the war the monetary system was scarcely considered except by a few financiers and currency experts, and most business men regarded the value of money as being determined by processes akin to the operation of natural law. Two decades of monetary uncertainty and of enforced or experimental intervention throughout the world have changed this attitude, and, in consequence, there has been widespread discussion and criticism of the monetary policy of Governments and Central Banks.

The main objects of a country's monetary system are to serve the convenience of its inhabitants and ensure reasonable stability of economic conditions by an appropriate credit policy. These are internal affairs, and, as such, do not enter into the scope of economic foreign policy. There are, however, important international repercussions of a country's monetary policy, as a consequence of foreign trade and financial operations. Also, a country must decide whether to join in an international monetary system, with a common element such as gold linking national currencies together at fixed rates of exchange, or whether it prefers to pursue a more independent policy. It is to these external aspects that attention is directed in the present chapter.

PRE-WAR POLICY

Only a brief summary of British pre-war monetary policy is here necessary. The gold standard was established in its purest and most automatic form, although there was always considerable management in its operation. This standard had been maintained for over two hundred years, with an interruption only during the Napoleonic Wars. Gold was the monetary standard of many other countries, but its effectiveness as an international standard was largely due to the fact that London was the undisputed monetary and financial capital of the world, with the consequence that there was comparative singleness of purpose under British monetary leadership—a condition not fulfilled since the war.[1] Also the gold standard countries raised no great obstacles to the operation of the system, but maintained a reasonable adjustment between their price levels while preserving exchange parities. Generally, when a country's balance of payments was adverse, the movement of the exchanges led to a movement of balances, gold was exported, its discount rate was raised, credit was restricted, and its whole economic relations, including prices and wages, were influenced to correct the trade balance. The restoration of equilibrium was facilitated by converse adjustments in the countries receiving gold.

The gold standard was abandoned during the war, and Great Britain adopted methods of war finance involving Government control of the supply of money, the pegging of the dollar-sterling exchange, and measures of inflation which were continued during the post-war boom of 1919–20, with the consequence that by 1920 the value of the pound measured by its purchasing power over wholesale commodities had fallen to about one-third of its pre-war value.[2]

---

[1] The Genoa Conference, 1922, recognised the need in post-war conditions for continuous cooperation between the central banks of the chief countries to ensure the smooth operation of an international monetary system. In fact, while there has been much cooperation between the central banks, especially of Great Britain, France, and the United States, there has also been rivalry or absence of agreement upon the objects and methods of an international monetary system. Strain and breakdown have resulted. "Cooperation in the big issues of international monetary affairs has been, let us frankly admit, a dismal failure" (Sir Henry Strakosch in "The Road to Recovery Supplement," Economist, January 5, 1935).

For a detailed review of the implications of the Genoa Conference resolutions, see R. G. Hawtrey, The Gold Standard in Theory and Practice.

[2] During the war the Treasury was given power to issue notes, with full discretion to decide upon the amount and manner of issue. The Treasury issue remained separate from that of the Bank of England until 1928.

A process of deflation then began which was especially severe during 1921 but which, though subsequently much more gradual, continued until the autumn of 1931. This greatly increased the real burden of the War Debt and added largely to the volume of unemployment. Within two or three years, deflation had brought the pound to within only a small margin of its pre-war parity with gold, and restoration of the gold standard became the object of British monetary policy.[1]

THE POST-WAR BRITISH GOLD STANDARD, 1925-31

Support for this policy was almost unanimous, few voices being raised against it, though there were differences of opinion about the date when the return to gold should be made. Alternative monetary systems were discussed mainly in academic circles, but the psychological factor was decisively on the side of gold, and, as was well expressed by Mr. Reginald McKenna, "So long as nine people out of ten in every country think the gold standard is the best, it is the best."

The return to gold, which was announced in the 1925 Budget Speech, gave great satisfaction.[2] It was considered to be a further step towards "liquidating the war" and returning to the stable and prosperous conditions enjoyed before 1914. Other countries would be likely to, and did in fact,

[1] The Government's early post-war currency policy was based upon recommendations made by the Cunliffe Committee in its Report on Currency and Foreign Exchanges after the war (Cd. 9182 of 1918), the final stage in their application being the passing of the Currency and Bank Notes Act, 1928. By this Act, the Treasury note issue introduced during the war was amalgamated with that of the Bank of England, the whole being henceforth controlled by the Bank. The fiduciary issue was fixed at £260 million, but elasticity was introduced, the Bank being given the right temporarily to issue, subject to agreement by the Treasury, additional notes without gold cover. This right was exercised in August 1931, an additional £15 million being issued, the fiduciary issue standing at £275 millions from that date until April 1933.

[2] From April 28, 1925, the Bank of England was empowered to deliver gold for export against any form of legal tender.

follow this lead.[1] Britain's international trade would benefit. The pound could again "look the dollar in the face." Restoration of the former parity was thought to be an act of honesty and the honouring of obligations, temporarily broken by war exigencies, and an enhancement of British financial prestige and credit was expected to result. Creditors would be paid 100 per cent, but debtors to Britain would also be required to pay 100 per cent, and as on balance Britain owed less than was owed to her, self-interest joined hands with honesty. Nevertheless the general attitude was that expressed in *The Economist* at the time: "Great Britain has made its gesture to the world in the grand manner. 'Gentlemen, the war, with its temporary interruption of our mutual affairs, is over. We have the honour to pay in our accustomed manner if so be that your account is in credit in our ledgers.'"

At the time of the return to gold the pound was overvalued by about 10 per cent. It was hoped that this would be adjusted by a rise in prices abroad, but instead the trend was downwards, thus increasing the strain upon Great Britain. British gold costs were too high in comparison with those in other countries, with the consequence that foreign competition, already severe owing to industrial developments abroad, was intensified, and the British ratio of exports to imports was adversely affected. Forced to sell at world prices, the profits of British undertakings were reduced and unemployment remained at a high level.[2] Wage rates were maintained, interest rates and other costs showed little reduction, so that British gold costs remained inflexible and unadjusted.

[1] Speaking on this subject in the House of Commons, Mr. Winston Churchill, the Chancellor of the Exchequer, stated that Holland and the Dutch East Indies would return to gold simultaneously with Great Britain, Canada was substantially on gold, and Sweden's currency was based on gold; South Africa, Australia, and New Zealand would soon revert to the gold standard, German and Austrian currencies were linked with gold, while Hungarian currency was linked with sterling.

[2] For a discussion of the effects of "profit deflation" and other factors during this period, see *A Treatise on Money*, by J. M. Keynes, vol. ii, pp. 181-9.

In the absence of elasticity in money costs it was hoped that it would be possible to reduce costs of production by increased efficiency in relation to foreign competitors, but this would inevitably be a gradual process, and equilibrium was still not restored when the situation was aggravated by the onset of the world depression in 1929. British difficulties were increased by instability of the French, Belgian, and Italian currencies during the period from 1925 to 1927 and by the return of these countries to gold at rates beneficial to their own export trade but involving additional strain upon sterling. The general effect was that British production expanded more slowly between 1925 to 1929 than that of France, Germany, and the United States, while her share in world exports diminished. Certainly the expectations of those who believed that a return to gold would give a stimulus to British industry and trade were not realised.

Nevertheless, although the strain remained severe upon British industry and trade, with low rates of profit and a large volume of unemployment, no serious proposals were made to devaluate sterling or abandon gold. Thus, in 1929, the Balfour Committee said: "It is unthinkable that any appreciable body of opinion would favour a fresh departure from the gold standard."[1] Although British difficulties were much increased by the world depression this attitude was maintained right up to the moment when suspension of the gold standard was forced upon the country in September 1931. The Macmillan Committee which issued its Report in June 1931, less than three months before suspension, recommended "that this country should continue to adhere to the international gold standard at the existing parity," largely because of the importance to Great Britain of her international banking and associated services. They had no hesitation in rejecting proposals to devaluate sterling because of the bad effect this would have upon confidence. They found many defects, however, in the operation of the gold standard and favoured maintaining the existing inter-

[1] Final Report.

national standard only as the best starting-point for an evolution from the historic gold standard to a sound and scientific monetary system.

Before discussing the circumstances and consequences of suspension, a review must be given of the post-war trend of the balances of British international payments.

BALANCE OF INTERNATIONAL PAYMENTS

A country's power to maintain exchange stability and its capacity to lend or borrow abroad, whether at short- or long-term, depend upon the balance of its international payments and upon its credit. If it is able and willing to maintain a favourable balance of trade it can both control the external value of its currency and lend abroad. If, on the other hand, because of inability or unwillingness, its balance of payments is unfavourable, the stability of its currency largely depends upon the extent to which the deficit can be met by the repatriation of its capital and by borrowing from abroad, which is determined by its credit. Its monetary policy is partly controlled by but also greatly affects its balance of payments.

For a considerable period before the war Britain's balance of visible trade was unfavourable, there being an excess in the value of imports over exports. The deficit was, however, more than covered by the net return from external investments and from shipping, financial and other services, and a considerable balance was available for short- or long-term investment abroad. During the first post-war decade this situation was continued, although with a smaller favourable balance of payments than before the war. In 1931, however, it was reversed, the balance becoming heavily unfavourable. This was due to the serious decline in exports and in the income from investments and from shipping and financial services, while at the same time a high rate of imports was maintained. This inevitably imposed a severe strain upon sterling, which was increased by a temporary lack of foreign confidence in British credit. Suspension of the gold standard resulted in September 1931, and the subsequent depreciation of sterling together with tariffs caused a considerable reduction of imports and tended to bring Britain's international balance of income and expenditure into equilibrium. However, the continuation of the world depression caused a low rate of visible and invisible exports which prevented the balance from becoming strongly favourable again. Consequently sterling remained sensitive, and this chiefly determined the Government's monetary policy and also its imposition of restrictions upon foreign lending.

These changes in the balance of payments are shown by the Board of Trade statistics tabulated opposite. Recent years, except 1935, yielded no surplus for investment abroad.

Suspension of the Gold Standard

Reference has been made to the strain upon British industry and trade after the return to the gold standard in 1925, and to the adverse effects of the world depression upon the balance of payments. By 1931 the situation was serious. It was aggravated by the fact that, when the United States ceased lending abroad during and after the Wall Street boom, Great Britain made considerable short-term foreign loans, which, as the depression deepened, became frozen just at the time when she needed liquid resources to strengthen her own exchanges. Also foreign banks with frozen assets in Central Europe withdrew funds from London to strengthen their position at home. Confidence in sterling was further shaken when the May Committee on National Expenditure recommended drastic economies if a large deficit in the national budget was to be avoided.

The cumulative result was a run on the pound during the summer of 1931 which rapidly grew to alarming dimensions, more than £200 million being withdrawn from London in about two months, and the Bank of England's gold

ESTIMATED BALANCE OF PAYMENTS, 1913, AND 1924 TO 1935

(In Millions of Pounds Sterling)

Year	Excess of Imports over Exports*	Estimated Net Income from				Estimated Total Credit or Debit Balance
		Shipping	Overseas Investment	Short-term Interest and Commissions	Other Sources†	
1913	158	94	210	35	—	181
1924	324	140	220	60	—10	86
1925	384	124	250	60	4	54
1926	475	120	285	60	19	9
1927	390	140	285	63	16	114
1928	358	130	270	65	30	137
1929	366	130	270	65	39	138
1930	392	105	235	55	36	39
1931	408	80	170	30	24	—104
1932	287	70	150	25	—9	—51
1933	263	65	160	30	8	—
1934	294	70	175	30	17	—2
1935	261	75	185	30	8	37

* Including merchandise and bullion.
† Including estimated net balance of Government receipts from and payments made overseas.

reserve fell to £130 million.[1] With a view to supporting
sterling the Bank of England borrowed £50 milion and the
Government £80 million on short term from Paris and New
York. The drain, however, continued, and in September
1931 the Government was forced involuntarily to suspend
the gold standard.[2] This was the first break with gold in
peace-time. It was not a planned act of policy but was the
consequence of unexpected circumstances. Neither the
Government nor the Bank of England desired the change,
which they made great efforts to avoid. The Bank of England
has been criticised for keeping the Bank Rate at $4\frac{1}{2}$ per cent
during the height of the crisis, instead of raising it to 6, 8
or even 10 per cent.[3] The Bank was, however, averse from
adopting this course, believing that a higher Bank Rate
would not stop the run on sterling. On the contrary a
raising of the Rate would probably have been interpreted
abroad as a further indication of the real weakness of the
British position, tension would have increased and the
drain of funds been accelerated.

Since September 1931 sterling has been a managed paper
standard, and there have been no formal limitations upon
Britain's monetary freedom. The experience has been of
great value as an experiment in currency management, free
from a metallic basis. Responsibility for the management
has been shared by the Government and the Bank of England.
After the abandonment of the gold standard "the relationship between the Treasury and the Bank of England had
to be necessarily closer than ever. Indeed, the whole policy,
the whole management of sterling is one which is discussed
continuously between the representatives of the Treasury
and the representatives of the Bank of England."[4]

The immediate effect of suspending the gold standard was

---

[1] During July, August, and September 1931 gold exports amounted to
£34 million.

[2] This was done by passing the Gold Standard (Amendment) Act.

[3] The Rate was raised to 6 per cent simultaneously with suspension.

[4] Statement by Mr. Neville Chamberlain in the House of Commons,
December 21, 1934.

a fall in the value of the pound. This reduced the capital and interest value of British investments overseas, but it eased the burden of the borrowers, thus diminishing the risk of default by those experiencing difficulty in meeting their obligations. The depreciation of sterling brought relief to British exporters, and also resulted in a reduction of imports. Expansion of British exports was, however, smaller than had been expected, as many countries increased their import restrictions. Importation was further curtailed by the new tariffs, and, as already shown, the net result of the monetary and fiscal changes was greatly to reduce the adverse balance of payments. The tariff also added considerably to the public revenue.

Confidence in sterling was largely restored when it was seen that, with a balanced national budget, fears of runaway inflation were groundless, and when repayment of the amounts borrowed at the height of the crisis in Paris and New York was made quickly and without difficulty. Improvement of the trade balance also increased confidence in sterling. At first prices rose rapidly, the wholesale index in November 1931 being 7 per cent higher than two months earlier. Then the effect of the continued fall in prices in gold standard countries caused British wholesale prices to decline until the summer of 1932, after which they fluctuated within narrow limits until the devaluation of the dollar gave a stimulus to a new rise.

British monetary policy has been criticised for accentuating the fall in gold prices and prolonging the depression in gold standard countries. However, sterling, judged as a measure of the value of commodities, remained remarkably steady throughout the four years following suspension of the gold standard. The cost of living was almost the same in January 1936 as in September 1931, the wholesale price index rose by about 10 per cent during the same period, while the intervening fluctuations were not great.[1] Thus

[1] The wholesale prices of primary commodities rose by more than 30 per cent, this being of great benefit to raw material producers in the Dominions and other countries.

the managed paper pound was reliable as a standard of commodity value, while wholesale prices measured by gold fell by more than 25 per cent during the same period. The corresponding exchange depreciation of sterling in terms of the French franc and other gold currencies was about 40 per cent. When for internal reasons the United States devaluated the dollar by a similar percentage a large part of the world had broken away from a standard which had failed to satisfy one of the chief purposes of a monetary unit.

Shortly after suspending the gold standard Britain made a big contribution to recovery and to the restoration of economic equilibrium by bringing about a substantial reduction in interest rates. The high long-term rates of interest since the war, due largely to extensive borrowing by Governments and speculators and to credit restriction resulting from the uncertainties of the financial outlook, had proved unremunerative to a large part of the business community desiring capital for new productive investment.[1] The slump greatly reduced Government and speculative borrowings, and vast amounts of short-term funds became available. This, together with lack of demand by producers and traders, resulted in a fall in short-term interest rates to exceptionally low levels.

The British Government and the Bank of England supported this trend by a policy of cheap and abundant money, at first to facilitate the conversion operation in the summer of 1932, by which a large amount of war loan was converted from a 5 per cent to a 3½ per cent basis. The Bank of England had rapidly lowered its rate to 2 per cent in June 1932, while throughout the years 1933 to 1935 market rates averaged below 1 per cent. The Government's lead was followed by conversion of local government loans and a rise in the prices of gilt-edged securities, and by the end of 1934 the yield on British Government securities was less than 3 per cent, a rate not much more than that

---

[1] For a discussion of this question, see J. M. Keynes, *A Treatise on Money*, vol. ii, pp. 377–87.

ruling before the war. In many other countries long-term rates fell during the same period by about 20 or 25 per cent. At these lower rates borrowing for production becomes more attractive, and, with improvement in confidence, internal and external capital investment tend to expand. This would both increase British industrial activity and the export trade, and prepare the way for restoration of monetary equilibrium between the various countries.

The abundance of money was increased by extensive purchases of securities and gold by the Bank of England and of securities by the joint stock banks. This policy of expansion led to a rapid growth of bank deposits, the amount in the autumn of 1935 being about £300 millions greater than four years earlier.[1] This additional purchasing power at the disposal of the public, which provided a basis for stimulus to industry and trade, was little used except to raise the value of gilt-edged and other fixed-interest securities.

The policy of cheap and abundant money, maintenance of price stability, and release from an oppressive gold parity had favourable results. In addition to lowering interest rates, it ended deflation, and this increased business confidence.[2] Production and employment improved and the export trade showed some recovery. Confidence in sterling was maintained. In brief, the managed paper pound has been a success. Whereas the return to gold in 1925 gave no stimulus to British industry, its abandonment in 1931 had favourable effects. In 1935 the volume of British industrial production was distinctly greater than in 1929, while the number of insured persons in employment was above the 1929 average, although, with an increase in the number of persons available for work, the numbers unemployed were nearly double those in 1929. By contrast, industrial production in France and

[1] The advantages which Britain has derived from this policy are outlined in a speech delivered by the Right Hon. R. McKenna at the Ordinary General Meeting of Shareholders of the Midland Bank on January 26, 1934; see *Midland Bank Monthly Review*, January–February 1934.

[2] A large increase in confidence had already taken place in the winter of 1931–32, before deflation ended.

the United States was about 30 per cent below the 1929 level. In Germany, despite rearmament activity, and in Italy, notwithstanding preparations for the Abyssinian campaign, industrial production did not reach the pre-depression level.

The Government has been criticised chiefly for not supplementing the expansionist monetary policy by a large-scale programme of development works. No doubt this would have been inexpedient while sterling was under a cloud, but after the beginning of 1933 a more comprehensive national programme of development works financed at low rates of interest would have been of advantage. The Government, however, expressed strong opposition to such proposals. Thus, at the World Economic Conference, Mr. Runciman stated that Great Britain had found public works to be the most unremunerative way of dealing with unemployment. The Government had terminated its scheme for dealing with the unemployed by capital expenditure and would not reopen these schemes no matter what might be done by other countries. The method was far too costly and the policy was being abandoned once and for all. This emphatic declaration closed the door to cooperation with the United States in a programme for forcing prices rapidly to a higher level. In 1935, however, some change in the Government's attitude towards public works became evident, and various schemes were included in its election programme.

The mechanism of monetary management has been strengthened by the establishment of an exchange equalisation fund to provide a safeguard against a recurrence of speculative movements such as aggravated the 1931 crisis. This new system is now reviewed, and an account is then given of the British Government's attitude towards the reconstruction of an international monetary system.

THE EXCHANGE EQUALISATION ACCOUNT

The Exchange Equalisation Account was instituted under the Finance Act, 1932, to counteract some of the currency movements which had aggravated the monetary crisis of the previous year. These included the temporary accumulation in London of large short-term balances, and there was danger of inadequate liquid funds being available to meet exceptionally large withdrawals. London was being used from time to time as a temporary refuge for funds which were moved about from one international financial centre to another. Fear of monetary depreciation or political uncertainties in one country caused funds to be moved for safety to other centres, from which they would be repatriated when stability had been restored. Extensive speculation was associated with these mass movements, and their general effect was to increase monetary and financial instability. At the beginning of 1931 the amount of short-term capital capable of being moved at short notice from one centre to another "had reached the amazing total of £2,000 million," and, although this figure was exceptionally high, the amount has remained very large in subsequent years.[1] Movements might take place at inconvenient times with serious effects upon the exchanges and additional difficulties to trade and investment.

The object of the Account is to ensure greater stability of the sterling exchanges by building up liquid resources when sterling is strong owing to temporary factors, to be drawn upon when these factors are operating in the reverse direction. For this purpose the Bank of England might have increased its purchases and sales of gold and of foreign currencies, but this would have involved risk of loss which is more appropriately borne by the Government. While the influence of temporary factors is diminished by the operations of the Account, long-range trade and investment movements continue to affect the level of sterling. Considerable short-term capital movements also form part of the normal working of the international monetary

---

[1] The 1931 figure was given in a report of the Bank for International Settlements and quoted by Mr. Neville Chamberlain in a speech in the House of Commons on May 4, 1933.

system, and the Account must distinguish them from the
excessive movements against which compensatory measures
are necessary. "The purpose of the Account is not at all
directed against a permanent alteration in the relative
exchange value of the pound."[1] The chief temporary
influences which the Account is used to compensate are
seasonal fluctuations, speculative operations likely to
disturb the exchanges, and movements of refugee capital.

The resources originally available for the Account
amounted to £150,000,000, but practical experience during
the first year showed the necessity for a larger sum,
and on the request of the Chancellor of the Exchequer to
Parliament in May 1933, the total amount was increased
to £350,000,000. The resources of the Account take the
form of Treasury Bills which can be sold in the market
as required by exchange transactions up to this maximum
amount. Until the sterling credits had been used to buy
some amount of foreign currencies or gold, the Account
could take no action to check a fall in sterling, though it
could prevent or restrain a rise by selling sterling.

In many foreign countries, especially in the United States,
criticism has been directed against the Account, there
having been misrepresentation and misapprehension about
its purpose. The suspicion was engendered that the Account
was being used to depress the value of sterling with the
object of helping British exporters to capture trade from
their competitors in other countries. The complaint was
made that it was being operated to injure the trade of the
United States by keeping sterling at an artificially low rate
in relation to the dollar. Support for the contention that
the object of the Account was to depress sterling was derived
from the conditions prevailing at the time when the Account
was instituted. The distrust of sterling in 1931, accompanied
by withdrawals of funds from London, had given place in
the early months of 1932 to a strong flow of funds to London

---

[1] Speech by Mr. Neville Chamberlain in the House of Commons on
May 4, 1933.

and to a rise in the value of sterling. The Account served to restrain the flow of unwanted funds, to discourage speculation for a rise in sterling, and to secure foreign currencies as a reservoir against future withdrawals of capital.[1]

That it is erroneous to regard the British Government's policy as being to depreciate sterling in the interests of British trade is indicated not only by British official statements but also by evidence given in March 1934 by Professor Sprague of Harvard University before the United States House of Representatives' Committee on Banking and Currency.[2] He stated that it was never the purpose of the Account to depreciate the pound, but merely to keep it as steady as possible in view of existing conditions, and he referred to the fact that, in November 1932, as a result of operations not to *lower* the value of sterling but to *prevent* its depreciation, the supply of dollars and francs in the Account was almost exhausted. This compelled temporary suspension of operations and in consequence the pound fell to $3.15.[3] Early in 1933 when doubts began to be entertained about the future value of the dollar the pound rose to $3.45, at which point the Account was used to regulate the upward movement by selling sterling for dollars, which were then used to acquire gold. During a large part of 1934 the Account was a seller of French francs; francs were, however, bought in November 1934 and again in 1935 and 1936 during periods of weakness resulting from political and economic difficulties in France.

The suggestion has also been made that the Government uses the Account to manipulate the value of sterling with

---

[1] The effect of the initial purchases of foreign currencies was to establish a somewhat depressed value of sterling. This gave some justification, though slight, to foreign criticisms of an effect, though not of the purpose, of the account.

[2] Professor Sprague had been Economic Adviser to the Bank of England for several years until early in 1933.

[3] This fall was due to the continued adverse balance of payments, seasonal drain, and withdrawal of foreign funds from London when low money rates prevailed, following the success of the War Loan Conversion.

the object of returning to the gold standard. This was denied by the Chancellor of the Exchequer in reply to a question in the House of Commons on January 30, 1934. However, the diminution in the fluctuations of sterling resulting from the operation of the Account increases currency stability, thus removing one of the obstacles to the re-establishment of an international monetary standard. The operations have also facilitated the maintenance of a free market for sterling during a period when many other currencies have been strictly controlled. In a sense the fund is at present of the nature of a "suspense account," until the country decides upon its permanent monetary policy.

Misunderstandings about the purpose of the Account have arisen largely because of the secrecy observed in its operations, and of the absence of published statements showing the condition of the fund at different times. This secrecy is in contrast with the availability of information about monetary operations in the days of the gold standard, and official statements, even if not up-to-date, are desirable. Under present conditions, however, publicity would furnish information of value to speculators, whose manipulations would then be more difficult to counteract. Accountancy considerations also make it inadvisable to publish regular statements showing the current position of the fund; at any given date the Account may show a paper profit in sterling which might not be realised if the assets were sold and the Account wound up.

Criticism from abroad may also be due to the fact that in certain periods a higher value of sterling than that ruling at the time might better suit the monetary situation of some foreign country. But the equilibrium value of sterling depends upon a complexity of factors in many countries and not merely upon the conditions of one country alone. On the other hand, misinterpretation abroad may sometimes be due to genuine errors of judgment by those operating the Account in attempting to forecast the natural trend or appropriate level of sterling. Although the transactions of the Account are conducted by experts in foreign exchange dealings, supermen would be needed to avoid all mistakes in weighing appropriately the many economic and also the less calculable political and psychological factors influencing the world's monetary relations.

The British Government's initiative in establishing an Exchange Equalisation Account was followed by the United States Government instituting a similar fund. This was considered by many as providing the United States with a weapon to counteract any injury likely to be inflicted by the British fund. A conflict of monetary policies and the use of the two funds as fighting forces would have greatly aggravated monetary instability and involved further deterioration in international economic and political relations. Such a contest of currency instability and competitive depreciation of currencies in order to snatch temporary advantages in international trade would be a form of economic warfare which countries could not undertake without disaster. Conversely, the resources available in the two funds can be used to increase the stability of the currency exchanges, if policies are in harmony. They can be definitely beneficial rather than injurious if worked in a spirit of cooperation. Actually the American fund has been used less extensively than the British Account, but conflict of policies has been avoided. On the whole, Washington has wanted to prevent the dollar from appreciating when London has been anxious to prevent sterling from depreciating. Without any formal cooperation, therefore, the two funds have tended to achieve the same purpose. There was a marked diminution in the fluctuations of the dollar, sterling, franc and many other exchanges during the course of 1934 and 1935, although in certain periods the franc exchange was disturbed by fears that France would not be able to maintain the gold parity.

In view of monetary uncertainties in the future the Account cannot be regarded as a temporary measure to

meet a short-period emergency but as an instrument
be retained as an essential part of the machinery for
monetary regulation. Though it may be inactive for considerable periods when exchange rates are stable, it will
remain useful in reserve for times of strain. It may be
noted that the establishment of the Account involves an
extension of Government responsibility for the monetary
policy of the country, which is, however, still mainly
regulated by the Bank of England. The Account supplements
the action of the Bank of England in buying and selling
foreign currencies and gold.[1]

Policy for Reconstructing an International Monetary System

The breakdown of the gold standard in Great Britain and
in other countries closely associated by trade and financial
relations with Great Britain resulted, as already indicated,
in the development of an informal "sterling area," and
attempts were made to increase monetary stability within
this area. Many of the countries were members of the
British Commonwealth, and the Ottawa Conference, 1932,
provided an occasion for discussing the main lines of Empire
monetary policy. The Conference reached an agreement in
terms which, however, were inevitably vague in view of
the uncertainty of the monetary outlook at the time.[2]

The Empire Governments declared at Ottawa that in
their view a rise throughout the world in the general level
of wholesale prices was in the highest degree desirable, and
stated that they were anxious to cooperate with other
nations in practicable measures for raising wholesale prices.
They agreed that monetary action alone would be inadequate

---

[1] A Survey of *The British Exchange Equalisation Account*, by N. F.
Hall, was published as a supplement to the *Economist* on May 5, 1934
(subsequently issued as a book), and an article on the same subject by
F. W. Paish was published in *Economica*, February 1935.

[2] Canada, though a party to the Agreement, was for some time more
closely associated with the dollar than with sterling.

as the level of prices was being depressed by non-monetary factors. Among monetary measures, low interest rates and abundance of short-term money were mentioned as favourable conditions for revival of enterprise and trade, but inflation with the object of financing public expenditure was deprecated. They then declared that the ultimate aim of monetary policy must be the restoration of a satisfactory international monetary standard, having in mind not merely stable exchange rates between all countries but deliberate management of the international standard in such a manner as to ensure the smooth and efficient working of international trade and finance.

The principal conditions precedent to the re-establishment of any international monetary standard were (1) a rise in the general level of commodity prices to a height more in keeping with the level of costs, including the burden of debts and other fixed charges, and (2) an adjustment of the political, economic and financial factors which had caused the breakdown of the gold standard, including war debts, excessive tariffs, exchange restrictions, and other obstacles to trade. International cooperation should be secured with a view to avoiding wide fluctuations in the purchasing power of the standard of value.

The Ottawa monetary agreement has subsequently remained the basis of British policy. Its clauses are capable of varying interpretation, Great Britain being less favourable to a big rise in commodity prices than some of the Dominions, especially Australia and New Zealand. She has also been anxious to avoid inflationary measures for financing public works, preferring to rely upon the gradual effects of cheap money.

The international monetary situation was soon made still more complicated by President Roosevelt's dollar policy, which, in the spring of 1933, increased the monetary divisions of the world by adding a fluctuating dollar standard to the gold and sterling standards. The inauguration of this policy, with its emphasis upon a big rise in commodity prices and subsequent stability of prices rather than of gold, took place at the moment when Mr. Ramsay MacDonald, the British Prime Minister, as President of the World Economic Conference, was visiting Washington with a view to securing some measure of agreement as basis for the deliberations of the Conference. Already in January 1933 the Preparatory Committee of the Conference had pronounced itself in favour of restoration of the gold standard, and this was supported by the British Government. The time of return and the parities were, however, to be determined separately by the proper authorities of each country. The Washington conversations resulted in the publication of a joint statement by Mr. MacDonald and President Roosevelt indicating the need for monetary stability, but without specifying the kind of stability desired; a rise in prices by concerted international action was also envisaged.

The World Economic Conference met at an inopportune moment when the United States was preoccupied with measures to raise her internal price level, and when she regarded agreement upon an international standard as of quite secondary interest. While the future of the dollar was so uncertain and the French were unwilling to devaluate the franc, Great Britain could not throw in her lot either with the dollar or with gold. Both sides manœuvred for her support. She had such close economic relations with her neighbours in Europe that a wide divergence of her currency from gold was undesirable. On the other hand, her own interests, together with those of Canada and also of other Commonwealth countries, required freedom to make adjustments to variations in the dollar. The British Government's first preference seems to have been for the gold standard, but, apart from the commercial and financial difficulties which would have arisen from a fixed parity between sterling and gold while the dollar was fluctuating, several of the Dominion Governments were opposed to an immediate return to gold, favouring a policy directed towards a substantial rise in prices. Britain, therefore, decided to remain independent and to steer a middle course, and the Conference broke down without any agreement being reached on the future relations between sterling, gold, and the dollar.[1]

When the World Economic Conference failed to agree upon monetary policy, the chief countries of the British Commonwealth issued a declaration reaffirming the principles adopted by the Ottawa Conference, and supporting the ultimate restoration of a satisfactory international gold standard.[2] Reference was made to the success which had attended the British Commonwealth's policy of raising prices, especially of primary products, and it was considered important that this rise should continue. It was thought impracticable to state in precise terms the ultimate price level at which to aim, but any price level would be satisfactory which restored the normal activity of industry and employment, which ensured an economic return to producers of primary commodities, and which harmonised the burden of debts and fixed charges with economic capacity. "The Governments of the British Commonwealth should persist by all means in their power, whether monetary or economic, within the limits of sound finance in the policy of furthering the rise in wholesale prices" until equilibrium had been re-established. The raising of prices by expansion of Government programmes of capital outlay was considered to be a matter for each Government. When equilibrium had been reached, measures should be taken to stabilise the position and prevent inflation which would cause disturbance in the opposite direction.

Pending the restoration of an international gold standard, the Empire countries recognised the importance of stability of exchange rates within their own area and agreed to keep this objective in mind in determining their monetary policy.

---

[1] The Conference adopted resolutions defining the rules necessary for the successful operation of the gold standard.

[2] The Declaration was signed by the representatives of the United Kingdom, Canada, Australia, New Zealand, South Africa, and India. It was not signed by the representative of the Irish Free State, who referred the matter to his Government.

Such inter-Imperial stability would, it was agreed, be aided by the pursuit of a common policy of raising price levels, and by the fact that the British Government was free from commitments to other countries upon the future management of sterling. The Empire countries, forming the nucleus of the sterling area, indicated that the area could be extended by the adhesion of other countries adopting a similar policy; they did not intend, therefore, to pursue a policy of exclusiveness.

Of special interest in this declaration is the emphasis upon the level and stability of prices, an appropriate and stable level of prices evidently being considered more important than stability of exchange rates or stability in terms of gold. The gold standard would be restored only if it would be likely to ensure reasonable stability of world prices. This contrasts sharply with the former policy of concentrating upon the maintenance of exchange stability.

Subsequent declarations of policy by the British Government have merely reiterated the general principles reviewed above.[1] For some time after the suspension of the gold standard the Government seemed to favour, and even to expect, an early return to an international standard based on gold, with sterling suitably devalued. Thus, an early restoration of exchange stability was clearly contemplated when the project for a World Economic Conference was launched, as this was to be one of its principal tasks. The realisation of this hope was indefinitely deferred by the unexpected instability of the dollar, and by the intensification of economic nationalism in many countries. Since then, the British Government has shown no urgent desire for the re-establishment of an international standard in the near future. The purpose of policy has been to secure a value for sterling which is the most satisfactory taking account of all the circumstances, both internal and external, and to strengthen the foundations of exchange stability

[1] For example, a statement made by the Chancellor of the Exchequer in the House of Commons on July 4, 1934.

within the sterling area. The measure of stability achieved
has been hailed with satisfaction, and the independence and
freedom of monetary action untrammelled by rigid relationships with the dollar and with gold is recognised as having
advantages in present circumstances.

The sterling area, though founded upon no formal agreement, is so extensive that sterling is the chief of the world's
currencies. Each country within the area is free to pursue
its own independent monetary policy, but the group, the
chief components of which are the British Commonwealth,
the Scandinavian countries, the Argentine, other South
American countries, Portugal, Egypt, and China, is largely
held together by close community of commercial and financial
relations. Stability within the sterling area is not incompatible with the gradual restoration of greater stability
with the dollar and with gold; indeed it makes an important
contribution towards the restoration of a common standard.
During 1934 and 1935 the relative fluctuations of sterling,
the dollar and gold became much smaller and disequilibrium
was reduced, although some of the gold standard countries
still experienced difficulty from the relative overvaluation
of their currencies, and it was uncertain whether they could
withstand the strain or would be forced to devaluate, thus
prolonging the period of international currency instability.

The ultimate objective of British policy is declared to
be the establishment of an international monetary system
based upon gold. There is, however, a growing tendency to
favour the gradual establishment of *de facto* stabilisation
of exchange rates and of the volume of money incomes,
which would ensure reasonable price stability, while preserving freedom from binding international obligations.
No anxiety is shown for an early return to gold, but instead
there is hesitation to resume the rigidities of the gold
standard.[1] Satisfaction with sterling as a managed currency

[1] Speaking in the House of Commons on December 21, 1934, Mr. Neville
Chamberlain said that "in the present circumstances of the time we can not
afford to run the risk that we would run if we did take away from ourselves
our freedom to move the pound where we want to, and we must wait until

is increasing, and what is now desired is to retain its advantages while fitting into an international system so as to facilitate international trade and finance. This requires that other countries shall apply a monetary policy broadly similar to that of Great Britain. Only in this way can the two objectives of internal monetary stability and stable exchanges be secured. Also, by contrast with the position in 1925, when restoration of sterling to its pre-war parity with gold was almost universally supported and was widely regarded as a point of honour, there is now little demand by advocates of the gold standard for restoration of the old parity. Instead, a substantial devaluation is generally assumed. The new standard will be based upon gold at a higher value than before. Now that no great financial country can claim the virtue of having maintained its pre-war parity without a break, the prestige associated with this parity has much diminished.[1] Also, compared with the 1914 parity, sterling is as good as the dollar and much better than the franc.

Apart from devaluation it seems improbable that the gold standard will be re-established in its old form. It is recognised that the early restoration of an international standard is impracticable in view of disequilibrium between costs and prices in the chief currency areas. This is greatest in the gold standard countries and least among the sterling area countries.[2] To link sterling with gold while the franc is so considerably overvalued would involve the risk of a fall in prices and intensified depression. Also, an international standard cannot operate satisfactorily while France

there is such a change in the price levels as might bring the dollar and the franc into greater harmony one with the other. . . ." At the Annual Meeting of Westminster Bank, January 1935, the Chairman, Mr. Rupert Beckett, stated that, having regard to the uncertainties of other currencies, to attempt to stabilise now would be dropping our currency anchor on shifting sands.

[1] Holland and Switzerland succeeded in retaining the pre-war gold parity during this period.

[2] See an article on "The Sterling Area" in the *Economist*, November 24, 1934; also Sir Henry Strakosch's paper on "The Road to Recovery," published as a Supplement to the *Economist*, January 5, 1935.

and the United States, both creditor countries, remain highly protectionist, sterilise a large part of their gold reserves, and only spasmodically exercise their power to lend abroad. In 1925 only one parity was seriously considered, but now there are various alternatives. Then, Britain returned to gold by an act of national policy with the expectation that other countries would follow her example, but now she must know what other countries intend to do. An international agreement is essential if rates of exchange are to be mutually satisfactory and to avoid placing some countries at a disadvantage.

When conditions permit of international monetary stabilisation, any agreement reached is likely to be for an experimental period. It must include a common understanding upon the objects of monetary policy and methods of operation of an international standard, with special reference to maintaining appropriate relations between debtors and creditors and between costs and prices. There is now a much larger body of opinion than in 1925 in favour of ranking price stability and internal economic equilibrium before exchange stability. The British Government favours much more conscious management of an international standard than before the war or during the period from 1925 to 1931. Deliberate management of an international standard to ensure the smooth working of international trade and finance was included in the Ottawa agreement as an objective of policy. That monetary management, with gold subordinated, will be the dominant feature of British monetary policy, both national and international, is also indicated by later official declarations that the avoidance of fluctuations in the purchasing power of gold arising from monetary causes is one of the essential conditions under which the United Kingdom would feel justified in returning to the gold standard.[1]

---

[1] Declaration made by Mr. Neville Chamberlain at the World Economic Conference, June 1933, and repeated by him in the House of Commons on July 4, 1934.

CHAPTER III

FINANCIAL POLICY

By the vast sums of capital which she has invested abroad
Britain's contribution to the economic equipment of undeveloped areas has been greater than that of any other
country. The benefits have been mutual; new areas have
enjoyed rapid progress by the utilisation of their rich natural
resources, while Great Britain has earned good returns upon
her investments and has benefited from expansion of trade.

The questions of chief interest in considering financial
policy are the objects in view and the extent to which
the Government has encouraged, restricted, or controlled
the direction of capital investment. In particular, has home
investment been favoured, and have some countries been
accorded advantages which have been denied to others in
their dealings with the British capital market? Are facilities
accorded to industries abroad which are complementary to
British production, but not to those which are competitive?
Does the Government use loans as bargaining counters in
securing political support or commercial preferences, or
require that they shall be used in the purchase of British
manufactures? Also, has anything been done to protect
British capital once it has been invested abroad?

PRE-WAR POLICY

Before the war, non-intervention as the basic principle of
policy was as widely operative in the financial as in the
commercial field. Official restrictions upon the free movement
of capital were almost unknown. The Government had, of
course, opportunity in informal and often private personal
consultations to express its opinion upon proposed issues
of foreign loans. Private financial interests were, therefore,
well informed about political aspects. Indeed, they desired

to obtain from the Government the fullest information upon the political situation, but, though they would give careful consideration to the views of the Foreign Office and the Treasury, they were entirely unfettered in reaching their decisions. Also, decisions to lend and the conditions of loans were determined primarily on economic grounds. Foreign lending largely for political reasons, similar to certain French loans to Russia, played a negligible part in British international financial relations.

The Government preferred to be free from any responsibility for foreign loans, recognising that thus they would avoid conflict with foreign Governments, and also that, if a loan which they had openly supported proved to be unsound, they would be exposed to attack by the investing public. Several colonial loans were, however, issued with the British Government's guarantee, one foreign loan was guaranteed jointly by the British and French Governments, and another by the British, French, and Russian Governments.[1] The Government's attitude towards the financial activities of the City is indicated by a statement made in the House of Commons in 1914 by Sir Edward (afterwards Lord) Grey, Secretary of State for Foreign Affairs. He said that British financiers ran their business quite independent of politics, adding: "I do not say that there are no cases in which loans have a political character and in which financiers come to the Foreign Office and ask if there is any objection to them. But generally speaking . . . these are things in which the Foreign Office does not interfere."[2] In no sense, therefore, was foreign investment controlled by the Government as an instrument of British foreign policy. Nor was the admission of foreign securities to Stock Exchange dealings controlled by the State. This was in marked contrast with the declared policy of certain foreign Governments, e.g. France, which directed foreign investment in the

[1] Jointly guaranteed loans were issued for Turkey (1855) and Greece (1898), while the chief guaranteed Colonial loans were for Egypt (£9,424,000 in 1885) and Transvaal (£35,000,000 in 1903, and £5,000,000 in 1909).

[2] *Parliamentary Debates*, House of Commons, 5th Series, LXIV.

political as well as the economic interests of their country.[1]

Indications may be given of one or two exceptions to the general rule. They arose chiefly in the Near East (Turkey), and in China where several foreign Powers were struggling to extend their political and economic influence. During the negotiations for certain loans to China the British Government intervened to ensure that the loans should be conditional upon the granting of political and commercial concessions by the Chinese Government. In 1912 a Chinese loan was floated in disregard of the British Government's opposition, but, although in some financial circles the Government was considered to be interfering unduly in private financial affairs, its influence prevented the success of the loan. Already during the previous decade, the British Government's unfavourable attitude for political reasons towards transportation and other developments in Turkey, including the Baghdad railway project, influenced London financial interests against the floating of Turkish loans. In addition to their own general willingness to support the Government's policy, financiers recognised that a loan issued in opposition to the Government's wishes would not be likely to prove attractive to the investing public. Apart, however, from a few such exceptions, the pre-war financial foreign policy of Great Britain was consistent with her system of *laissez-faire*.

POST-WAR CHANGES

During recent years the Government has been much more active than before the war in bringing its influence to bear upon financial houses in the City concerned in the investment of British funds abroad; also the method of guaranteeing loans has been used more extensively than in pre-war days, while embargoes have been placed upon international lend-

---

[1] In some countries Government regulation of the admission of foreign securities to official listing for Stock Exchange purposes has long been exercised.

ing, and other positive measures have been adopted for the regulation or control of investment policy.

For more than a decade after the war the changes were tentative and haphazard, and it was only in the depths of the world depression that a modified *laissez-faire* system was superseded by extensive Government regulation. A more deliberate policy has now replaced the former practice of occasional intervention when required by special circumstances. Indeed, during the early post-war years an attempt was made to restore the pre-war system so far as conditions would permit. But the circumstances had changed to such an extent that Government intervention was inevitably greater than before the war and this prepared the way for the development of an active policy of control, the objects of which have, however, generally been economic rather than political.

Britain no longer controls the international capital market, but is faced with rival lending centres, especially the United States and France. Resources available for lending abroad are less than before the war, owing to the challenge to British commercial supremacy and the effects of economic nationalism upon British trade. There has been a growing demand that home industries and public authorities should have preference in the capital market over foreign borrowers, and that any capital lent abroad should be invested in ways directly advantageous to British industry. Also, the automatic mechanism of the gold standard no longer adjusts balances of payment, including international capital operations, by gold movements and bank rate changes.

Although these changed conditions have led to increase in Government intervention and influence, the final decisions and nominal responsibility still rest with the business community. In practice, however, though by different methods, control in Great Britain is as strict as in countries where it is exercised more formally. Although the Government frequently exercises its influence without statutory authority, and although it might legally be within the competence of private financial institutions to promote operations in opposition to the Government's wishes, such a course would in practice invite failure. As the Government's influence is often exerted through the Bank of England, the transformation of the Bank into a public authority, as is proposed by the Labour Party, would convert the present system of Government influence into one of formal responsibility, which might sometimes be a source of embarrassment.

The general effect of economic and political conditions and of Government intervention has been a decline during post-war years in the proportion of new capital lent to foreign countries. The proportion is smaller than in pre-war years, and the post-war trend has been downwards since about 1924. Loans to British Dominions and Colonies have been well maintained at over 25 per cent of the total amount of new capital issues, while the proportion issued for investment at home has increased. (See table on page 73.)

The effects of the war caused foreign lending to be exceptionally low during the years 1919 to 1921. It attained its highest post-war level during the period from 1922 to 1926, the peak year being 1924. Excluding the year 1925, during which the Government used its influence against foreign lending so as to avoid additional strain upon the sterling exchanges at the time of Britain's return to the gold standard, the capital raised in Great Britain for foreign countries in this period was about 25 per cent of the total of new issues; in the exceptional year 1925 it was 13·8 per cent. From 1927 onwards it has never exceeded 16½ per cent, and since 1932 it has been almost negligible. Though considerable recovery from the low levels of the depression years is probable, foreign lending is unlikely for some years at least to reach the level attained between 1922 and 1926.[1]

The only post-war years free from considerable restrictions

[1] Statistics of new capital issues in the United Kingdom since the war are tabulated on page 73.

upon foreign lending were 1922 to 1924 and 1926 to 1928.[1] Significant in the first of these periods was the issuing of a number of foreign loans with British Government encouragement or guarantee.[2] The League of Nations Loan to Austria in 1923 carried a British Government guarantee, while the Government was interested in the success of the loans to Greece and Hungary issued in 1924 under League of Nations auspices. The Government also incurred responsibility for the German Dawes Loan in 1924. As already indicated, the scale of new British issues for foreign countries diminished from about the middle of the first post-war decade, that is before the onset of the world depression, when foreign loans again came under an embargo. The amount of new foreign issues was considerable in 1930, but a large part of the total involved no transfer of funds abroad. Thus large issues for the Japanese and Brazilian Governments were for refunding indebtedness or earlier loans due for repayment. The Young Loan for Germany was issued in connection with the Hague reparations settlement, and as the Loan was not to exceed the amount received in reparations by the British Government the operation involved no export of funds. An Austrian Loan was also authorised in 1930. Subsequent changes are reviewed in a later section which deals with recent regulation of new foreign issues and its effects.

BRITISH CAPITAL INVESTED ABROAD

The total amount of British capital invested abroad immediately before the war has been estimated at about £4,000 million. About one-quarter of these investments was sold during the war and the proceeds used to pay for imports

[1] In 1929, as in 1925, the Government and the Bank exerted influence to restrict the amount of British investment abroad when pressure on sterling was specially great.

[2] Several loans for relief purposes were made in the first three post-war years by the British Government out of its own resources, without calling for public subscription, to the Governments of Austria and of some of the South-Eastern European countries.

of munitions, food, and raw materials, especially from the
United States. Foreign investments, therefore, formed a
valuable national reserve. Although since the war Britain
resumed capital investment abroad the pre-war level has
not been attained.

At the end of each of the years 1929 to 1933 the total
amount of British capital invested abroad in marketable
securities was as follows:[1]

1929 ..	.. £3,438 million		1932 ..	.. £3,355 million
1930 ..	.. £3,425 million		1933 ..	.. £3,386 million
1931 ..	.. £3,410 million			

The distribution of the 1933 total was as follows:

	£ million
Dominion and Colonial Governments and Municipalities ..	1,147
Foreign Governments and Municipalities	333
British Companies operating abroad[2]	1,211
Foreign and Colonial Companies[2]	695

Approximately two-thirds of the 1933 total was invested
in the British Dominions and Colonies, nearly 17 per cent
in South America, 6½ per cent in Central America and the
United States, a similar proportion in Europe, and the
remainder in the Far East. There was a persistent decline
during the six years from 1928 to 1933 in the nominal
amount of British capital invested in foreign government
and municipal loans, both absolutely and relatively to the
amount in Dominion and Colonial government and municipal
loans, the ratio of foreign total loans of this class falling
from 26 per cent in 1928 to 22·5 per cent in 1933.[3]

The investment of so large a proportion of British overseas
capital within the Empire is partly because British investors
have confidence in the potentialities of and knowledge about

[1] From articles by Sir Robert Kindersley in the *Economic Journal*,
June 1933, September 1934, and September 1935. In addition to these
amounts there are other investments, e.g. in property, mortgages, and
securities not dealt in on the British Stock Exchanges; they totalled about
£280 million in 1933.

[2] Nominal share and loan capital. The foreign and colonial companies
are those whose securities were dealt in on British Stock Exchanges.

[3] See Sir Robert Kindersley's article in the *Economic Journal*, September
1935, p. 368.

conditions in the Dominions and Colonies. Language, race, and similarity of political, financial, and legal systems are factors, as is also the granting of trustee status to many Dominion and Colonial loans. Further, the loans have usually been in developments complementary to British industries and have made substantial demands for British products. This has, indeed, been one advantage in lending more to Empire countries than to some foreign countries in which developments would be more competitive than complementary.

The recent tendency to increase the proportion of funds invested within the Empire is due chiefly to a desire, in view of economic nationalism and political insecurity abroad, to strengthen economic relations within the Empire, and this is now supported by the Government's policy of restricting foreign loans.[1] Other factors are the effects of certain defaults in discrediting foreign loans; also foreign countries are less dependent upon the London capital market now that the rivalry of other creditor centres has increased.

OBJECTS AND METHODS OF INTERVENTION[2]

In this section brief reference is made to objects and methods of intervention mainly during the first post-war decade, subsequent sections dealing in somewhat greater detail with more recent developments. Mention has already been made of Government relief loans immediately after the war to Austria and certain distressed countries of South-Eastern Europe. Although these loans were made mainly to help

[1] The Macmillan Committee favoured a policy of using funds available for investment in foreign countries primarily for British owned enterprises rather than for loans to foreign governments and municipalities which absorb capital while doing little for British industry and commerce.

[2] For a detailed discussion of these questions see *Memorandum on Recent British Measures affecting International Finance*, submitted by the British Coordinating Committee to the Second International Studies Conference, on the State and Economic Life, of the League of Nations International Institute of Intellectual Cooperation, London, May 1933.

in the feeding of starving populations, the political motive was not absent, as it was thought that, unless these populations received relief, they would become a prey to communist propaganda, and this would aggravate the chaos in Central Europe.

The Government has made somewhat more extensive use of a practice adopted only rarely in pre-war days of giving its guarantee to certain loans. As already stated, the British Government, largely for political reasons, joined with several other Governments in guaranteeing the League of Nations Austrian Loan in 1923.[1] This method of joint guarantee by several Governments avoids the danger of special political advantage which may arise if only one country makes a loan. It is also largely free from the risk that a borrowing country, in endeavouring to secure specially favourable terms, may play off one financial centre against another.

The British Government's guarantee has been chiefly used for loans for public utility and transport developments in British Colonies and Mandated Territories,[2] and, under the various Trade Facilities Acts, 1921 to 1926, for loans the proceeds of which would be used in fixed capital construction likely to promote employment and would be spent on British products. Such loans could be issued to borrowers either within Great Britain or abroad.[3] Powers under this legislation came to an end in 1927, when a total of £73 million had been issued with the British Government's guarantee. The loans were raised mainly by transportation, public utility, and industrial companies in Great Britain and other parts of the Commonwealth; only very few loans for foreign countries or undertakings were guaranteed.

[1] Its support of other League of Nations loans and of the Dawes and Young loans was also based upon political and economic considerations, although these loans did not carry its guarantee.

[2] A total of about £24 million has been lent since 1919, mainly to the Sudan, Tanganyika, and Palestine.

[3] The 1924 Trade Facilities Act empowered the British Government to pay three-quarters of the interest up to five years upon such part of Dominion and Colonial Government public utility loans spent in Great Britain, total payments by the British Government being limited to £5 million.

A number of the companies to whose loans the guarantee was attached are controlled by Colonial Governments. One or two of the undertakings have experienced such financial difficulties during the depression that the British Government has been called upon to pay the amounts in deficit, but this is exceptional. The guaranteeing of overseas loans to be spent upon British products was somewhat similar in purpose to the system of export credit guarantees given to facilitate trade with certain countries in which risks were abnormally great.

British Dominion and Colonial Governments have long enjoyed advantages over foreign Governments when borrowing in London, as a result of the trustee status of their loans. This status, which was first accorded in 1900 by the Colonial Stock Act, greatly extends the market and tends to reduce fluctuations in the price of the securities. Borrowing is facilitated at terms generally more favourable than those at which non-trustee loans can be issued. Indeed, it was often claimed in the days before Britain was able to give extensive tariff preferences to Empire products that the facilities granted for raising funds in London were an appropriate return for the trade preferences accorded to British manufactures by Dominion Governments. The advantages of trustee status have undoubtedly strengthened the tendency, which has now been operating during several decades, for a larger proportion of new British capital invested overseas to be loaned to Governments within the Empire. The facilities have even stimulated an unduly rapid rate of borrowing by certain Governments during post-war years, thus imposing burdens which their populations experienced difficulties in supporting. Such excessive mortgaging of the future has, however, been exceptional, and the general effect of the loans has been a development of resources and equipment and a higher standard of life in the Dominions and Colonies, as well as remunerative investment for British capital and increased demand for British manufactures.

Action is taken by the British Government for the protection of British funds invested abroad. The method of direct intervention is adopted only where the Government is in a position of some responsibility to subscribers; where other loans are in default, negotiations with the borrower, whether Government or private undertaking, are conducted by unofficial organisations representing British holders, for example, the League Loans Council and the Council of Foreign Bondholders, with more or less support from the Government according to its political or economic interest in the loan. The Government at all times watches closely the interests of British holders of bonds of defaulting foreign Governments.[1] As the Government prefers to avoid accusation by British lenders of its responsibility for their losses, and dislikes having to take direct action in the protection of their interests, the number of loans involving its guarantee or moral obligation to intervene is small.

Reference is made in a later section to the special measures adopted by British Governments when faced with German default on the Dawes and Young Loans and with the inability of German traders, owing to exchange restrictions, to pay British exporters for goods supplied. The Government's general policy is indicated by its attitude at the World Economic Conference, 1933, towards proposals for the adoption of a plan for adjusting the burden of international indebtedness. Debtor countries urged, with support from some creditors, that capital and interest payments should be scaled down in accordance with general principles; for example, that money obligations should be reduced in proportion to the fall in the prices of the principal exports of the debtors. Also, arrangements should be made so that the creditor countries would import a sufficient balance of goods from debtor countries to permit transference of loan interest by the debtors.

The British Government was opposed to any permanent

[1] Statement by Mr. Neville Chamberlain, House of Commons, November 15, 1934.

reorganisation of debts during the depression. It hoped that the difficulties of debtors ~~was~~ largely temporary and that a return of economic prosperity would enable them to meet their obligations. A scaling down of debts at the lowest point of the depression would be unfair to creditors. The policy favoured was one of temporary adjustments varying according to the conditions of each individual debtor. "No universal rule can be applied to them, and the natural method of procedure is by negotiations between the debtors who know their own difficulties and creditors whose assent is required to any derogation from their natural rights."[1] A rigid uniform procedure was deprecated in view of wide variations in the conditions of different debtor countries. This policy of temporary piecemeal adjustments is the one pursued by the British Government, both in its own direct negotiations and in its support of unofficial settlements. In arranging trade agreements with certain debtor countries, particularly the Argentine, the Government has taken into consideration not only the interests of British producers and exporters but also of British investors.

Recent Regulation of New Foreign Loans

The financial crisis of 1931 resulted in a great decline in the amount of new long-term capital issues and especially in the proportion lent to foreign countries. From the time of the crisis until the end of 1932 lending to foreign countries was negligible, while total issues were much below those in any previous year since the war; they were only about 40 per cent of the issues in 1929 and 1930. The fall was mainly due to the uncertainties of the period, those with capital being unwilling to lend while potential borrowers were either too weak to obtain funds on reasonable terms or preferred to postpone increases in their commitments.

[1] Statement by Mr. Neville Chamberlain on June 26, 1933, to Sub-Commission 1 of the Monetary and Financial Commission of the World Economic Conference.

At first the Government relied upon its influence to discourage the floating of any loan of which it disapproved, as well as upon the inevitable decline in the amount of new issues, especially to foreign countries, resulting from the difficulties of the period. When, however, the War Loan Conversion operation was announced in June 1932, Mr. Neville Chamberlain, Chancellor of the Exchequer, with a view to ensuring the success of the scheme, appealed to the capital market to refrain from making new issues until conversion was completed. Although no compulsion or statutory sanction was involved, the market fully complied with the Chancellor's request. The Conversion having been successfully completed at the end of September 1932, the restraint was withdrawn, subject however to two exceptions, the more significant being the retention of the "embargo" upon foreign loans.[1] This embargo applied to "issues on behalf of borrowers domiciled outside the Empire, or issues the proceeds of which would be remitted directly or indirectly to countries outside the Empire."

The purpose of the restriction was indicated by the Treasury to be prevention of additional strain upon sterling by export of capital at a time when the British balance of payments was unfavourable or not sufficiently favourable for considerable sums to be lent abroad. With the same object in view the ban was laid not only upon new foreign issues but, in May 1933, was extended to cover purchases of large blocks of securities from foreign holders for re-sale in Great Britain by public issue or other means. The Chancellor of the Exchequer intimated that he disapproved of such operations, considering them to be against the public interest, and the Government requested financial houses to dissuade business men from promoting them. The Treasury even referred to the purchase of foreign securities by indi-

---

[1] The other exception was any operation involving underwriting or invitation to the public to subscribe new cash for the purpose of optional replacement of existing securities by new issues. This restriction was subsequently relaxed, being limited to optional conversion of trustee securities.

viduals as being inopportune in the conditions then prevailing; as, however, foreign exchange operations were not restricted, ordinary investment by individuals in foreign securities or purchase of British securities held by foreigners abroad was not interrupted. On the other hand the disapproval of large-scale purchases of securities for repatriation and of new foreign issues was fully respected, being virtually a command. Consequently, a number of British companies were prevented by Government opposition from completing favourable capital transactions, the objection being that the export of funds to foreign countries would be involved.[1]

The Government's policy was not without its critics, who claimed that the embargo upon foreign lending was unnecessary or even injurious.[2] In particular, opponents pointed out that loans to foreign countries would be likely to result in purchases of British products; they also contended that the prevailing insecurity and instability in the economic world alone would be a sufficient safeguard against a boom in investment abroad. A resumption of foreign lending would, they thought, provide a stimulus to world recovery.

A considerable period elapsed before the Government modified its policy, although some indication of the kind of change which might be expected was given in April 1933, when the Government exceptionally granted permission for the issue of a Danish Government Loan of £1,000,000 to finance the construction of the Seeland-Falster Bridge by a British firm using British steel. More than a year later, on July 19, 1934, the Chancellor of the

---

[1] Treasury sanction was obtained by several British companies for the repatriation of large blocks of their shares held in the United States, a more liberal attitude being adopted by the Treasury during 1935 than in previous years. The companies which secured sanction include Boots Pure Drug, General Electric, Associated Electric Industries, and Electrical and Musical Industries, a total amount of more than £6 million being involved.

[2] See, for example, an article on "The New Capital Market: The Case for Ending the Restrictions," *Midland Bank Monthly Review*, October–November 1933.

Exchequer announced that the "embargo" would be relaxed in favour of two classes of foreign borrowers, one being borrowers in countries within the sterling *bloc*. This was the first official public reference to the sterling *bloc*, and the new policy was designed to strengthen monetary relations in this group of countries. The Chancellor was henceforth prepared to consider sterling issues by a country within the sterling *bloc* where the loan was required to increase the sterling assets of that country and so to minimise fluctuations in the exchanges.[1] He would also consider sterling issues on behalf of any borrower, whether within the sterling *bloc* or not, if the proceeds were calculated mainly to produce direct benefit to British industry.

Little use has yet been made of these facilities, mainly no doubt because, in the unstable world economic conditions prevailing in 1934 and 1935, foreign loans offered little attraction to British investors. For this reason, indeed, there is considerable support for the view that a complete abandonment of the embargo would not cause serious strain upon sterling. Its relaxation is, however, useful in making possible some resumption of foreign lending while safeguarding the sterling exchange, providing a means of strengthening the sterling *bloc*, and improving the prospects of British exports. Short-term lending is less restricted, and early in 1936 the Government approved a loan to France of £40 million to be repaid nine months later.

The fall in new capital issues, especially for foreign countries, resulting from the world depression and the embargo is shown by the statistics tabulated on page 73. New lending was well maintained during 1930, but in each of the five following years total issues remained considerably below those in any other year since the war. The year 1931 showed a big drop in the amount and proportion of loans to foreign countries, and in 1932 these loans were almost

---

[1] The first issue arranged under this new policy was a loan of about £1,150,000 to a Norwegian company, which had the effect of strengthening the Norwegian exchange.

NEW CAPITAL ISSUES IN THE UNITED KINGDOM*

Year	Amounts Invested (£000 omitted)				Percentages of Total Issues		
	Home	British Dominions and Colonies	Foreign Countries	Total	Home	British Dominions and Colonies	Foreign Countries
1911–12†	38,000	67,000	95,000	200,000	19·0	33·5	47·5
1919–21†	204,098	53,913	21,171	279,182	73·1	19·3	7·6
1922–26†	106,067	69,202	51,958	227,227	46·7	30·4	22·9
1927	176,043	87,744	50,927	314,714	55·9	27·9	16·2
1928	219,135	86,110	57,274	362,519	60·5	23·7	15·8
1929	159,402	54,412	39,935	253,749	62·8	21·5	15·7
1930	127,356	70,046	38,757	236,160	53·9	29·7	16·4
1931	42,588	36,832	9,246	88,666	48·0	41·6	10·4
1932	83,817	28,873	348	113,038	74·1	25·6	0·3
1933	95,059	29,814	7,996	132,869	71·5	22·5	6·0
1934	106,741	40,391	3,058	150,190	71·1	26·9	2·0
1935	161,934	18,038	2,852	182,824	88·6	9·4	1·6

* Statistics, based upon issue prices, published in the *Midland Bank Annual Review*. British Government borrowings for purely financial purposes, all redemption and bonus issues, and issues by private companies, as well as short-term bills, are excluded. Refunding issues, which were numerous from 1933 to 1935 are, therefore, not included. The amount of new capital issues invested abroad does not indicate the trends of private investment and may be supplemented or counterbalanced by the purchase or sale of investments abroad.

† Annual averages. Pre-war figures approximate.

non-existent.[1] More than half of the £7,996,000 borrowed by foreign countries in 1933 involved no drain upon resources, as nearly £4½ million went to the Austrian Government for funding short-term borrowings from the Bank of England which had been first arranged in the summer of 1931 and subsequently renewed. The remainder consisted mainly of the Danish Government Loan of £1 million already mentioned and a number of small privately arranged borrowings by companies operating in South America. A loan was also permitted to enable a British undertaking to be bought from American interests which had acquired control. In 1934 and 1935, notwithstanding announcement of the policy of permitting certain foreign loans, the Government maintained stringent control over the market, and the total of issues for foreign countries remained small. In making comparisons of amounts issued during the last three or four years with those issued between 1919 and 1929, allowance should be made for the fall in prices which increased the relative real value of issues in recent years.

The policy and practice of British long-term lending since 1931 may be summarised as follows:

(1) Foreign lending was first prohibited, then, since July 1934, restricted (a) to countries within the sterling *bloc* requiring funds to minimise exchange fluctuations, and (b) to countries which will use the proceeds of loans mainly in a manner directly beneficial to British industry.

(2) Borrowers within the British Empire, being free from these restrictions, are treated preferentially. Within the Empire the declared policy is one of equality between Home, Dominion and Colonial borrowers, this differing somewhat from the policy of Britain first, the Empire second, and foreign countries last, which is applied in commercial relations.

It may be noted that loans to Dominion and Colonial

---

[1] From early July to the end of September 1932 during the War Loan Conversion operations the new capital market was closed to all issues, whether Home, Dominion, or Colonial or foreign.

borrowers impose a strain upon the sterling exchanges equal to that caused by a foreign loan of similar amount, unless it be assumed that the foreign borrower would use the proceeds in ways less directly beneficial to British industry. Also, in consequence of restricting foreign loans, capital is available in somewhat larger amounts and at lower rates for borrowers within the Empire. This point is not, however, of any great importance at a time when large supplies of idle funds are seeking suitable fields for investment. Finally, an increase in foreign lending would require willingness of the Government to adopt a commercial policy sufficiently liberal that borrowers could increase their exports to Great Britain for the purpose of making interest payments and ultimately of repaying their loans.

Exchange and Clearing Agreements

Exchange and clearing agreements being often related both to trade and to the meeting of foreign capital obligations by debtor countries might have been reviewed in certain of their aspects in the chapter on Commercial Policy. It is examined here because capital obligations have been prominent in the negotiations and agreements between Great Britain and Germany, and the relations between these countries so far represent the chief British interest in a system which has been extensively applied between Continental European countries during recent years.

The objects of exchange and clearing agreements may be briefly explained. They are to ensure that payments due from the importers of a creditor country to exporters in a debtor country which is failing to meet its trade debts or capital obligations shall be primarily reserved:

(a) for paying traders in the creditor country for goods exported to the debtor country, whether for goods previously exported but not paid for or for goods exported subsequent to the conclusion of the agreement.

(b) for paying interest and other sums due on loans made to the debtor country.

Alternatively, or in addition, exporters to a debtor country may be credited with the currency of that country, and this can be used for the purchase of its goods for export; or each country may use the proceeds of its sales to the other country solely for buying the products of that country.

Some agreements are designed mainly to secure payment of past debts, while others are intended largely to ensure continuance of trade with a country experiencing exchange difficulties and imposing exchange restrictions. Countries which import considerably more from a debtor country than they export to it are in a favourable position for negotiating agreements, being able practically to dictate terms. Agreements are concluded between Governments, that of the creditor country intervening to protect the interests of its traders and investors. The agreements themselves vary considerably in detail, the main distinction being between exchange agreements, which are voluntary, and clearing agreements, under which traders are required to use the clearing accounts. Voluntary agreements are usually preferred by debtor countries, as they involve less control of their affairs. Compulsory agreements suffer from the defects that while they may result in some increase in trade between the two countries concerned, part of this trade is along uneconomic channels, while triangular trade is restricted and higher prices are paid for less suitable goods than when countries can buy in the best market.

The British Government's consideration of clearing arrangements and negotiation of exchange agreements with Germany has resulted from Germany's transfer difficulties. Although these difficulties were relieved by the virtual abandonment of reparations in accordance with the settlement reached at the Lausanne Conference in 1932, they again became acute in 1933 and 1934 owing to the effects upon German trade of the prolonged world depression and of her own internal economic policy. In the summer of 1933, restrictions were placed upon payments of interest to foreign creditors on most of Germany's long-term debts, but full payment was maintained on the Dawes and Young Loans. These Loans, which totalled 2,399 million Reichmarks or about one-quarter of Germany's long-term obligations, were regarded as being in a special category. While other loans to Germany were made by the private investor at his own risk, the Dawes and Young Loans had been issued under the auspices and with the active encouragement of the Governments of the Allied Powers, which were consequently in a position of some responsibility to the investors for preventing default.

When, therefore, a year later, Dr. Schacht, President of the Reichsbank, announced that the Reichsbank intended to suspend from July 1934 until further notice all cash transfers on German medium- and long-term debts abroad, including the Dawes and Young Loans, the British Government made a strong protest,[1] and promptly introduced into Parliament a Bill—the Debts Clearing Offices and Import Restriction Bill—which was rapidly passed, giving the Government power to set up an exchange clearing system for the protection of British financial interests and prevention of discrimination against British creditors.[2] German exports to Britain being largely in excess of her imports from Britain, she was in a weak position in face of a unilateral

---

[1] See Cmd. 4620, giving the texts of Notes dated June 15 and June 20, 1934, exchanged between the German Ambassador in London and Sir John Simon, Secretary of State for Foreign Affairs, on the proposed suspension of transfers. Sir John Simon's Note includes the following passage: "The Dawes Loan was raised at a time when Germany was in a state of economic collapse, and the lenders who subscribed to that Loan were given the most absolute right to payment in all conditions. The Young Loan was accepted as an unconditional obligation by the German Government, and if no special security was asked for, it was because the Young Committee recommended that 'the basis of security' was the solemn undertaking of the German Government to which no further guarantee can add anything whatsoever."

[2] The German Government, in announcing suspension of cash transfers, stated that the equivalent in Reichsmarks of the loan service was placed at the disposal of the creditors.

clearing system[1]; the trade balance excess in Germany's favour was over £14 million, sufficient to cover the interest on all German loans issued in London more than three times and the interest on the Dawes and Young Loans more than ten times. In England the view was strongly held that Germany was not making a fair attempt to meet her obligations. The threat of coercion in obtaining payment by a unilateral clearing scheme was immediately effective, and the German authorities agreed to transfer the interest on these loans for the ensuing six months.[2] In return the British Government agreed not to exercise against Germany during this period its powers under the Debts Clearing Offices and Import Restrictions Act. Dr. Schacht, however, continued to stress Germany's need of a full and prolonged moratorium, and he largely blamed reparation policy and protectionist obstacles to German exports for the exchange difficulties of his country.[3]

The British Government also intervened on behalf of British exporters of cotton and wool yarn and coal to whom several millions of pounds sterling were due for deliveries to German importers, but which the German traders were unable to pay because of their Government's exchange restrictions. The question of future trade between the two countries was involved in the negotiations, as British exporters of cotton and wool yarn decided to suspend export of goods to Germany until arrangements had been made for payment of past commercial debts. British traders resented what they considered to be the German Government's deliberate policy of preventing payment by imposing

[1] This weakness vis-à-vis Britain was qualified by the fact that in her trade with the British Empire as a whole Germany had an excess of imports over exports.

[2] On other long- and medium-term loans Germany agreed to pay in interest-bearing scrip for 100 per cent of the coupon values, or in cash six months in arrears for 40 per cent of the coupon values. Interest payments were continued under Standstill Agreements covering a large sum of German short-term bank debts. On November 1, 1934, the German Government agreed to continue payment of interest on the Dawes and Young Loans as from January 1, 1935.

[3] See, for example, a speech by Dr. Schacht on August 30, 1934.

stringent exchange restrictions; they were satisfied that their German customers were generally ready to meet their foreign obligations to the best of their ability. On the other hand, Dr. Schacht considered that British exporters had only themselves to blame, as they had continued their deliveries while debts were piling up and while foreign exchange allotments to German importers were being progressively reduced.

On August 10, 1934, an exchange agreement between the two Governments to promote future trade provided a method by which British exporters of goods to Germany would receive payment, even though the Reichsbank continued stringent foreign exchange regulations.[1] No provision was made for payment of past trade debts.[2] The scheme was intended to ensure that British exporters to Germany would have the first share of the proceeds of German exports to Britain.

Under the Agreement a German importer of British goods paid reichsmarks into a special account in the Reichsbank to cover such part of his liability as he was unable to meet in sterling. This special account was in favour of the Bank of England which sold the reichsmarks for sterling to British importers of German goods so that they could pay their debts in Germany. The sterling obtained by these operations was then paid to the British exporter. The scheme was to be temporarily suspended whenever the amount of unsold reichsmarks, which were given the name "Sondermarks," exceeded five millions.

The scheme was voluntary, depending for its success upon the extent to which British importers of German goods and German importers of British goods used the account in paying for their purchases. It was expected that, as Great Britain ordinarily imports much more from Germany than she exports to Germany, the demand for

[1] The text of the Agreement was issued as a White Paper (Cmd. 4673).
[2] It was this which led British cotton yarn exporters unanimously to decide on suspension of further business with Germany until they had been paid for previous exports.

sondermarks would be adequate for the working of the scheme, and that new British exports to Germany would be financed without increasing the strain upon the German foreign exchange. This expectation was not realised, the demand for sondermarks was less than the supply, and the scheme was soon suspended owing to an excessive accumulation of unsold sondermarks, British importers not making adequate use of the fund.[1]

New negotiations resulted in an agreement announced on November 1, 1934, to liquidate past commercial debts and to promote future trade; it also terminated the previous "Sondermark" agreement. During the negotiations it seemed probable that the only solution would be to set up a clearing system, but the German Government then put forward an alternative solution which was adopted.[2] Its main features were: (1) Agreement by the German Government to earmark for payment for British exports to Germany 55 per cent of the sterling obtained by the sale of German goods to the United Kingdom. This should be more than adequate if the past relation of British imports from and exports to Germany is maintained; (2) Immediate provision by the Reichsbank of at least £400,000 to discharge existing commercial debts; and an undertaking, which was fully observed, to liquidate any balance of indebtedness within twelve months, if necessary by earmarking a further 10 per cent of the value of German exports to the United Kingdom; (3) No immediate restriction by the German Government upon the issue of foreign exchange certificates necessary to obtain payment for British exports to Germany, but, in the event of the German Government subsequently deeming it necessary temporarily to control their issue, special consideration would be shown to exports of particular

---

[1] One explanation was that British importers of German goods have their purchases invoiced in sterling, and their German creditors prefer payment in sterling.

[2] See Cmd. 4726. A clearing scheme was drafted and approved, and was held in reserve to apply if the alternative arrangement should prove unsuccessful.

importance to the United Kingdom—coal and coke, herrings, yarn, tissues, and textile manufactures. In announcing this new agreement to the House of Commons, Mr. Runciman, President of the Board of Trade, did not take an optimistic view of the experiment, and warned British traders to proceed with caution. It has, at least, the merit of avoiding the more rigid mechanism of a clearing system, and on the whole it has worked well.

The negotiations and agreements with Germany have been reviewed at some length because they represent a technique which is new in British economic foreign relations.[1] Some arrangements along these lines seem inevitable in the circumstances. But though they may be unavoidable in the present conditions of crisis and readjustment of international trade, they should be regarded not as permanent instruments of policy but as temporary transitional arrangements to be abandoned as healthier conditions of trade are restored.

Conclusions

During post-war years Britain has had a smaller amount of capital available for investment abroad, and has experienced greater competition from other financial centres. Even before the depression only about half as much was available for overseas investment as in pre-war days. New capital investment has been increasingly controlled, with restrictions operating chiefly against foreign borrowers, in consequence of which a larger proportion is invested within the Empire. Since 1931, foreign lending has been almost at a standstill and restrictions upon the capital market seem to be based upon a more deliberate policy than before. The objects of Government intervention have been mainly economic rather than political.

The chief changes in policy having been introduced during

[1] In 1935, in view of strain upon the lira, a trade and exchange agreement was reached between the British and Italian Governments. A clearing agreement with Spain came into effect in January 1936.

F

the depression, the question arises whether the new policy is only temporary, due to exceptional crisis conditions. As in other fields, however, the impression is conveyed that permanent changes are being made. Greater control over capital investment is consistent with present trends away from *laissez-faire*. Though no doubt present restrictions will be considerably relaxed as economic conditions become more stable, it seems likely that a conscious governmental regulation of British capital resources will be retained in place of the former freedom. The National Government is unlikely to abandon control. At the World Economic Conference, 1933, Mr. Neville Chamberlain indicated the need for maintaining a greater measure of control, with the objects of avoiding in future the unfortunate experiences of imprudent international lending and borrowing during previous decades, and of restoring confidence to investors. A Labour Government would also be likely to exercise control over new capital resources, there being wide support in the Labour Party for the setting up of an investment board to distribute funds between home, Dominion, Colonial, and foreign investments according to a coordinated plan.

Capital investment policy cannot be applied in isolation from commercial and monetary policies. Restrictions upon imports increase the difficulties of overseas debtors in meeting their obligations, while the volume of capital available for investment abroad is largely determined by the effects of commercial policy upon the relation between imports and exports. Both again are influenced by monetary policy, while variation in the exchange value of sterling increases or decreases the burden of existing debt upon borrowers, and the value of securities to investors.

There is one further question of outstanding interest. Britain has long had a balance of payments which afforded a substantial surplus for investment abroad. To maintain such conditions in perpetuity would scarcely be in the best interests of the country. There are periods when it would be advantageous to use for consumption rather than for reinvestment the income from past loans and even to repatriate some of the capital invested abroad. More investment at home or less national saving and a higher standard of living might be preferable to a high rate of capital export. Britain, which was first in the field in the industrial revolution and whose houses and industrial towns were built before the development of modern ideas of planning, needs the application of an extensive programme of industrial and social reconstruction, and, for a period, the advantages of capital developments at home may outweigh those of investment abroad. A complete reversal of former policy is unlikely, and attractive developments abroad, especially if they would be likely to create a demand for British manufactures, will continue to be financed from the British capital market. But British investment abroad is not likely to resume its earlier high rate. This will involve some adaption of economic and commercial relations and the application of a trade policy which will permit of a surplus of imports appropriate for a higher rate of use at home of the fruits of former investment abroad.

CHAPTER IV

COMMERCIAL POLICY

Three aspects of British commercial policy may conveniently be given separate treatment, although they are intimately inter-related. The present chapter deals with those features of policy which determine direct commercial relations with foreign countries. It outlines pre-war tariff policy and reviews post-war changes, including the general abandonment of free trade in 1931–2.[1] The principles applied in recent bilateral agreements and present attitudes towards the most-favoured-nation principle are examined. The two following chapters deal successively with Britain's policy of Imperial commercial preferences and with British Agricultural Policy, attention being directed to those aspects which affect foreign countries.

PRE-WAR POLICY

The outstanding characteristics of British commercial policy before the war were freedom of British markets to the trade of the world, and the securing of unconditional most-favoured-nation treatment from foreign countries for British products. The year 1860 saw the crowning of the edifice of economic liberalism of which Huskisson, Peel, Gladstone and Cobden had been the architects and builders. The corner-stone was the Cobden Treaty with France. From then onwards until the war, customs duties on goods imported into Britain were solely for revenue purposes, and were imposed upon a few commodities produced only abroad, or if produced within the country a corresponding

---

[1] A valuable review of pre-war and post-war policy up to the year 1932 is given in *An Historical Survey of British Commercial Policy*, a Memorandum prepared by the British Coordinating Committee for the International Studies Conference, London, 1933, organised by the International Institute of Intellectual Cooperation.

excise duty was collected so that, except for transportation costs, the foreign producer was in a position of equality with his British competitors in the British market.[1] Preferential treatment for the products of British Colonies was abandoned, while the British Government for a time insisted, against the wishes of the Colonies, on opening the doors throughout the Empire equally to the trade of all the world.[2] Thus, the policy applied was consistent, logical and doctrinaire, this being perhaps unique in the recent history of British political practice.[3]

Although British free traders supported the application of their doctrine by Great Britain alone, whatever other countries might do, it was widely believed at the time that British leadership in adopting free trade would be followed by other countries and that economic internationalism would rapidly be established on a world scale. The belief that a free-trade era was dawning seemed in process of realisation during the decade following 1860, when substantial tariff reductions were secured by agreements negotiated between most European countries. Unconditional most-favoured-nation treatment was extensively adopted, and Great Britain shared in the benefits of increased liberty of trading. Even when the Tories were returned to power in 1874 they gave little attention to tariff reform, which, in Mr. Disraeli's opinion, was "not only dead but damned."

Free-trade aspirations were, however, to meet with disappointment. Even in 1860, while Great Britain, by the application of the unconditional most-favoured-nation prin-

---

[1] With the passing of Gladstone's Budget in 1861 import duties were levied only on tobacco, alcoholic drinks, sugar, flour, gold and silver plate, playing cards, and dice.

[2] These questions of Imperial Preference and the Open Door Policy are discussed in detail in Chapter v.

[3] There were only two or three minor deviations from free-trade principles before the war. The Russian Government's complaint that the Tariff Amendment Act, 1899, was in violation of the most-favoured-nation agreement by imposing countervailing duties against exports of Russian bounty-fed sugar to India was rejected on the ground that the duties merely restored equality by withdrawing the competitive advantages which the bounty gave to exports of Russian sugar.

ciple, extended to other countries the concessions she had granted to France by the Cobden Treaty, the French Government required reciprocal advantages from other countries if they were to enjoy the concessions accorded to Great Britain. The Franco-Prussian War of 1870 was a shock to confidence in Europe, and shortly afterwards a reaction against commercial liberalism rapidly developed on the Continent—a movement closely resembling the economic nationalism which has swept over all countries since the World War. Within a few years almost all Continental countries denounced their commercial agreements with Great Britain, and the new agreements were considerably less liberal, although Great Britain succeeded in including the unconditional most-favoured-nation clause. During the years immediately preceding the World War, Britain was a party to no less than eighty treaties and agreements which included the unconditional clause. A method of actual though not legal evasion of this clause was, however, evolved by including in reciprocal agreements between two countries detailed specifications of commodities ingeniously worded so that many concessions which were apparently of general application were in fact particular and exclusive, being of little value to other countries.[1] This practice, which was increasingly applied, involved real discrimination against Britain, which had nothing to offer, and favoured countries active in securing concessions by reciprocal agreements.[2] On balance, however, the clause was of considerable value to British trade.

At the time of the reaction on the Continent, tariff supporters in Great Britain began to revive after their almost annihilating defeat, but their recovery was slow

---

[1] A frequently quoted example of extreme specialisation is found in the German Tariff Act, 1903, which, with the intention of favouring export from Switzerland while withholding the favour from most other countries, provided a lower tariff on "large dappled mountain cattle or brown cattle reared at a spot at least 300 metres above sea level and which have at least one month's grazing each year at a spot at least 800 metres above sea level."

[2] Britain's only tariffs being for revenue, any concession she could have made would have upset her budgetary dispositions.

until Mr. Joseph Chamberlain gave them a stimulating lead, particularly by launching his tariff reform campaign in 1903. He laid special emphasis upon Imperial Preference, largely for its use in the political and economic consolidation of the Empire. The value was increasingly recognised of the complementary exchange of British manufactures for the food and raw materials produced by other parts of the Empire. With the growth of population in hitherto sparsely settled areas and with rapid development of transport facilities, Colonial markets attracted greater attention. The moment was, therefore, not unsuitable for raising the tariff issue, especially as British commercial supremacy was being increasingly challenged by the industrialisation of other countries, and her trade hampered by protectionist policy abroad. Nevertheless, the tariff proposals were decisively rejected at the polls both in 1906 and 1910, largely because of opposition to food taxes which were included in the programme, and up to the outbreak of the World War free trade seemed to be as firmly established in Britain as it had been at any time during the previous fifty years.

FROM 1914 TO THE GREAT DEPRESSION

Tariff policy during this period was marked by minor breaches in the walls of the free trade citadel, but, with a few significant exceptions, the main features of pre-war policy were retained, and the vast majority of goods continued to enter Britain free of duty. The first breach was made in 1915 when, with the objects of strengthening the sterling exchanges, relieving shipping, and securing revenue, the McKenna Duties of 33⅓ per cent *ad valorem* were imposed on certain so-called luxuries.[1] Though introduced as a war-time measure the duties were continued after the war. They were subject to the criticism that, being levied

[1] The commodities selected were private motor-cars, clocks, watches, cinematograph films, and musical instruments.

upon luxuries with the object of yielding revenue, they should logically have been accompanied by excise duties upon home production, but this step was not taken. The duties were, therefore, protective, and especially the "infant" motor-car industry, which had been far outstripped by that of the United States, made a rapid advance behind the shelter afforded, although it would have developed, no doubt more slowly, without protection.[1]

Immediately after the war the principle of Imperial Preference was applied by granting a rebate of one-sixth of existing revenue duties on imports into Great Britain of goods produced in Empire countries. In 1920 the dyestuffs industry, which had been developed with the aid of a subsidy during the previous five years, was given protection when war-time restrictions were removed, by the Dyestuffs (Import Regulation) Act, 1920, prohibiting imports except under licence, and a large dyestuffs industry has been established. The chief departure from free trade at this time was, however, the passing of the Safeguarding of Industries Act, 1921, which was openly protectionist. Under this Act, duties usually $33\frac{1}{3}$ per cent *ad valorem* were imposed in the first instance for five years for the protection of certain "key" industries considered essential for national defence and industrial security.[2] A system was also established by which any British industry could apply for the imposition of a safeguarding import duty not exceeding $33\frac{1}{3}$ per cent, and anti-dumping provisions were also included, covering exchange dumping as well as ordinary dumping.

By a procedure introduced in 1925 a safeguarding duty

---

[1] The advance was facilitated by the system of taxation upon owners of cars, the rates being considerably less on cars with low than on those with high horse-power. This favoured the British maker, as American companies mainly produced high-powered cars, which are more suitable for American conditions.

[2] Key industry duties were imposed upon scientific instruments and glassware, optical glass, certain chemicals, wireless valves, gauges, magnets, tungsten, ignition magnetos, hosiery latch needles (essential for the hosiery industry), etc.

would only be accorded if the applicant industry could satisfy a committee of enquiry appointed by the Board of Trade that:

(1) the applicant industry was of substantial importance;

(2) abnormal quantities of the class of goods produced were being imported;

(3) the prices of the imported goods were lower than those at which similar goods could be profitably manufactured at home;

(4) competition of the imports was causing or was likely to cause serious unemployment in the British industry;

(5) the exceptional competition was due to subsidies, bounties, or other artificial advantages, including currency depreciation, or to inferior labour conditions (wages, hours, etc.);

(6) the applicant industry is being carried on with reasonable efficiency and economy;

(7) the imposition of a duty would not cause serious unemployment in industries using the goods in production.[1]

Thus, protection was to be reserved for certain reasonably efficient industries in special need because of unfair foreign competition and most likely to benefit from restriction of imports, while the amount of protection was to be adapted to the circumstances of each industry. Parliamentary approval was necessary before a duty could be imposed. Empire products were exempt from the "key" industry duties, and enjoyed preferences on the safeguarding duties.

Evidently, few industries would find it easy to run the gauntlet of the above conditions, and in the application of the system certain of the conditions were not strictly enforced, duties being granted, for example, to safeguard industries of minor importance. The free traders, strongly represented in the House of Commons, were ever watchful, and, in practice, few industries were accorded safeguarding

---

[1] See *Safeguarding of Industries—Procedure and Enquiries*, Cmd. 2327, London, 1925.

duties.[1] Only about one out of every two hundred British workers was employed in safeguarded industries, while the goods liable to safeguarding and other protective duties, chiefly the McKenna duties, only amounted to 2 or 3 per cent of British imports.[2] In 1930 only 17 per cent of total imports (value) from all foreign countries paid any duty, including revenue tariffs. Therefore, although the new duties represented important changes of principle, they were, in practice, applied to a comparatively small range of commodities and industries. The stream of free trade, though no longer pure, was only slightly contaminated. This situation continued until the time of the world depression, the McKenna duties, safeguarding duties, and some of the revenue duties remaining the chief departures from freedom of trade. Thus the "revenue" duties levied upon artificial silk, petrol, and sugar afforded some protection to home industries.[3]

The extent of application of the various duties fluctuated with political changes. At the Imperial Economic Conference, 1923, the Conservative Party announced its support of a much more extensive policy of protection and Imperial Preference, but at the General Election of that year, which was fought on this issue, the electorate gave an unfavourable vote. In consequence of this defeat, a Labour Government came into power, which in 1924 repealed the McKenna duties, reduced the revenue duties on tea, coffee, cocoa, and sugar, and allowed certain safeguarding duties to lapse. The practice of granting a rebate of one-sixth on Empire

---

[1] Safeguarding duties were early imposed upon fabric gloves, glove fabric, domestic glassware, and incandescent gas mantles; after 1925, leather gloves, lace and embroidery, cutlery, translucent tableware, pottery, packing and wrapping paper, buttons, and wrought enamelled hollow-ware were added.

[2] *Statement submitted by the British Members to the International Economic Conference*, Geneva, 1927 (League of Nations document, C.E.I.29, 1st Series, p. 25).

[3] Customs and excise duties were imposed upon silk and artificial silk by the Finance Act, 1925, but certain advantages were conferred upon home producers; home refiners of sugar were somewhat favoured after 1928, and home-produced oil from shale or coal was free from duty.

products was retained, but the value of Imperial preferences was automatically diminished by the abandonment of some duties and the reduction of others. The Labour Government, however, resigned before the end of the year and the new Conservative Government quickly restored the McKenna duties. Amongst the reasons given for their restoration was protection of sterling after the return to the gold standard. The view was held that restriction of imports, especially of motor-cars and other so-called luxury goods from the United States, would reduce the demand for dollars and other foreign currencies, and consequently strengthen the sterling exchanges.

During the next few years the Government extended safeguarding duties to several more commodities. Also, in 1926, the operation of the key industry duties was prolonged for ten years. The Government did not, however, consider that it had a mandate from the electorate to introduce a general system of protection, and it avoided making any major changes. Thus proposals to apply the safeguarding system to certain big industries, particularly iron and steel and wool, were rejected, although the McKenna duties were applied in 1926 to commercial motor vehicles, and in 1927 to rubber tyres and tubes.

The 1929 General Election brought a Labour Government again into office, and during the next two years several safeguarding duties were allowed to lapse when the five-year period for which they had been originally imposed came to an end. Apart from this and one other minor measure,[1] the Government made no changes in the existing system. It did, however, make a big effort, under the leadership of the late Mr. William Graham, to secure greater liberty of trading by international agreement, but even the attempt in 1930 to secure a tariff truce had to be abandoned owing to lack of support. This failure did much to convince

[1] This was the repeal of the anti-dumping provisions of the Safeguarding of Industries Act. The McKenna duties, which the first Labour Administration had repealed, were retained for the revenue produced.

British opinion that, in the then existing political and economic conditions of the world, little could be hoped from multilateral action.

By this time the British Government was preoccupied with the consequences of the world economic crisis. Throughout the post-war period many British industries had been almost continuously depressed, and doubts had grown about the wisdom of Britain's traditional commercial policy. Yet, until the world depression few changes were made. This depression, however, greatly increased the numbers favourable to a change in policy and willing for the Government to venture upon a large-scale experiment in protection and Imperial Preference.

THE NEW COMMERCIAL POLICY

In the crisis of 1931 the National Government, which had succeeded the Labour Administration, appealed to the country for "a doctor's mandate" and was returned to power with an overwhelming majority in which Conservatives preponderated. The doctor's mandate was interpreted as empowering the Government to make substantial changes in commercial policy, and the Conservative section urged the immediate introduction of a comprehensive tariff system. Somewhat reluctantly the National Liberals and National Labour members acquiesced, many of them hoping that free trade would be abandoned only during the emergency and that the traditional policy would be resumed when the crisis was over. They agreed that the temporary imposition of customs duties would readjust the balance of trade, which the world depression had disturbed, by stemming the flood of imports, thus bringing them into a better relation with exports, and that the funds obtained would be a valuable addition to the national revenue at a time when the budget was unbalanced. They recognised that under the existing conditions of world depression, British industry was being disorganised by the dumping of foreign manufactures at abnormally low prices in the world's one great free trade market. Some of them also considered that the customs duties would redistribute the burden of taxation and, in so far as they were paid by the workers, would somewhat reduce real wages, thus lowering labour costs which were thought to be too high owing to recent alleged rigidity of money wages.

The Conservatives demanded tariffs for these reasons, but they also favoured permanence for the new policy, to protect British industry, to provide a basis for Imperial Preference, and to enable the Government to negotiate reciprocal agreements with foreign countries. They considered that Britain was too dependent upon foreign countries, that her industry and trade were unduly vulnerable, and that a readjustment of her economic structure to reduce these dangers was desirable.

Permanent changes were, in fact, made, although this did not become evident during the early months of the National Government's Administration. The first step taken was the passing of the Abnormal Importations (Customs Duties) Act, November 1931, by which power was given to the President of the Board of Trade to impose duties, where desirable in order to check an abnormal stream of imports, up to a maximum of 100 per cent on a large range of imports of wholly or mainly manufactured goods. A long list of these articles was covered by orders issued by the Board of Trade, the rates of duty all being at a flat *ad valorem* rate of 50 per cent, and remaining in operation until May 19, 1932, unless cancelled earlier. The Act was temporary, being passed for a period of six months, and this interval was used as a breathing space for the preparation of more considered and systematic measures.[1]

In February 1932 the temporary Act of the previous year was replaced by the Import Duties Act which, in the

[1] The Act was supplemented by another temporary measure, the Horticultural Products (Emergency Duties) Act, 1931, which imposed import duties upon fruit, flowers, and vegetables from foreign countries.

sequence of departure from free trade, was the next main step following the safeguarding of industries in 1921, and which is the foundation of the system now in force. The 1932 Act gave protection to home industries, and provided a basis for preferences within the Empire and for reciprocal agreements with or retaliation against foreign countries. A 10 per cent *ad valorem* basic tariff, stated by the Government to be mainly for revenue purposes, was imposed upon imports, from which, however, certain goods were exempted, chiefly certain foods and raw materials.[1] Existing duties under previous Acts were retained, except those under the emergency legislation of 1931.

The Act provided for the imposition, by Treasury Order on the recommendation of an 'Import Duties Advisory Committee, of higher duties than 10 per cent upon luxury goods and upon articles produced or likely to be produced within a reasonable time in Great Britain in substantial quantities in relation to British consumption.[2] In fixing these higher duties, consideration must be given to the advisability in the national interest of restricting imports into Britain and to the interests generally of British trade and industry. The taxation of luxury goods was consistent with the need for economy at the time of crisis. Higher tariffs on the second class of commodity provide for the protection and fostering of home production, on the ground that there are many articles imported from abroad which British manufacturers can produce at reasonable cost. With little or no lowering of her standard of living Britain could, it was believed, become less dependent upon foreign supplies, while the free trade argument that to restrict imports would most probably reduce foreign demand for British products had less force than usual at a time when

---

[1] For example, cotton, wool, flax and hemp, hides and skins, wooden pit props, rubber, wood pulp, paper for newsprint, iron ore, scrap iron and steel, shipbuilding materials, and sulphur. The chief exempted foods were wheat in grain, meat, and animals.

[2] Provision has been made for duties lower than 10 per cent in exceptional cases, but this power has been little used.

this demand had shrunk to an exceptionally low level. The conditions for the imposition of the higher duties were much less exacting than those of the Safeguarding of Industries Act, and the door was thrown open to a considerable expansion of protection beyond the 10 per cent basis.

The Act also empowers the Treasury on the recommendation of the Board of Trade to admit the goods of specified foreign countries duty free or at duties less than the full rate. In practice this power is limited by an obligation to maintain certain preferences for imports of Empire products. Subject to this limitation, however, the Government is enabled to bargain with foreign countries, and it soon concluded a series of bilateral agreements based upon reciprocal concessions. As is indicated later in this chapter, these agreements, together with the Ottawa system of Imperial Preference, weaken the case for maintaining the unconditional most-favoured-nation clause. The granting of concessions in bilateral agreements is disliked by various business interests, who complain that, having undertaken capital developments likely to be profitable if protected by tariffs imposed in accordance with recommendations of the Import Duties Advisory Committee, they are seriously injured when lower rates are conceded to foreign competitors.

In addition, the Government has power of retaliation, being authorised to raise tariffs up to 100 per cent above existing rates upon goods imported from any foreign country which discriminates against the products of the British Empire or of British Mandated Territories or Protectorates. Thus, the Act furnished the Government with the whole armoury of weapons for offence and defence, as well as with power to make concessions. In principle, the tariff schedules consist mainly of three levels: the rates fixed for foreign countries by the 1932 Act or on the Advisory Board's recommendations, lower rates resulting from reciprocal agreements, and still lower rates or even free entry for imports of Empire products. The lower rates fixed in reciprocal agreements apply to all foreign countries by the application of the unconditional most-favoured-nation clause; thus direct discrimination against foreign countries is avoided and in practice only two rates are in operation, the Empire rates and those for foreign countries, although the way is open for discrimination if the unconditional clause is abandoned. Higher retaliatory rates are kept in reserve, and it seems likely that they will be only rarely applied.

The Import Duties Advisory Committee has made a number of recommendations, the most interesting and comprehensive being its first series issued on April 21, 1932.[1] It decided in the first instance to fix uniform rates of duty upon fully manufactured articles, with lower rates in special circumstances, and higher rates on luxury or semi-luxury articles. Such a procedure was inevitable owing to the need for rapid decision, but the Committee intended subsequently, on the basis of detailed investigations, to raise or lower the initial rates of duty on individual commodities where necessary in the interests of British industry and trade.

The Committee considered the 50 per cent rate of duty imposed under the emergency measures of 1931 to be dictated by abnormal conditions, while even the $33\frac{1}{3}$ per cent duties imposed on certain commodities under earlier Acts were thought to be too high for application to a wide range of products in many industries because of the greater effect upon the cost of living and of adverse reactions upon other industries. The rate of $33\frac{1}{3}$ per cent had also been mainly applied to key industries or to those suffering from exceptional foreign competition. The Committee therefore decided upon an additional duty of 10 per cent *ad valorem*, making a total of 20 per cent as its basis for fully manufactured articles. Higher total rates of 25 or 30 per cent were fixed for luxury and semi-luxury goods, $33\frac{1}{3}$ per cent for bicycles and bicycle parts and certain chemicals, while for a few articles used as raw materials the total rate was 15 per cent. Duties were imposed on only a few articles

[1] Cmd. 4066. This document includes a useful summary of the duties in force before the passing of the Import Duties Act, 1932.

of food, pending the results of the Ottawa Conference. While declaring its intention to modify any rates which did not operate satisfactorily the Committee emphasised the need for stability in the rates and stated that it would not recommend any reduction in the general level of protection for at least twelve months, and in fact no general change has been made.

Special attention was given to the iron and steel industry. The Committee were agreed that a prosperous and highly efficient iron and steel industry is essential to British economic progress and national security, and that industries using iron and steel would suffer in the long run if, by insisting on easy access to foreign supplies at very low prices, the native iron and steel industry were overwhelmed, or even seriously contracted. Total duties of $33\frac{1}{3}$ per cent were therefore fixed for a number of iron and steel products. Subsequently, duties on some iron and steel products were fixed temporarily at 20 per cent and on others at $33\frac{1}{3}$ per cent, these being granted on condition that a scheme of reorganisation would be prepared which would establish the industry upon efficient lines, but after an interval the duties were accorded without a time limit, on an undertaking by the industry that it would consider measures of reorganisation.

Some steps have been taken to improve the organisation of industry, but complaints are made by users of steel, particularly motor manufacturers, that the iron and steel firms are more interested in high prices under protection than in reducing costs by more efficient production. Home production of iron and steel rose by 70 per cent and imports fell by 50 per cent between 1931 and 1934, largely as a result of the tariffs, together with sterling depreciation and trade improvement. In 1935 the prosperity of the industry further increased and for the first time British iron and steel manufacturers joined the European Steel Cartel. Before this step was taken the representatives of the industry experienced difficulty in securing satisfactory quotas, and the

British Government somewhat reluctantly came to the assistance of the British manufacturers by raising the tariff on imports to 50 per cent. Very satisfactory terms were then immediately granted by the Continental interests, and the additional tariff having served its purpose in the process of bargaining was suspended at the request of the British Iron and Steel Federation. A temporary arrangement was soon converted into an agreement for five years. Important features of this agreement with the Cartel are a low quota of iron and steel products for import into Britain from the European countries, the stabilisation of British exports to "neutral" markets at the 1934 proportion, and the reduction of British import duties on the products covered to a level not exceeding 20 per cent *ad valorem.*

From time to time changes in rates of duty on various commodities have been made on the Committee's recommendation. Any applicant is given opportunity to state his reasons for the revision of a rate, and other interested parties are invited to express their views. During the first three years of the Committee's work more than 300 formal applications were considered, and about 100 Orders were issued by the Treasury on the Committee's recommendations, imposing duties additional to the minima fixed in the Act. On a number of commodities the original *ad valorem* duties have been changed into specific rates, this being facilitated by price stability. Duties have been raised on certain commodities imported in increased quantities at prices against which British manufacturers were finding it difficult to compete, and where British productive capacity was not being fully used. Reductions have been made on commodities which cannot be made economically in Great Britain, while some commodities, little produced in Great Britain but useful to a British industry usually as raw materials, have been added to the free list. For machinery a special system of licences has been introduced by which considerable quantities are imported free of duty, usually of goods not manufactured in Great Britain. There has been surprisingly little criticism of the Committee's work either in Parliament or by business organisations, and it can undoubtedly be considered to have performed its functions successfully.

In the summer of 1932 a further important step was taken in the development of the new tariff system by the establishment of a wide range of Imperial Preferences in the Ottawa Agreements. These Agreements are discussed in Chapter v. Here, however, it may be noted that the Ottawa Agreements, by providing that the preferences would remain in force for five years, gave an appearance of permanence to the new policy. Consequently, a number of Liberals who had acquiesced in the introduction of tariffs to meet an emergency now refused to support the Government; Sir Herbert Samuel and other Liberals, together with Lord Snowden (National Labour), resigned their offices, and with their followers joined the Opposition. As the Government still had an overwhelming majority this caused little embarrassment and no interruption in its policy.

The year 1932 also saw the initiation of a new agricultural policy, which is discussed in Chapter vi. Its chief interest in the present chapter is that it was based upon the quota system of quantitative regulation of imports, this being considered at that time a better method than tariffs for giving a stable demand to home producers especially in a period of currency depreciation abroad and of world agricultural crisis in which prices had collapsed to almost panic levels. The adoption of this system is yet another indication of the extent to which free trade principles had been abandoned.

Although the British Government was applying the method of bilateral agreements in its relations with foreign countries, the World Economic Conference, 1933, offered some hope of tariff reduction by multilateral agreement. Actually, the political, economic, and monetary conditions necessary for a constructive international effort leading to removal of trade restrictions were absent. The Government of the United States was absorbed in its "New Deal," concentrating upon the domestic situation to the almost complete exclusion of international economic relations. Great Britain was also involved in a New Deal which attracted much less attention than the American experiment but which represented an almost equally fundamental change from her traditional policy. France determined to cling to the gold standard, and, as this was not acceptable to the United States, no monetary agreement was possible, and there was the further consequence that, in the absence of monetary stability, agreements about tariff levels could be of little value. In these circumstances the results of the Conference were inevitably meagre.

The Conference is, however, of interest in the present discussion because of the statements on commercial foreign policy made by the British Government's representatives. Their review of the purposes for which tariffs may be imposed was brief but comprehensive, including the yielding of revenue, maintenance of a country's standard of living, and the encouragement of forms of industry and production regarded as essential to the economic life of a country. Thus the door is widely opened for protection. The British spokesmen, however, favoured a reduction of excessive tariffs, and claimed that there is no justification for prohibitive tariffs to maintain industries which cannot be conducted economically and efficiently. Along the lines of the Ottawa Agreements they were of the opinion that, with certain exceptions, the protective element in any tariff should not exceed what is necessary to place efficient domestic producers in a position to compete with producers abroad. On the subject of import quotas a subtle distinction was drawn between quotas arbitrarily imposed as additional protection, and quotas established by international agreements to regulate production and marketing. These were stated to be the chief principles which the British Government was applying, and it regarded them as providing a suitable basis for international agreement. It considered its own tariffs to be neither excessive nor prohibitive and its quotas to be justified by their purpose of regulating production and marketing and to be free from the charge of arbitrary imposition. Other countries no doubt viewed their own systems with similar complacency.

There still remains for review the exercise by the British Government of its power to conclude trade agreements, based upon reciprocity with foreign Governments, and the use which it has made of the weapon of retaliation. The most-favoured-nation principle also claims consideration in the light of recent changes in commercial policy. These questions are discussed in the two following sections.

RECIPROCITY AND RETALIATION

The British Government immediately used its powers of tariff negotiation and has concluded a large number of bilateral commercial agreements incorporating reciprocal concessions.[1] Retaliatory or restrictive measures have been taken to combat French discriminations injuriously affecting British trade, and to counteract excessive Japanese competition alleged to be unfair to British trade particularly in colonial markets. In some of the negotiations, political as well as economic considerations have been involved. Thus, discussions with the object of reaching a trade agreement with Egypt took place during 1935 on the invitation of the British Government, which was inspired by the belief that a closer and more permanent association of the economic interests of the two countries would be the best foundation for happy political relations.

The principles and methods applied in the agreements vary according to the trading conditions prevailing between Great Britain and the country concerned. Where a foreign country's trade balance with Great Britain is favourable the British Government enjoys a bargaining advantage.

[1] During the first three years after the passing of the Import Duties Act, 1932, seventeen agreements were reached. During 1935 negotiations were undertaken or agreements reached with Italy, Egypt, and Spain, the total number of agreements at the end of the year being nineteen.

In these circumstances the agreements are directed towards securing greater equality of trade, the country increasing its importation of British goods, or being faced with a reduction of its exports to Great Britain. The principle applied is "Buy from those who buy from you," which represents a departure from the more natural triangular trade.[1] Its application, however, involves displacing the former foreign suppliers who then seek other markets, thus intensifying competition elsewhere. For example, the complaint has been made that agreements increasing the export of British coal to Scandinavian markets have benefited Northumberland and Durham at the expense of South Wales, which has encountered greater competition from Polish coal in Italy and France when Polish exports to Scandinavian countries were restricted by the agreements and were forced to seek fresh markets. Another principle said to have been applied is that of ensuring remunerative prices to efficient British producers by giving them first claim to the British market and adjusting imports to meet such market demand as British firms are unable to satisfy. As, however, the quantity demanded is continually changing, this principle could only be applied effectively by changing the import quota frequently or by making frequent changes in the tariff—a method which is unsatisfactory because of the uncertainty involved.

The terms of some agreements have been arranged on the British side to increase the trade and employment of severely depressed industries, especially coal, iron and steel, and textiles. With some countries an important purpose of the agreements has been to ensure that the sums received by the foreign country for her exports to Britain shall be largely earmarked to meet her trade and capital debts due to Britain. These agreements have, therefore, served in part as a debt-collecting device. Several agreements introduce

---

[1] Data compiled by the League of Nations show a general tendency during recent years for the importance of triangular trade to diminish relatively to bilateral trade.

the quota system or other quantitative regulations, this giving greater stability to markets and to the producers and being considered superior in some circumstances to tariffs, e.g. where there is risk that currency depreciation may diminish the protection accorded by the tariff. The quota system has been regarded as a means of planning trade. In all the negotiations the policy has been "Britain first, the Empire second, foreign countries last."

In securing advantages for British traders in foreign markets various concessions, chiefly reductions of tariffs, have been necessary. These and the reciprocal concessions of foreign countries have increased liberty of trade not merely between the two countries but over a much wider field by the operation of unconditional most-favoured-nation agreements. The granting of concessions has, however, been criticised by British industrial interests.[1] They complain that, by the operation of the most-favoured-nation clause, countries secure commercial advantages without making equivalent concessions; some of the agreements, however, mainly cover commodities in which the contracting parties each have a preponderating share of the other's markets, thus avoiding this difficulty. As already indicated, the criticism has been made that the confidence of British industrialists and their ability to adopt a policy of capital construction are diminished by uncertainty about the amount of protection they will enjoy. Tariff concessions made without consulting representatives of the British industries affected have called forth strong protests on the ground that without such consultations the Government is not in possession of the information necessary to form a judgment upon the balance of advantage.

The granting of any concessions to countries which have a favourable balance of trade with Great Britain is considered unnecessary; but in adopting this attitude the interests of British capital invested abroad tends to be overlooked, while Britain's weakness in bargaining with countries to which

---

[1] For example, by the Federation of British Industries.

she is on balance a debtor is not mentioned. Industrialists have claimed that the tariffs originally fixed on the basis of the Import Duties Advisory Committee recommendations were intended to give the minimum of necessary protection and that there should be no reductions below this level. Strong objections were raised against tariff concessions to Germany and on iron and steel duties in the Swedish agreement. Also concessions have been criticised as barring the way to further Imperial Preference. The Government's attitude, however, is that the findings of the Advisory Committee are subsidiary to matters of policy and that it is not possible altogether to take tariffs out of politics.

The first agreements were concluded in the spring of 1933 just before the opening of the World Economic Conference, the countries concerned being Norway, Sweden, Denmark, Germany, and Argentina. Of these countries Denmark had the most favourable balance of trade with Great Britain, for at no time during the last twenty years had she bought as much from Great Britain as she sold to her, while during several years before the agreement was concluded Great Britain had imported four or five times as much from Denmark as she had exported to that country. Already in 1931 the British Government had called the attention of the Danish Government and trade organisations to this disparity, and in consequence of these representations a "Buy British" campaign was initiated in Denmark and an Exhibition of British goods held in Copenhagen.

By the terms of the agreement Denmark undertook to increase the proportion of British coal to 80 per cent of her coal imports, and wherever possible in Government contracts to give a preference of 10 per cent to British iron and steel firms.[1] Danish tariffs on textile manufactures were reduced and other concessions made. The British Government made certain tariff concessions, but the general effect of British policy has been to impose restrictions upon

---

[1] An order was placed with a British firm for the construction of the Storstrom Bridge.

Danish trade, the dairy and pig product interests particularly being affected by the protection granted to the British farmer and the preferences accorded to Dominion producers.

The agreements with Norway and Sweden are on similar lines to that with Denmark; and here it may be noted that these countries together purchase considerably more from Great Britain than either France, or Germany, or the United States. The agreements are designed mainly to benefit the coal industry, and indirectly shipping. Norway undertook to purchase 70 per cent of her coal imports from Great Britain, while Sweden undertook to purchase 47 per cent. They agreed to reduce the duties on wool and cotton textiles and various other goods and to extend their free list. Norway, which was in a strong bargaining position as her visible trade with Great Britain was closely balanced, was able to secure important concessions for her fishing industry; Britain agreed to import not less than specified amounts of white fish and fresh herrings, the amounts being only about 10 per cent below average imports during the previous ten years.[1] Britain agreed to keep various timber products on the free list (e.g. wooden pit props and wood pulp) and to reduce the duties on wrapping paper and certain chemicals. Sweden also secured reduction of British duties on certain kinds of steel in which she was specially interested. Britain agreed not to control the quantity of imports of Swedish bacon, hams, butter, and eggs except so far as necessary in regulating the marketing of domestic production, and in these circumstances to allocate to Sweden an equitable quota of foreign imports on conditions not less favourable than those granted to other foreign countries.[2]

The German agreement is more restricted in scope than those with the Scandinavian countries, but, like them, its

---

[1] The amount specified was 240,000 cwt. of white fish and 500,000 fresh herrings annually.

[2] In any year British imports of butter were to be not less than 185,000 cwt., and if British imports totalled more than 8,100,000 cwt., Sweden was to be allotted a share in the excess.

main purpose on the British side is to benefit the coal industry. In return for a number of tariff concessions on goods in which she is specially interested Germany agreed to give licences for the importation of not less than 180,000 tons of British coal a month, exclusive of bunker and free port coal, and to increase the British quota in proportion to increased coal consumption in Germany.[1]

The agreements with Argentina, concluded in May and September 1933, are of interest in dealing with exchange difficulties as well as trade restrictions, the exchange question being of special importance both for meeting trade debts and also because of the large sums of British capital, amounting to well over £500 million, invested in Argentina. Under the terms of the first agreement the Argentine Government undertook that the full amount of the sterling exchange arising from the sale of Argentine products in Great Britain, after deduction of a reasonable sum annually towards the Argentine Public External Debts payable in other countries, would be available to meet the current requirements of Great Britain. In no event was Britain to be treated less favourably than any other country in regard to remittances of currency. Thus Britain is using her power as a large-scale purchaser of Argentine products to ensure payment of trade and capital debts due to her from Argentina. Indeed the agreement has been described merely as an instrument for debt collection.

The second agreement deals with reduction of trade barriers. The Argentine Government agreed to continue to admit coal and coke free of duty, to make substantial reductions in the duties upon textiles, and to make reductions, though on a smaller scale, upon machinery and vehicles,

---

[1] It was estimated that the higher quota of 180,000 tons would give employment to 3,800 miners and that many others would be employed in the work of transport; on the other hand, Britain's tariff concessions would result in unemployment for not more than 1,800 workpeople in the industries affected. The agreement has been criticised on the ground that the concessions to British coal could have been secured under the terms of the Anglo-German Trade Agreement of 1924, without reducing British duties.

pottery, chemicals, food and beverages, sports requisites, and other commodities. Argentina, being very largely dependent upon the British market for her exports of agricultural products, especially chilled and frozen beef, was greatly concerned about Britain's policy of fostering home production and granting Imperial Preferences. The Argentine Government, therefore, endeavoured to secure some guarantees for the continuation of her export trade. With this object, the agreement provides that the British Government will not impose restrictions upon imports of chilled beef from Argentina below the quantities imported during the year ended June 1932 (as arranged at Ottawa), unless, and then only in so far as, it appears to the British Government to be necessary in order to secure a remunerative level of prices in the British market. Such restrictions shall not be maintained if it appears that meat from Argentina is being replaced by increased imports of meat from other countries, thus neutralising the desired effect on prices. If a reduction of more than 10 per cent is proposed, the change will be made only after consultation with all the chief meat-exporting countries, including those in the British Commonwealth, and in effecting such reduction Argentina will be given fair and equitable treatment.

Actually the imports of chilled beef from Argentina in the year ended June 1932 were exceptionally low, representing a reduction of 10 per cent on the average of the four previous years. In various ways the Ottawa arrangements gave considerable advantages to British meat producers and to Dominion producers of chilled beef and also frozen meat.[1] Argentina's allocation of frozen meat was heavily reduced, and it was expected that by 1934 her exports to Great Britain would have been reduced by

[1] Until recent years Argentina and other South American countries commanded almost the whole of the export trade in chilled meat, which sells at a higher price than frozen meat. Recently, however, Australia and New Zealand have developed methods of chilling meat suitable for the longer journey to Europe, and are, therefore, interested in expanding their export trade.

one-third of their former level, the gap being filled by Dominion and home-produced meat. In the event of further reductions being made, these would apply both to the Dominions and to Argentina. This policy of restricting the market for chilled and frozen meat has been criticised because these kinds of meat are mainly consumed by the poorer sections of the community upon whom, therefore, the burden of restriction falls.

In an agreement with Poland concluded in February 1935 valuable concessions affecting 50 per cent of British exports to Poland were secured largely in return for continuation by Britain of most-favoured-nation treatment to Poland and for an undertaking that if Britain decides to regulate the importation of agricultural produce Poland will be allowed to send not less than 41·4 per cent of the quantity of bacon she sold to Britain in 1932 and not less than $13\frac{1}{2}$ per cent of the total permitted imports of eggs from foreign countries.[1] Poland agreed to reduce her rates of duty on 340 articles and undertook not to raise the rates on 110 other articles; the most important reductions are on herrings, textile goods, motor vehicles and accessories, certain categories of machinery and chemicals, and other commodities not produced in Poland. British shipping interests in Polish emigrant and cargo transport are also given safeguards for equitable treatment.

The agreement with the U.S.S.R., which was concluded in February 1934, is of particular interest because of its attempt to regulate trade with a country operating a State trading monopoly and to apply in a special way the most-favoured-nation principle to such trade. The orthodox most-favoured-nation clause is scarcely applicable under these conditions and requires adaption. A main purpose of the agreement was to secure a closer balance between the Soviet Union's exports to and imports from Great Britain in place of the very large favourable balance which the

---

[1] Details of the agreement are given in the official British paper, Cmd. 4820.

Soviet Union had enjoyed in previous years.[1] With this object in view the Soviet Union undertook that the proceeds of her sales in Great Britain would be spent in this country in a gradually increasing proportion until at the end of about five years there would be an approximate equality of payments, both visible and invisible, between the two countries.[2]

A second feature of the agreement was provision against the danger that the Soviet Government not being subject to ordinary commercial considerations for individual commodities, might cut down its prices in any particular market to uneconomic levels. At Ottawa the Canadian Government especially had shown itself nervous of this risk and more generally of the Soviet Union's competitive power in the British timber and wheat markets, and had insisted upon a safeguarding provision in its agreement with Great Britain.[3] On the other hand, the Soviet Union demanded most-favoured-nation treatment from Great Britain. This was granted, but a provision was inserted in the agreement that if, as regards any particular commodity, prices of the Soviet Union's products fell so as to frustrate the preferences given to the Dominions or to be detrimental to British production, the agreement could be suspended in reference to such commodity. By this means dumping, which could so easily be practised by the Soviet trading monopoly, could be quickly stopped. Injurious price manipulation by State action, therefore, would be likely to result in termina-

---

[1] In the years 1931–3 Britain imported goods from Russia to a value of about £124 million, whereas her sales to Russia amounted only to about £40 million.

[2] Throughout 1934 the trade returns showed balances still very much in the Soviet Union's favour. However, referring in the House of Commons on July 18, 1935, to the operation of the agreement, Mr. Runciman, President of the Board of Trade, stated that the Soviet Union had far exceeded their undertaking, and that they had also made a great increase in their use of British shipping services.

[3] In consequence, the British Government denounced the Anglo-Soviet Trade Treaty and Protocol of 1930, by which an attempt had been made to apply the most-favoured-nation principle to State trading and to avoid discriminations and political considerations in the regulation of commercial and financial relations.

tion of most-favoured-nation treatment. Otherwise there is to be no discrimination against the goods of either country, and the subjects of either country are to enjoy all trading facilities, rights and privileges accorded to the subjects of any other country.[1]

In big timber contracts signed in 1934 and 1935 by the British Company, Timber Distributers, Ltd., a "fall clause" was inserted at the request of the British importers, providing that in the event of the market price falling below contract prices a repayment would be made to the British importers. This clause was deleted at the request of the Board of Trade consequent upon objections by the Canadian Government that the clause was a frustration of Article 21 of the Ottawa Agreement. It was claimed that the clause was unfair to other traders who observed the ordinary commercial practice of selling to meet day-to-day requirements. For several years before the Ottawa Conference, Soviet timber sales in one huge contract had been subject to the fall clause permitting reduction in prices to meet competition from other countries. In 1936 the huge contract method was abandoned.

Whereas the British Government has widely exercised its powers of negotiating agreements, the weapon of retaliation has rarely been used. It was brought into operation against the Soviet Union in 1933 at the time of the trial of the employees of Metropolitan-Vickers for alleged sabotage. Although the method of retaliation was economic its purpose was political and need not be discussed here. Retaliatory measures were adopted against France in 1934 towards the end of a trade dispute which had lasted over two years, while in the same year measures were taken against Japan which, though not involving formal discrimination, did, in fact, operate with specially restrictive effect against her trade.

The dispute with France originated in a surtax of 15 per cent imposed in November 1931 on imports from Britain

[1] Britain formally retained all her rights in respect of debts and claims against the U.S.S.R., the recognition of which was one of the conditions for the resumption of diplomatic relations between the two States in 1929.

to offset the advantage gained by British exporters from the depreciation of sterling after her departure from the gold standard. The British Government complained that the principle of countervailing currency depreciation was not applied equally against other countries, and at length the French Government agreed to suppress the surtax from the beginning of 1934.[1] Almost immediately, however, the French import quotas system was made much more restrictive.

The climax was reached when French quotas were made more liberal to Belgium and the United States in return, the French Government stated, for reciprocal concessions by these countries. The French pointed out that Britain herself had secured similar differential concessions from other countries, for example, an increase in her whisky quota to the United States in return for undertaking to increase her imports of American bacon, and a quota of 80 per cent of Danish coal imports to the disadvantage of other countries. In these circumstances the French considered that the British Government was unfair in its condemnation of the French quotas and in taking its stand on the most-favoured-nation principle.

Faced with strong British protests the French Government decided to remove the discrimination from most products. But there still remained discrimination against many classes of cotton textiles and certain other goods, and, in consequence, the British Government issued an Import Duties (Foreign Discrimination) Order in February 1934 imposing an additional duty of 20 per cent *ad valorem* on certain classes of French goods, the order being framed with a view to effecting a reduction of imports from France approximately equivalent to the reduction of British exports to France, estimated at about £500,000, resulting from the French differential quotas.[2] During the dispute

---

[1] It had been removed from coal in February 1932.

[2] Statement by Mr. Runciman in the House of Commons, February 15, 1934, which indicates in detail the extent of French discrimination against Great Britain.

British difficulties in negotiation were increased by the fact that, at the time, her trade balance with France was favourable, thus weakening her bargaining power.

The dispute was finally terminated in July 1934 when the French Government agreed to apply the quota system without discrimination against British trade, and Great Britain removed the 20 per cent retaliatory duties from French imports. Each country undertook, with a few specified exceptions, to observe the most-favoured-nation principle. Further, in the interests of the coal trade, which represents nearly one-half of British exports to France, the British Government, in return for certain tariff reductions, secured an undertaking that France would maintain her imports of British coal at not less than 49·5 per cent of the average imports of coal into France from all sources during the years 1928 to 1930.[1] The British concessions included lower duties on raw silk and artificial silk (50 per cent reduction), cut flowers, certain vegetables and a few other products, and an undertaking not to increase the duties on brandy and sparkling wines. The lower duties on raw silk and artificial silk were welcomed by British manufacturers using these goods as their raw materials, but only in order to prevent a breakdown of the negotiations was the Treasury induced to sacrifice the £2½ million of revenue involved.[2]

Recent British trade policy towards Japan differs somewhat from that expressed in the agreements already reviewed. Its purpose is not so much to secure reciprocal concessions or to secure a closer balance of trade, but to restrict Japanese competition. This competition increased very rapidly during the years 1932–4, causing a great reduction in Britain's exports of cotton textiles and artificial silk fabrics. Early

[1] The agreement was to remain in force in the first instance until the beginning of April 1935. Subsequently the quota was raised to 52·6 per cent.

[2] Other countries, including Germany, enjoyed the benefit of the lower duties by the operation of the most-favoured-nation clause, and complaints have been made that British manufacturers have been adversely affected as a result of large increases in imports from Germany of hosiery goods made of artificial silk.

in 1934 representatives of these British and Japanese industries met to discuss an agreement for the regulation of trade, but without result. The British Government then intervened. It could do nothing about foreign markets, and the British Dominions, being masters of their own commercial policies, were not likely to increase their preferences to Great Britain, as most of them had favourable trade balances with Japan which they were afraid to risk. The British Government was, however, able to arrange for various British Colonies and Protectorates to impose restrictions upon imports, and from May 1934 a quota system based upon average imports during the years 1927-31 was applied to all foreign cotton and artificial silk goods imported into these territories.[1] This policy of regulating imports aroused opposition in some of the Colonies, which maintained that their interests were being sacrificed in order to help Lancashire manufacturers, and the plan was put into operation only upon insistence by the Colonial Office. Though not formally a discriminatory infringement of the most-favoured-nation clause the effect of the system was specially restrictive upon Japanese trade, involving a reduction to about one-half of the sales during the two preceding years, and the effect of the policy has been to increase considerably Lancashire's exports to the areas concerned.[2] It has, however, been criticised on the ground that it deprives the natives of the Colonies of cheap supplies.

The policy applied in the reciprocal agreements with foreign countries in recent years, the adoption of the quota system, and the great extension of Imperial Preference have considerably altered the significance of the most-favoured-

[1] This was possible without denouncing the existing Anglo-Japanese Commercial Treaty; in West Africa, however, the system could not be applied owing to the operation of the Anglo-French Convention. In some Colonies it was opposed by the unofficial members of the Legislative Councils and was put into effect by the votes of the official members, or by direct authority of the British Secretary of State for the Colonies.

[2] An increased amount of Japanese grey cloth has, however, been sold to British exporters, has been put through the finishing processes in Britain and then exported to the Colonies free from the quota restrictions and at the lower tariffs enjoyed by British goods.

H

nation principle and the British Government's attitudes towards it have lately changed. It is, however, still retained as an important feature of British policy. The application of this principle may now be reviewed.

THE MOST-FAVOURED-NATION CLAUSE

Strong support of the most-favoured-nation principle in its unconditional form has long been a feature of British commercial policy, but recently a tendency has developed to modify its application. The clause has been included in almost all British commercial treaties and agreements, with the object of promoting trade, ensuring equality of treatment, and preventing discrimination, thereby fostering good international relations.[1] In pre-war years the principle operated with mutual advantage, though even then its application was not free from difficulties; these have increased since the war, especially during the depression. In 1929, it was still possible to conclude that most-favoured-nation treatment was accorded to British trade in almost all important markets, and that, with relatively insignificant exceptions, British goods were "admitted into foreign countries on terms at least as favourable as those applicable to similar goods imported from other foreign sources."[2] Since then the situation has deteriorated, largely as a consequence of the increasing use of the quota system. The value of the principle has diminished as a result of high tariffs imposed by certain countries, of tariff specialisation, and of the growing practice of arranging reciprocal trade agreements between two or more countries. Its operation has been hampered by

[1] The unconditional clause usually runs as follows: "Articles produced or manufactured in the territories of either of the two parties imported into the territories of the other (from whatever place arriving) shall not be subjected to other or higher duties or charges than those paid on the like articles produced or manufactured in any other foreign country." Import prohibitions or restrictions are dealt with along similar lines with a view to preventing discriminations, and by including such a provision any discriminatory quota plan can be attacked as an infringement of the agreement.

[2] *Final Report of the Committee on Industry and Trade*, p. 14.

the extensive use of currency exchange restrictions and clearing manipulations by various countries. The clause can scarcely be applied where, as in the Soviet Union, a country's foreign trade is in the hands of a Government agency. Without infringing the letter of the clause such a country can transfer its purchases from one foreign country to another.[1]

British attitudes toward the clause have changed during the last few years partly as a consequence of the tariff policies adopted by other countries, but largely because since 1932 Great Britain has herself adopted the method of bilateral trade agreements based upon reciprocity. While British policy was largely free trade the unconditional most-favoured-nation clause brought her the advantage of concessions obtained by reciprocal bargaining between other countries. These other countries in principle recognised that Britain had a reasonable claim to enjoy the benefit of their agreements as she imposed no restrictions upon their trade; the benefits were, however, usually less appropriate to her trade and industrial structure than they were to the parties negotiating the agreements. It was also widely agreed that low tariff countries could make a reasonable claim to benefit, but objections were raised to countries with high tariffs enjoying advantages for which other countries had made sacrifices, without themselves granting any concessions.

The problem is complicated by differences in tariff systems,

---

[1] An attempt was made to ensure most-favoured-nation treatment for British trade with the U.S.S.R by including in the agreement of 1930 a provision with the object of ensuring that the goods, shipping, trading organisations, and trade of each of these countries should not in any respect be placed in a position of inferiority as compared with those of any other countries. The countries undertook to be guided by commercial and financial considerations alone; there should also be no discrimination against the U.S.S.R. in the measures taken by the British Government in the granting of trade credits. The agreement was terminated by the British Government after the Ottawa Conference in view of the obligation there accepted to apply certain safeguards against State trading, but, as indicated earlier, a new agreement applying the most-favoured-nation principle was concluded in February 1934.

some countries making a usual practice of conducting reciprocal negotiations while others fix a single tariff without
discrimination against any country, and in return they
claim most-favoured-nation treatment to ensure their own
freedom from discrimination. Where the single tariff is
high this claim, though formally valid, is often unfair in
practice, and has increased the objections to the clause in
its unconditional form.

For a number of years the United States with a high
single tariff schedule, the rates of which were often almost
prohibitive, strongly asserted her right to unconditional
most-favoured-nation treatment, although this was considered in many other countries to be unreasonable. In 1934,
however, she announced a new policy of reciprocal bilateral
treaties, and agreements of this type were soon concluded
with Cuba and Brazil, involving mutual advantages which
are denied to certain other countries. This change in
American policy, which is in effect a reversion to her practice
before 1923, is yet another step in the practical abandonment
of the unconditional most-favoured-nation system. During
recent years the clause, instead of being accepted as a means
of promoting trade, has been regarded as an obstacle to the
removal of restrictions by making States reluctant to engage
in bilateral, regional, or multilateral negotiations. There is
growing dissatisfaction with its operation, and it is being
widely evaded and disregarded.[1]

The difficulties may be illustrated by recent British
experience. In negotiating bilateral trade agreements with
various countries Great Britain has given reciprocal advantages in order to secure easier access to their markets for
her manufactures. Japan, the United States, Germany, and
other manufacturing countries, without giving any *quid pro
quo*, immediately claim the same facilities in virtue of the

---

[1] An interesting discussion of the operation of the clause under current
conditions took place at the Conference on The State and Economic Life,
held in London, May–June 1933, under the auspices of the League of
Nations International Institute of Intellectual Cooperation. (See the
Record of the Conference, pp. 45–85.)

automatic operation of the most-favoured-nation clause. A bargain by which Britain secures a lowering of the tariff on textile goods entering Argentina may lose most of its value to Lancashire if the benefits accrue equally to American and Japanese products. Conversely, Argentina must share with other producers of food and raw materials the advantages which she has secured by the agreement with Great Britain. In such circumstances the incentive to lower tariffs by mutual concessions is much diminished. There has, therefore, been a tendency to reduce the number of agreements and to restrict their scope. Nevertheless, each agreement promotes the trade both of its signatories and of other countries, and Great Britain benefits from agreements to which she is not a party, the system thus affording compensations which at least partly offset its disadvantages. Safeguards are, however, necessary as a protection against countries which neither directly nor indirectly relax their restrictions, while benefiting from the relaxations of others.

While Britain's tariff policy has made her sometimes wish to refuse unconditional most-favoured-nation treatment to certain countries it has weakened her claim to be granted such treatment by other countries. So long as she pursued a free trade policy or imposed import duties only upon a few commodities she had a strong claim to unconditional most-favoured-nation treatment. Now that she has put substantial tariffs upon a wide range of commodities and has accorded considerable preferences under the Ottawa Agreements to the Dominions of the British Commonwealth the strength of this claim is considerably diminished. The self-governing Dominions enjoy complete independence in their tariff policy, but Great Britain in her treaties with foreign countries has always drafted the most-favoured-nation clause in a way which precludes these countries from the right to benefit from any inter-Imperial preferences which she grants. Such preferences are regarded as valid exceptions, being domestic affairs, and, although they are disliked by foreign countries, no official protest has been

directed against them. The Ottawa Agreements would have
been impracticable if foreign countries could have shared in
their advantages by the application of the most-favoured-
nation clause.

The British Government has avoided taking any general
measures to introduce a revised clause in its commercial
treaties. Revision would involve the risk of losing advantages
which the clause still affords, it would increase the danger
of more discriminations against British trade, and the
complicated task of revising a large number of commercial
treaties would have to be undertaken. Every additional
tariff discrimination would involve additional work for the
customs officials in dealing with imports from different
countries, while the strain upon international commercial
relations would be increased. In view of these considerations,
the Government has shown preference for piece-meal
adjustments rather than for the adoption of a new procedure
to be generally applied, and has rejected proposals for the
appointment of a committee to examine the operation of
the clause with a view to its revision to meet the world
conditions of to-day.[1] Mr. Runciman has indicated that the
Government prefers to decide each case on its merits instead
of laying down a general rule. The inclusion or omission

[1] Such proposals were made during 1934 by the Manchester Chamber of
Commerce and the National Union of Manufacturers, which were dissatisfied with the working of the clause and favoured its revision. The
Manchester Chamber of Commerce and somewhat later the Association of
British Chambers of Commerce, in consultation with other organisations
of industrialists, undertook detailed investigations into the operation
of the clause and published statements of their findings. The investigations
were facilitated by the supply of information by the Board of Trade.
The Manchester Chamber, while unfavourable to the perpetuation of the
unconditional clause, supported change by stages on the principle of
expediency; it did not advocate general denunciation of most-favoured-
nation engagements, but urged the Government not to grant such treatment to countries which entirely failed to meet the reasonable requirements
of Britain, i.e. non-cooperating countries. The report issued by the Association of British Chambers of Commerce indicates that British difficulties
have arisen almost entirely in respect of quota restrictions. While raising
various general problems of commercial policy, the report makes no
constructive proposals for a modification of the Government's policy
towards the clause.

of the clause, whether in its unconditional or modified form, is "a question of expediency which cannot be settled except with reference to the circumstances of a particular negotiation." There is, therefore, to be no rigid adherence to the unconditional form.

The new policy is indicated in the following statement by Mr. Runciman in the House of Commons on May 4, 1933: "Countries entitled under existing treaties to most-favoured-nation treatment will enjoy the benefits of any reductions which are accorded by the arrangements now being negotiated, but the Government propose in due course to undertake negotiations with other foreign countries, and they will certainly not be prepared to continue indefinitely to accord full most-favoured-nation treatment to countries which show themselves unwilling to meet the reasonable requirements of this country in regard to the treatment of United Kingdom goods." This policy was also proclaimed by the Government's spokesmen at the World Economic Conference. Until this time British Governments had consistently advocated the retention of the unconditional clause in commercial agreements.[1] The announcement of the new policy has not, however, been supplemented by any indications as to methods for determining which countries fail to meet the reasonable requirements of Great Britain, or what measures of discrimination are to be directed against them. No "black list" of countries which discriminate unfairly against British trade has been made public.

Great Britain has continued to demand most-favoured-nation treatment from other countries and to raise objections against discriminations. This was made the subject of a special declaration by the Ottawa Conference, 1932. British opposition to projects for European Economic Union has been based partly upon the fact that it would involve arrange-

[1] At the time of the Conference the most-favoured-nation clause was included in agreements with about forty countries, but in a large majority of the agreements the clause could be denounced after not more than twelve months' notice.

ments in conflict with the unconditional most-favoured-nation principle. Britain has been widely criticised for opposing the tariff agreement proposed at Ouchy in 1932 between Belgium, Luxembourg, and the Netherlands. The chief ground for this opposition was that the agreement would have involved a technical violation of the most-favoured-nation clause. These countries were willing to undertake:

(1) not to increase their existing tariff levels against any country;

(2) to reduce their tariffs between themselves by a considerable amount in successive stages over a period of five years;

(3) to invite any other country to enter the agreement on similar terms;

(4) to admit to the agreement not only countries observing similar conditions to those adopted by the original participants but also countries which, without complying with the specific conditions, had tariff rates at least as low as the reduced rates fixed in the agreement.[1]

Such an agreement can scarcely be styled as discriminatory in view of the third principle, which throws it open to all countries willing to observe the same conditions. To admit such regional agreements as internationally recognised exceptions to the unconditional most-favoured-nation clause might go a long way towards removing some of the chief difficulties, and might rescue the clause from the danger of complete abandonment. Abandonment would involve a vast complicated network of discriminations based upon exclusiveness which would create much international irritation and would impose still further restrictions upon international trade; these could largely be avoided by the application of the principles proposed in the project between the Netherlands and Belgium.[2]

---

[1] This provision could not be applied with precision because of the practical difficulty of measuring relative tariff levels.

[2] Certain exceptions to the unconditional principle have long been recognised, e.g. where two countries form a *zollverein*, or where countries with close political associations of long standing with traditionally intimate

The British Government has not hesitated to protest when a country has discriminated against British trade; it has demanded equal treatment and has adopted retaliatory measures, if necessary, with the object of enforcing its demands. Such measures were directed against France in 1933 when her quotas were considered to be unfair to British trade, and after months of retaliation a new and more favourable agreement was concluded. Retaliations were directed against Japan in 1934. The British Government has also used the most-favoured-nation principle not only in trade negotiations but to prevent discrimination against Britain by countries practising exchange control. Thus, the Anglo-Argentine Convention of May 1933 provides that in no event shall Britain receive less favourable treatment than any other country in the allocation of foreign currency by Argentina in meeting its commercial and financial obligations.

RESULTS AND CONCLUSIONS

Only preliminary conclusions can yet be drawn about the results of the new protectionist policy. Its effects during the depression, for which sufficient data are now available, must be distinguished from its long-range effects, which cannot yet be fully appreciated. The outstanding feature in the period immediately following the imposition of tariffs was the heavy fall in imports from foreign countries, this being caused partly by the tariffs and depreciation of sterling and partly by lack of confidence during the depression. On the other hand, imports from Empire countries were well maintained, partly as a result of preferential treatment, and partly because these countries supply the British market with immediate necessaries to a greater extent than foreign countries; the demand for less essential commodities could be postponed during a period of lack of con-

trading relations accord special privileges to one another (e.g. Spain and Portugal, Norway and Sweden). Preferences within the British Empire are not regarded as derogations from the principle.

fidence. The reduction of imports from foreign countries was advantageous at the time of an adverse balance of payments.

The effect of the duties on imports from foreign countries has been to increase somewhat the proportion of British requirements produced at home, while, as is indicated in the next chapter, the policy of Imperial Preference has increased the proportion of British food and raw materials imported from Empire countries, which have gained at the expense of foreign countries. Data are not available satisfactorily to show the increase in the proportion of home production, but the following indexes of the volume of production, imports and exports indicate the trend.

INDEX NUMBERS OF THE VOLUME OF BRITISH PRODUCTION, IMPORTS AND EXPORTS*

(1924 = 100)

Year	Production	Imports‡ Retained	Exports of British Products‡
1930	103·1	113·6	86·0
1931	93·3	116·9	65·8
1932	92·9	102·7	66·1
1933	98·3	104·2	67·7
1934	109·4	110·3	72·6
1935	115·3†	111·1	78·4

* Compiled from statistics published in the *Board of Trade Journal*.
† First nine months.   ‡ Based on values at 1930 prices.

These figures show that between 1933 and 1935 British production expanded more rapidly than either imports or exports, and they, therefore, indicate an increased proportion of home production to external trade.[1] The reduction in the volume of exports is not so serious as might be expected, because the selling prices of British exports did not fall during the depression in so great a proportion as those of

[1] Since 1932 the iron and steel industry particularly has shown rapid expansion of production,

the foodstuffs and raw materials which form the bulk of her imports.[1] Between 1924 and 1934 average import values fell by 46 per cent and average export values by only 34 per cent. There is danger, however, that the relatively high prices of British exports may cause further reduction in purchases by foreign countries.

Materially, Britain was more prosperous at the end of 1934 and throughout 1935 than in 1930 or even than in 1928.[2] During this period production surpassed that of the previous peak year 1929, but the volume of external trade lagged behind. Although Britain's industrial activity may increase somewhat further by production at home of still more goods hitherto imported from abroad, she is already manufacturing a large part of the commodities which she can produce at costs not widely different from foreign costs. A further substantial advance in the home production of her requirements would involve increasing economic loss, and Britain must, therefore, look to greater recovery in foreign trade if the rate of increase in her standards of living, which was interrupted by the depression, is to be resumed.

Statistics of Britain's imports and exports show that her trade with foreign countries now forms a smaller proportion of her total trade than a few years ago, the most marked change having taken place since the protectionist policy was adopted. The proportion was about 70 per cent in 1913 and nearly 68 per cent in 1929, but it had fallen to about 60 per cent in the years 1933 to 1935. In 1934 and 1935 imports from foreign countries represented 62 to 63 per cent of total imports, while exports to foreign countries represented 53·1 per cent of total exports in 1934 and 52

[1] Already in the decade 1921 to 1930 exports represented only about 18 per cent of the national income compared with about 22 per cent in the years immediately before the war. (Address by Sir A. W. Flux to the Insurance Institute of London.)

[2] Allowance should, however, be made for an increase in the population of nearly 3 per cent since 1928. Also, prosperity would have been at a much higher level if progress had not been interrupted by the depression.

per cent in 1935; these export percentages were somewhat less than in 1929 when the proportion was about 55 per cent. The values of British imports and exports are tabulated below, separate figures being given for trade with European countries, other foreign countries, and Empire countries.

BRITISH IMPORTS AND EXPORTS*

(£ *million*)

Year	IMPORTS			
	From European Countries	From other Foreign Countries	From Empire Countries	Total
1913	320·0	257·1	191·5	769
1929	466·4	395·5	313·7	1,221
1933	241·3	184·8	231·3	675
1934	256·5	204·3	254·2	731
1935	264·8	207·2	266·1	757

Year	EXPORTS OF BRITISH PRODUCTS			Total Exports (Including Re-exports)
	To European Countries	To other Foreign Countries	To Empire Countries	
1913	195·1	134·8	195·3	635
1929	235·5	169·3	288·3	839
1933	131·4	72·9	144·4	417
1934	136·7	73·6	166·0	447
1935	141·4	80·1	184·1	481

* The figures of exports to each group of countries are of British products, excluding re-exports, but the total includes re-exports. The value of re-exports was £110 million in 1913 and also in 1929, £49 million in 1933, £51 million in 1934, and £55 million in 1935. The trade with European countries includes that with their Dependencies, while that with Empire countries excludes trade with the Irish Free State; the totals, however, include trade with the Irish Free State.

The table shows an increase in imports and exports in 1934 for the first time since 1929, trade with each group of countries contributing to the change, though in varying proportions. Total trade in 1935 was still only 60 per cent of its value in 1929, imports having fallen 38 per cent and exports of British products 41·5 per cent. As a result of changes in price levels the fall in the volume of trade between 1929 and 1933 was less than in its value, while the increase since 1933 has been greater in value than in volume. The volume of trade, especially the export trade, remains much below the 1929 level.

The reduction of imports during the depression was achieved chiefly at the expense of foreign countries. Imports of manufactured articles suffered the greatest reduction during the depression, food and raw material imports being well maintained, especially in volume, although their value was affected by the substantial fall in prices. Among manufactures, iron and steel and machinery showed the greatest reduction, this being partly offset by increased home production. It is significant that notwithstanding the adoption of protection and depreciation of sterling, which caused an immediate fall in imports in 1932, British exports show a greater proportionate reduction than British imports. This should be considered in relation to the decline in Britain's capacity to lend capital abroad.

Trade with foreign countries in the sterling area, especially the Scandinavian and Baltic countries and the Argentine, gained somewhat relatively to that with gold *bloc* countries. This reflected the factor of currency stability, but it was also facilitated by the trade agreements. British trade with countries with which trade agreements are in operation shows a considerably greater expansion during recent years than that with other foreign countries. The fall in exports to gold *bloc* countries was largely due to the drastic import restrictions imposed by these countries. Between 1929 and 1934–5 trade fell more with non-European foreign countries than with foreign countries in Europe, their products usually competing more directly with those of Empire countries. Imports from foreign countries outside Europe in 1934–5 were about 28½ per cent of total imports, and exports about $18\frac{1}{2}$ per cent of total exports, compared with $35 \cdot 4$ per cent and $23 \cdot 9$ per cent respectively in 1929. The rise in the value of British exports in 1934 and 1935 was due mainly to purchases by Empire countries. These countries gained more from non-European than from European countries.

The importance of Empire countries in supplying British requirements and as customers for British products is indicated by the following figures. They show that, in 1935, four out of the first six suppliers of Britain's needs were in the Empire.

CHIEF BRITISH CUSTOMERS IN 1935		CHIEF SUPPLIERS OF BRITISH IMPORTS IN 1935	
	£ million		*£ million*
India and Ceylon	41·0	United States	87·5
South Africa	33·6	Canada	56·0
Australia and Papua	29·4	Australia and Papua	54·3
United States	22·9	India and Ceylon	51·1
Canada	21·4	Argentina	44·0
Irish Free State	20·2	New Zealand	38·1
Germany	18·9	Denmark	32·0
France	16·7	Germany	30·0
Argentina	15·3	Netherlands	23·1
Denmark	13·8	U.S.S.R.	21·7
New Zealand	13·4	France	21·6
Netherlands	11·7	Irish Free State	18·7

Britain's balance of trade is least favourable with the United States and Soviet Russia, which sold to Britain in 1935 respectively nearly 4 and about 6 times the value of their purchases from her. Argentina and New Zealand follow with imports of British products about one-third of their sales to Britain;[1] account must, however, be taken of their need of heavily favourable balances of trade to meet their capital obligations to Britain; then come Canada and Denmark, which sold to Britain around $2\frac{1}{2}$ times the value of the commodities which they bought from her. Both the United States and the Soviet Union are consider-

[1] In 1934 the Argentine bought 22·5 per cent of her imports from Britain, while the percentage which she bought from the United States was 14·8; in 1929 these percentages were almost reversed.

able purchasers of re-exports from Britain, but especially with the United States they do not greatly modify the very favourable balance of trade. With the Soviet Union, as already cited, a trade agreement has been negotiated which provides for a substantial correction of the balance of trade over a period of years.[1] No trade agreement has yet been negotiated with the United States, notwithstanding the heavy balance in her favour.

The importance of British tariffs on imports from foreign countries is indicated in the table on page 128, which shows the percentages of imports free of duty before the new policy was introduced, and the position under the Import Duties Act and after the Ottawa Agreements came into force. The percentages have been only slightly modified by Additional Import Duties Orders which have increased the tariffs on various commodities and by certain reductions effected by trade agreements or on recommendations of the Import Duties Advisory Committee. The percentages show that since the Ottawa Agreements came into force about one-quarter of British imports remain free of duty, while about one-half pay new duties of 10 to 20 per cent; of the remainder nearly 8 per cent are subject to new duties of over 20 per cent, and 17 per cent are subject to the old revenue, key industry or safeguarding duties. Imports of a substantial part of the commodities still on the free list are restricted by other methods.

The effect of protection upon prices has been less than was anticipated. Both wholesale prices and the cost of living fell slightly in 1932 and 1933, but they took an upward turn in 1934, and again in the latter part of 1935 when the wholesale index rose above and the cost of living reached the 1931 level. The maintenance of low prices was due largely to the poor demand for commodities throughout the world resulting from the depression. The restoration of

[1] This covers British re-exports to the Soviet Union, and in 1934 and 1935 the Soviet Union increased threefold compared with 1933 the value of her purchases of re-exports from Britain.

BRITISH IMPORTS AS AFFECTED BY THE NEW TARIFF POLICY*

Countries	1930 Percentage of Imports Free of Duty	1932, Before Ottawa				1932, After Ottawa			
		Percentage of Imports Free of Duty	Imports Subject to New Duties of			Percentage of Imports Free of Duty	Imports Subject to New Duties of		
			10 per cent	11–20 per cent	Over 20 per cent		10 per cent	11–20 per cent	Over 20 per cent
European Countries ..	88·4	20·1	40·2	21·6	6·5	17·9	29·9	31·9	8·7
United States	70·5	29·8	25·5	12·2	1·0	20·5	30·0	13·4	6·6
Latin America	85·0	67·9	16·7	0·4	—	56·3	22·5	3·0	3·2
All Foreign Countries ..	83·0	30·2	32·9	15·3	4·6	25·2	28·3	21·8	7·7

* Data published in the *Economist*, October 1932. The percentages make allowance for the first few Additional Import Duties Orders issued.

more active conditions in world markets will allow the normal effect of import duties upon prices to be felt.

During the depth of the depression the introduction of protection helped to correct the unduly adverse balance of trade, and the duties produced a substantial revenue at a time when other sources of income were difficult to find. The new policy has caused an increase in the relative importance of home production of British requirements,[1] but against this must be set losses of production for export, and of income from shipping and from financial services associated with external trade. The trade agreements have enabled Britain to use her bargaining power, including the threat to withdraw most-favoured-nation treatment, to require certain foreign countries whose balances of trade with Britain were very favourable to buy a larger proportion of their imports from her. This she was able to do at a time when the system of triangular trade was not working effectively and when there was no certainty that importation of foreign goods by Britain would result in a corresponding demand for British products. Market conditions during the depression may have been partly responsible for some of the changes in the direction of British trade which have been reviewed above, but monetary and commercial policy have been more important factors. With a return of more normal business conditions Britain is likely to increase her trade in manufactured specialities, both imports and exports, with foreign countries, while retaining a moderate tariff level, being a little less dependent than formerly upon overseas trade, and maintaining an increased proportion of her trade within the Empire.

[1] Details of the results are given by industries in *Import Duties Act. Report on the Inquiry (1933)*, published by the Board of Trade in November 1935.

CHAPTER V

IMPERIAL TRADE POLICY

This chapter deals with those aspects of British Imperial trade policy which directly affect foreign countries. It includes a review of changes in policy since about 1860, special attention being directed to recent developments, particularly the Ottawa Agreements and the question of the open door in relation to Imperial Preference. Policies which only indirectly affect foreign countries or which are essentially internal affairs of the Empire are excluded. Thus the recent Anglo-Irish trade war, resulting from strained political relations, and the economic settlement reached at the end of 1934 by the Governments of Great Britain and of the Irish Free State are not reviewed.

TRENDS FROM ECONOMIC INTERNATIONALISM TO ECONOMIC IMPERIALISM[1]

The year 1860 marked the triumph of unqualified internationalism as the central principle of British trade policy. Five years earlier, in accordance with the British Government's free trade policy, British exports to colonial markets ceased to enjoy any preferences and henceforth competed on equal terms with foreign products. In 1860, when the remaining preferences for the products of British Colonies were removed, the whole Empire was thrown open without differentiation to the world's trade. Future generations may look back with astonishment and envy at this unique economic adventure.

The new policy and the ideal upon which it was founded were not long unchallenged, the opposition coming first from the Colonies. The abandonment of preferences for their

---

[1] The course of this transition runs parallel to the changes in commercial policy reviewed in the previous chapter.

goods in the British market had been resented by colonial producers. They favoured protection and Imperial Preference, and those Colonies which enjoyed a sufficient measure of tariff autonomy applied a protective policy. Their autonomy was, however, limited by the British Government's power to conclude treaties with foreign countries providing for no discrimination in any part of the Empire against their trade. This provision was included in treaties with Belgium in 1862 and with Germany in 1868, and was extended to other countries by the application of the most-favoured-nation principle. Therefore, even those Colonies which were approaching self-government were unable to grant trade preferences, either to Great Britain, or to one another, or to any foreign country. Against their wishes Britain adhered to the policy of the open door.

During the 1880's the Colonies, experiencing dfficulties from foreign tariffs, renewed their demands for Imperial Preference. Under the leadership of Canada, those Colonies which were most advanced in self-government insistently urged that they should be granted complete fiscal autonomy in order that they might introduce preferences for Great Britain and other parts of the Empire into their tariff systems. Finally, at the Colonial Conference, 1897, the British Government withdrew its opposition to this development, and, by subsequently denouncing the Belgian and German treaties, removed the legal obstacles to fiscal autonomy. The leading Colonies soon exercised their new powers, and by 1907 they had all put into practice the principle of Imperial Preference.

The closing years of the nineteenth century also saw a growth of interest in the potentialities of Empire trade, both in supplying Britain with food and raw materials and in offering markets for British manufactures. This interest was focussed by Mr. Joseph Chamberlain in his campaign inaugurated in 1903 for the protection of British industry and preferences within the Empire. As is indicated in Mr. J. L. Garvin's *Life of Joseph Chamberlain*, the nation was becoming disturbed about its economic future, the long age of easy commercial supremacy was over, free trade was being rendered increasingly difficult by the restrictive policies of other countries, and, therefore, the expansion of sheltered markets under the flag grew more and more attractive. Mr. Chamberlain's plan was to consolidate the Empire into an economic union and he was willing to tax British imports of food from foreign countries in order that valuable preferences might be accorded to Empire producers.

The whole policy of protection and preferences advocated by the tariff reformers was decisively rejected at the General Elections of 1906 and 1910, largely because of opposition to taxation of food. Faced with these verdicts the British Government, much to the disappointment of the Dominions, made no attempt before the war to reciprocate the preferences accorded by all the Dominions to British exports. The war, however, marks the beginning of a transition. Imperial cooperation was developed in many fields, and Empire products were given favourable treatment under the British war-time system of licensing imports. In 1917 the Imperial War Conference supported a policy of Imperial Preferences as a means of giving all possible encouragement "to the development of Imperial resources and especially of making the Empire independent of other countries in respect of food supplies, raw materials, and essential industries." A policy of preferences was also recommended by the Committee on Industrial and Commercial Policy, which reported in 1918. Except for the advantages given to Empire products under the licensing system, the first application of these recommendations by the British Government was in the Finance Act, 1919, which provided for rebates for Empire products of 33⅓ per cent of the tariffs on various goods subject to the McKenna duties, and for an Empire preference of one-sixth of revenue duties on imported goods. Two years later, Empire products were entirely exempted from the key industry and depreciated currency duties imposed under the Safeguarding of Industries Act.

In practice these concessions were of little value as few commodities were involved, and these were largely manufactured articles which were unimportant among the exports of Empire countries to Great Britain. The concessions were, however, significant as representing a change of principle and as the forerunners of further favours, but no major development of policy took place for a decade.[1] Before reviewing the new orientation which followed the crisis of 1931 an outline of the British policy of the open door is given.

OPEN-DOOR POLICY[2]

For the purposes of this section, an open-door policy is deemed to be applied when a country, by its own free unilateral decision, allows the traders of other countries to buy or sell, without any discrimination, in its colonial markets on terms equal to those applied to its own dealers.[3] The open door, therefore, involves equal conditions of access to supplies of food and raw materials produced in a colonial area, and equal opportunity to sell goods in its markets.

From 1855 until almost the end of the century, Britain applied the open-door policy throughout the Empire, while until the war this policy was, with minor exceptions, maintained in the non-self-governing Colonies. As already indicated, the system of preferential duties upon British goods imported by the Colonies was abandoned in 1855, British and foreign traders, henceforth, being treated alike. Also, by the

[1] Mention may be made of the short-lived Empire Marketing Board which undertook an extensive campaign of publicity with the object of increasing sales of Empire products by the voluntary preference of consumers.

[2] An interesting memorandum on "The Open Door and Reciprocity," by Professor (now Sir) Alfred Zimmern, was submitted to the International Studies Conference organised by the League of Nations International Institute of Intellectual Cooperation, London, May–June 1933.

[3] Other aspects of open-door policy are not discussed, though it may be noted that Britain, along with other countries, has benefited from open-door treaties by which certain countries have undertaken to maintain equal conditions of trade for all the signatory States.

Belgian treaty of 1862 and the German treaty of 1868 the British Government agreed that the traders of these countries would not be subject to higher duties in British Colonies than those applied to British traders, and this undertaking was automatically extended to other countries by the operation of the most-favoured-nation clause. About twenty years later Britain concluded treaties with several countries providing for equality of treatment in specified Crown Colonies, chiefly in Africa, in return for similar treatment in some of their colonies. Throughout this period the British Government maintained the open-door policy both in Crown Colonies and in Colonies already exercising considerable powers of self-government, which were shortly to achieve complete autonomy. The doors were kept open without the consent of, and sometimes with strong opposition from, the areas concerned. Also commercial treaties applicable throughout the Empire were concluded by the British Government. Where trade was restricted by colonial tariffs, British and foreign goods were treated alike.[1]

The year 1897 marks the division of the Empire into two groups, the first comprising those Colonies which gained complete fiscal autonomy, including powers of trade discrimination, and the second comprising those which remained subject to British control. In that year, in deference to Canada's desire to grant tariff preferences to Great Britain, the British Government gave notice to terminate the Belgian and German treaties, which were formal obstacles to any modification of the open-door policy. In giving notice, Lord Salisbury stated that the obligation to maintain the open door was a barrier against the internal fiscal arrangements of the British Empire and was inconsistent with the close ties of commercial intercourse which subsisted, and should be consolidated, between the Mother Country and

---

[1] One or two exceptions may be noted. By arrangements made in 1854 and 1871 Canada, with the acquiescence of the British Government, accorded more favourable tariffs to United States than to British trade. During this period the British Government agreed to preferences between the various Provinces of Canada, and between the Colonies of Australia.

the Colonies. This implies that tariff arrangements within the British Empire are of purely domestic concern and that mutual preferences between any of its components are quite consistent with maintenance of most-favoured-nation agreements with foreign countries. The British Government has since maintained this view; it was reiterated and applied as a basic principle at the Ottawa Conference, 1932, and it has not been formally challenged by foreign Powers. Also after the termination of the Belgian and German Treaties those Colonies with fiscal autonomy soon accorded preferences to Britain and to other parts of the Empire, but the British Government, though no longer bound to maintain the open-door policy in Crown Colonies and Protectorates, did in fact continue to apply it for a number of years.

The open-door policy was used to justify territorial extensions of the British Empire, particularly at the time of the partition of Africa. Thus, in a speech in Birmingham in 1896, Mr. Joseph Chamberlain stated that in the development of new colonial territories Britain acted "as trustees of civilisation for the commerce of the world. We offer in all these markets over which our flag floats the same opportunities, the same open field to foreigners that we offer to our own subjects, and upon the same terms. In that policy we stand alone. . . . All other nations seek at once to secure monopoly for their own products by preferential and artificial methods." It was argued, too, that Britain was compelled to take part in the scramble for Africa in order to avoid having all the doors closed to her trade.

Mention may be made of a few exceptions to Britain's otherwise strict application of the open-door policy; they serve mainly to emphasise the extent to which this policy was effective. In 1904 an export duty on tin ore from the Federated Malay States was modified to give preference to ore shipped for smelting in Great Britain;[1] the preference did not, however, apply to other parts of the British Empire. The raising of Rhodesian customs duties in 1906 gave preferences

---

[1] This preferential system is still in operation.

to British products in accordance with an Order in Council
of 1898 which specified the maximum duties to be levied
on imports from Britain. In 1913 an agreement negotiated
between many of the West Indian Colonies and Canada
came into operation providing for preference in the Canadian
market for sugar exported by these Colonies. Empire wines,
especially those from Australia, were given preference in the
Falkland Islands as a result of the system of tariff classifi-
cation adopted. For these infringements of the open-door
principle, which were less in the interests of Great Britain
than of the Colonies, the British Government was ultimately
responsible in view of its constitutional power to override
any policy of which it disapproved, even though favoured
by colonial opinion.

The war caused a great change of opinion, and increasing
support was forthcoming in Britain for a preferential
Empire policy, and abandonment of the open-door system.
Towards the end of the war, on the initiative of the British
Government, a substantial export duty was imposed by
the West African Colonies upon all palm kernels shipped
by them to foreign countries; kernels exported to and
crushed in Great Britain or any other part of the Empire
were exempt. This preferential arrangement was adopted
in the interest of Great Britain rather than that of the
Colonies, and was directed chiefly against Germany which,
before the war, had imported a large part of the West
African palm-kernel exports. This was the first serious
departure from the open-door principle in the interests of
the Mother Country during sixty years. Two further derogations took effect in 1919. The Legislative Council of India,
with a view to helping the Indian tanning industry, imposed
an export duty of 15 per cent on untanned hides and skins,
but granted a rebate of two-thirds of the duty on those to
be tanned within the British Empire.[1] A differential export
duty on tin shipped from Nigeria with preference for the
Empire was imposed on instructions from the Colonial

[1] India had gained fiscal autonomy in 1917.

Office. Of these three raw-material preferences, those on palm kernels and hides and skins were abandoned after a short period, but that on Nigerian tin has been retained.

The open-door principle has been mainly violated not by differential export duties on raw materials, which encounter most opposition from foreign countries and are evidently injurious to the interests of colonial producers, but by preferences on British goods imported by the Colonies. Contrary to its earlier practice the British Government since the war, acting through the Colonial Office, has favoured the establishment of such preferential import duties by the Colonies. As early as 1922 preferential tariff systems were widely applied in various parts of the Empire, twenty-five or more Colonies being involved. In a number of Colonies, however, the open door was maintained in accordance with treaty provisions, while in mandated territories ("A" and "B" Mandates) equality of treatment to all States Members of the League of Nations is a legal obligation under the Covenant.[1] Even apart from these exceptions, the Colonial Secretary cannot directly order the Colonies to grant preferences. His authority varies considerably in the different Colonies, in some of which the influence of local opinion and its representation in the legislative councils is considerable. Colonial Office instructions, however, carry great weight, and in the last resort local opinion can formally, if not always in fact, be overridden by the official element.

As indicated below, the Ottawa Conference resulted in a large extension of preferences in the Colonies for the products of Great Britain and the Dominions, which themselves made concessions to colonial products. In place of the uncoordinated preferences of the previous decade, which applied to not more than about 6 to 8 per cent of colonial trade, the open-door principle was systematically abandoned, except where treaty obligations stood in the way.

[1] In practice there seems to be no example of discrimination in these mandated territories against non-members of the League.

The Ottawa Agreements

The Agreements reached at the Ottawa Conference in August 1932 were made possible by the Import Duties Act of the same year by which Britain adopted an extensive protective system. She was then for the first time able to offer a wide range of preferences to the Dominions and Colonies, and the structure of the New Protection was completed at Ottawa on the principle of "the home producer first, Empire producers second, and foreign producers last." Except for this preferential rank, the negotiations and agreements with the Dominions were essentially similar to the bilateral trade agreements with foreign countries reviewed in the last chapter. The chances of success were distinctly greater than those of the World Economic Conference held during the following year; currency relations were less uncertain, trade was less competitive within the Empire than between the leading manufacturing countries, while association as members of the Commonwealth facilitated the negotiations.

Nevertheless, the Agreements were reached in an atmosphere of realism without a trace of sentimental Imperialism. Indeed, the so-called "sordid bargaining," hard dealing, and bitter struggles were thought by many to involve serious danger to good relations within the Empire. Both Great Britain and the Dominions rejected the idea of Empire Free Trade as quite impracticable. The war had destroyed any possibility of such a system by causing the Dominions rapidly to develop manufacturing industries when British supplies were difficult to obtain, and henceforth the production of Britain and the Dominions included an appreciable competitive element alongside their complementary trade. The Dominions, desiring to maintain and develop their manufacturing industries and fearing almost equally the competition of British and foreign goods, were unwilling to make substantial reductions in their tariffs. On her side, Britain disliked raising considerable tariffs against foreign supplies of food and raw materials, on account of the unpopularity of taxes on food-stuffs and of the effect of such tariffs upon costs of production and therefore upon the export trade; yet tariffs upon these commodities were necessary if really valuable preferences were to be accorded to the characteristic products of the Dominions and Colonies.

The general purpose of the Agreements was stated by leading British and Dominion statesmen to be the development of more trade and freer trade throughout the Empire as a step to more trade and freer trade throughout the world. For example, Mr. Baldwin, the leader of the British Delegation, stated the general objective of the Conference to be "the expansion of Empire trade, to be brought about as far as possible by lowering the trade barriers between the several members of the Empire." Both he and Mr. Bennett, then Canadian Prime Minister, repudiated any idea of isolating the Empire from the rest of the world by tariff walls designed to shut out foreign trade. The Empire was to become an area of greater liberty of trading, but such an area could be extended whenever other countries were prepared to reduce their restrictions. The Agreements were not, however, entirely consistent with these principles. Thus Britain agreed to maintain or impose duties on a considerable range of foreign food-stuffs and raw materials in order to grant preferences to Empire producers. Her obligations to maintain specified tariff rates considerably restricted her freedom to negotiate agreements with foreign countries for reciprocal lowering of tariffs. The Agreement between Great Britain and Australia included a provision stating that for meat the policy of the British Government is, first, to secure the development of home production, and, second, to give the Dominions an expanding share of imports into the United Kingdom. This would involve at least a *relative* restriction of foreign sales to Britain. There was also considerable support for the view that for many commodities the resources of the Empire were adequate for its needs and that trade should be organised so as to use these resources; if fully acted upon this would imply for these commodities a policy of self-sufficiency and exclusiveness.

Eleven separate preferential agreements were concluded at Ottawa, but four of them were between two Dominions or between a Dominion and Southern Rhodesia and need not be reviewed here. Those in which Great Britain was directly involved were with Canada, Australia, New Zealand, Newfoundland, South Africa, Southern Rhodesia, and India; the British Government also negotiated many reciprocal preferences between some of the Dominions and the non-self-governing Colonies. All the Agreements were to remain in operation for five years, except the Indian Agreement, which could be terminated by giving six months' notice. The present account deals with the general principles upon which the Agreements were based, details being given only for purposes of illustration. Some of the undertakings summarised below were not included in all of the Agreements.[1]

Essentially the Agreements provide that, in return for increased preferences over a wide range of commodities in the Dominions, the British Government would continue the exemption of Empire products from the duties imposed under the Import Duties Act 1932, that is, would accord them free entry, and would maintain at least the existing duties of 10 per cent on specified foreign products.[2] Britain even agreed not to reduce these general *ad valorem* duties of 10 per cent without the consent of the Dominion Governments, thus limiting her fiscal freedom for the five years covered by the Agreements. She also undertook to impose or increase duties on foreign supplies of commodities, chiefly certain foods and raw materials in which the Dominions were specially interested but which had hitherto been untaxed, in order to increase the preferential advantages enjoyed by the Dominions in the British market.

---

[1] For example, the commodities upon which preferences were maintained or increased vary according to the trading interests of each Dominion.

[2] These included timber, fresh and canned fish, canned meat, barley, wheat, flour, macaroni, leather, tallow, lead, zinc, copra, and asbestos.

These new or increased duties include two shillings a quarter on wheat, fifteen shillings a hundredweight on butter, 15 per cent *ad valorem* on cheese, together with specific duties on various raw fruits, canned apples, dried fruits, condensed milk, eggs, honey, cod-liver oil, chilled and frozen salmon, copper, rice, linseed, and other products.[1] Except for these changes the Agreements involved few tariff increases on foreign products, while Britain secured increased preferences by the lowering of Dominion tariffs. A few commodities were added to the British free list, e.g., shellac, jute, and Indian hemp. The British Government further undertook to maintain for ten years specified margins of preference on the revenue duties paid by foreign importers of tobacco into Great Britain.

The British Government introduced two main safeguards when granting increased Empire preferences, the first to avoid injury from shortage or limitation of supplies, and the second to give opportunities for expansion of home agricultural production. Thus the new duties on foreign wheat, copper, lead, and zinc can be removed at any time if Empire producers are "unable or unwilling to offer those commodities on first sale in the United Kingdom at prices not exceeding the world prices and in quantities sufficient to supply the requirements of the United Kingdom consumers" (Canadian Agreement). The danger envisaged has not been experienced in the conditions of world depression, with abundance of supplies, which have persisted throughout the period since the Agreements came into operation; the testing-time will come when prosperity results in a great expansion of demand.

For certain foods Britain was unwilling to give *carte blanche* to the Dominions. As already stated, the British Government's meat policy is to restrict foreign entry and to give the Dominions an expanding share of imports into Great Britain, but only in so far as this is consistent with

---

[1] Of these wheat, copper, and linseed had previously been on the free list.

the development of home production. In the operation of
the Agreement Australia has laid great emphasis upon the
right of the Dominions to this expanding market.[1] With a
view to raising meat prices to remunerative levels, Britain
undertook to regulate her imports of frozen mutton and
lamb and of chilled and frozen beef, while the supplies of
bacon and ham coming on to the British market were to
be regulated quantitatively.[2] In the interests of the home
producer Great Britain also reserved her right to review at
the end of three years the basis of the preferences for dairy
products, poultry and eggs, and either to impose a preferential duty on imports from the Dominions while maintaining the existing margin of preference, or, in consultation
with the Dominions, to adopt a system of quantitative
regulation.

The British Government secured the acceptance of two
general principles dealing with the protection of Dominion
industries. Canada, Australia, and New Zealand agreed that
"protection by tariffs shall be afforded against United
Kingdom products only to those industries which are
reasonably assured of sound opportunities for success."
The application of this principle would restrict the growth
of competitive industries and would facilitate the preser-
vation of complementary trade. The second principle deals
with the tariff levels to be fixed for the protection of suitable
industries. Protective duties against British products in the
Dominions "shall not exceed such a level as will give United
Kingdom producers full opportunity of reasonable competition on the basis of the relative cost of economical and
efficient production, provided that in the application of
such principle special consideration shall be given to the
case of industries not fully established." This implies a
reconsideration of existing tariff schedules, and the Do-

[1] Australia's attitude on this question is reviewed in the following
chapter.
[2] These undertakings are considered in the next chapter. In any arrangements made to regulate British imports of bacon and ham Canada is to
have free entry for not less than 2½ million cwt. per annum.

minion Governments undertook that Tariff Boards would be responsible for the revision of rates. The British Government secured the right to request the Boards to review the duties charged on any specified commodities with a view to giving effect to these two principles, and British producers are entitled to be heard if they consider that the principles are being violated by existing or proposed tariffs.

In practice, both principles are difficult to apply. There are many industries about which it cannot definitely be decided that they have no reasonable chance of success in a Dominion until the experiment has been tried, by which time capital has been invested and opposition is raised to the abandonment of high protection. Also, leaving aside the difficulty of determining when an industry suited to Dominion conditions is still an "infant" requiring special protection, the principle that tariffs should be levied at rates which are just sufficient to compensate for differences in cost of production would, if generally applied, destroy the whole basis of trade. Actually, in the operation of the Agreements this principle has been found unworkable. For example, the Canadian Tariff Board after conducting detailed inquiries into British and Canadian costs of production of various commodities, including a review of information submitted by British firms, was unable to reach satisfactory conclusions about relative costs in the two countries. In attempting such comparisons one of the difficulties is that only very rarely are identical commodities produced in two countries, while account must also be taken of the inter-related costs of the whole production of a firm and not merely of the costs of a single product.

During the negotiation of the Agreements Canada showed great concern about Russian competition in the wheat and timber markets of Great Britain and pressed strongly for the formulation of satisfactory safeguards. It was generally recognised that Russian trade being a State monopoly was not necessarily operated in the same way as ordinary competitive trade and that for a time certain products might be offered in certain markets at prices considerably below costs of production, either to capture trade from some other country or for non-economic reasons. The British Government, however, wished to avoid an open clash with the U.S.S.R., which would result if she agreed to discriminate against Soviet trade. Finally, after difficult negotiations, a clause drafted in general terms without mentioning the U.S.S.R., was inserted in the Canadian Agreement providing that, if either Government is satisfied that preferences granted by the Agreement in respect of any particular class of commodities are likely to be frustrated by the creation or maintenance of prices through State action on the part of any foreign country, that Government will prohibit the importation of such commodities from the foreign country concerned for such time as may be necessary to ensure the effectiveness of the preferences. This involved termination by the British Government of her most-favoured-nation agreement with the U.S.S.R., which had been in force since 1930. At the Ottawa Conference the Governments had undertaken to free themselves from existing treaties which might interfere with any mutual preferences granted within the Commonwealth, and had agreed not to enter into any treaty obligations in the future which would interfere with such preferences.[1]

In the Agreements the method of fixing minimum margins of preference was adopted. This may have certain advantages, but it limits freedom to negotiate reciprocal agreements with foreign countries and is, therefore, an obstacle to obtaining concessions for British trade. Again, British trade policy as applied in the Ottawa Agreements is somewhat inconsistent with her monetary policy; foreign as well as Empire countries are encouraged to join and cooperate in the sterling area on terms of equality, whereas the British tariff system, by favouring Empire countries,

[1] Not only was it necessary to cancel the Anglo-Soviet Treaty, but the Union of South Africa took steps to terminate its obligations under a treaty with Germany which provided that any favourable treatment accorded to Great Britain would be enjoyed also by Germany.

discriminates against all foreign countries, whether members of the sterling area or not.[1]

The question may be raised whether measures should be taken to protect British producers against unfair competition from inside as well as outside the Empire, or whether such measures should be directed only against foreign countries. Unfair competition resulting from sweated conditions, subsidies, currency depreciation, or dumping at prices below costs of production may originate in Empire countries and be as injurious to British manufacturers as if it came from foreign countries. To prevent injury from such competition the withdrawal of preferential treatment from the Empire country concerned or even a policy of discrimination against it might be necessary. In practice, however, it seems to be assumed that special measures for protection against unfair competition will be directed only against foreign countries.

Britain's right to arrange preferences within the Empire and to abandon the open-door policy in colonial areas has not been challenged. Other countries have acquiesced in an interpretation of the most-favoured-nation clause which permit of exclusive tariff preferences and maintenance of margins of preference within the Empire. With the adoption of the new Imperial trade policy Britain cannot any longer claim that the flag and the political associations of the Empire confer no exclusive advantages. The more these advantages are increased the greater will become the jealousy of foreign Powers and the stronger the incentive for them to weaken or destroy the Empire. On the other hand, an Empire closely bound together by economic as well as racial and cultural interests is more likely to unite in resisting attack and will be stronger to achieve success than if economic relations are weak and uncoordinated.

An immediate political consequence of the Ottawa Agreements was the resignation from the National Govern-

---

[1] This is modified by the bilateral agreements concluded with foreign countries, many of which are in the sterling area.

ment of Lord Snowden and of Sir Herbert Samuel and a number of his Liberal Party colleagues. At the beginning of 1932 they had resigned as a protest against the tariff policy of the Government but had been persuaded to withdraw their resignations on the understanding that the principle of Cabinet or Ministerial responsibility would be waived.[1] Even this concession would not induce them to continue their support of the Government when the Ottawa Agreements were concluded. The Samuelite Liberals considered that the Agreements would be a hindrance rather than a help to trade recovery, that they added new obstacles to world trade, particularly by quotas and new duties on foreign products, that the British Parliament was surrendering rights by binding itself not to reduce certain duties without the consent of the Dominions, that the British Government had limited its power to negotiate freer conditions of trade with other countries, that the taxation of essential food-stuffs imposed new burdens on the mass of the people, and that strain would be imposed on Empire unity and friendship by the endless bickerings which the operation of the Agreements would involve.

Lord Snowden's resignation, which was couched in typically vigorous language, referred to the return from Ottawa of the British Delegation "after weeks of acrimonious disputes and sordid struggles with vested interests, with agreements wrenched from them to avert a collapse of the Conference and an exposure to the world of the hollowness of the talk of Imperial sentiment in economic affairs." After stating reasons similar to those advanced by the Liberals against the Agreements he claimed that the Dominions were to have a free market in Great Britain while retaining their protective and often prohibitive duties against British trade, and he concluded that free traders

---

[1] In the General Election of 1931 the formula on tariffs adopted by Mr. Ramsay MacDonald and Mr. Baldwin was "an examination by the National Government of the policy of tariffs, with an open mind and without hampering pledges, and to put it into force if it was found to be the best means of restoring a favourable balance of trade."

could not be expected to acquiesce, even passively, "in such a policy of national humiliation and bondage."

OPERATION OF THE OTTAWA AGREEMENTS

In reviewing the operation of the Ottawa Agreements two main aspects may be considered, first, the application of the principles adopted by the Conference, and second, the actual trends of trade resulting from the preferences. Largely in return for specified preferences in the British market, Canada, Australia, and New Zealand, as already stated, undertook not to protect unsuitable industries and not to fix tariffs so high that British producers would not have full opportunity of reasonable competition on the basis of relative costs of economical and efficient production, special consideration, however, being given to industries not fully established. The application of these principles, which was expected to result in substantial reductions of tariffs on British manufactures, is here outlined. Other principles included in the Agreements to ensure to Dominion farmers a reasonable share of the British market in relation to the new schemes for reviving British agriculture are reserved for consideration in the following chapter.

The principles for avoiding excessive protection of Dominion industries against British goods have received varied application in different Dominions, and difficulties have arisen in their interpretation. These have been greatest in Canada and Australia, which, being the most industrial-ised of the Dominions, compete most keenly with British manufactures. The principles, being vague, are capable of varying interpretations. While committed to lower rates on British than on foreign goods the Dominions can still protect their own manufacturers in industries likely to be successful under Dominion conditions, and, although certain industries may be manifestly unsuitable, many others must have their chance and can demand protection. Though the protection afforded to Dominion industries should not be prohibitive but should be based upon relative costs, in order to give British manufacturers full opportunities of reasonable competition, it is difficult in practice to agree upon relative costs. Also exceptions can be made by Dominion Tariff Boards in protecting industries not yet fully established. This opens the door to high protection for many industries. On the other hand, the tariffs should fall progressively, and finally be removed altogether, as Dominion industries reach levels of costs equal to those of British industries, including costs of transporting British goods to the Dominions.

It is of interest to note that the principle of reasonable competition based on relative costs has not been adopted for determining the levels of British tariffs on food-stuffs and other primary products imported from the Empire. If operated in the same way as the Dominions apply the principle to British manufactures, the tariff rates against Dominion products would be considerably higher even than those now in force on food and raw materials imported from foreign countries.

New Zealand, less developed industrially than Canada and Australia and more dependent upon the British market, has given a more liberal interpretation to the Ottawa principles. Her Tariff Commission considers that British manufactures should have a fair deal, this being understood to mean that prohibitive duties should be ruled out and that, while recognising that relative costs cannot be compared with mathematical accuracy, the duties on British imports must be based upon differences in production costs in the two countries, and must aim at equalising these costs. Their recommendations, which were adopted in July 1934, resulted in extensive tariff reductions and abolition of duties, thereby increasing the preferences on British goods.[1]

The New Zealand Government, in considering means of increasing Britain's purchasing power over New Zealand

---

[1] In addition to the abolition of duties on more than twenty classes of commodities, reductions ranging from 10 to 50 per cent were effected on a large number of manufactures. On a few categories the Commission recommended small increases of duty.

products, had already inquired whether the British Government would be willing to consider granting special advantages for New Zealand products in the British market in return for a great lowering of duties on British manufactures imported by New Zealand. This would, however, have involved granting favours to one Dominion with consequent discrimination against others, and it would also have created difficulties for the manufacturing industries of New Zealand. No steps were taken to negotiate a reciprocal agreement along these lines.

The Canadian Tariff Board during 1933 and 1934 received representatives from British manufacturers who claimed tariff reductions in accordance with the competitive principle, and detailed investigations into costs of production in Canada and Great Britain were made. The hearings before the Board became a conflict between the Canadian and British manufacturing interests, and continued the struggles of the Ottawa Conference, where the Canadian industrialists had consistently opposed the competitive principle. Indeed, there developed a "Canada versus Britain" atmosphere of tension and strain.[1] Unfortunately, in attempting to compare costs of woollen goods, on which Canadian tariffs are very high, the Board found it impossible to obtain reliable data and came to the conclusion that this method could not be used satisfactorily for determining the levels of Canadian protective tariffs.[2]

Though strict scientific accuracy may be impossible of attainment, this should not stand in the way of substantial reductions from the very high tariffs in force, which could

[1] See the *Economist*, June 30, 1934.

[2] This was in an interim report, and the Board proposed to continue its investigations. It insists that comparison of costs must be made upon the basis of goods of the same kind and quality. In its inquiries in the woollen industry, however, it states that "a diligent search among the 150 woollen cloths in the British sample and the 100 woollen cloths in the Canadian sample revealed that not a single pair of cloths afforded a fair comparison, while an examination of the worsted cloths by a textile expert did not disclose more than six or seven pairs of cloths of approximately similar structure." Difficulties also arose from differences in methods of manufacturing and of cost accountancy in the two countries. The difficulties are, of course, greatest in industries in which production is complicated.

not be justified by reference to the relative cost principle even if interpreted most liberally on the Canadian side. But in the absence of a workable principle the amount of protection tends to be determined by political considerations, while high tariffs can be maintained by alleging that various industries are not fully established. Much, therefore, depends upon the spirit in which the principles are applied and the attitudes adopted towards the policy of high protection, but in practice Canada has not yet made substantial reductions. The coming into power of the Mackenzie King Liberal Government as a result of the 1935 elections may, however, lead to lower tariffs.

Australia also has maintained high protection, and for a period beginning in the summer of 1934 even increased the duties on certain classes of cotton yarn and piece goods on the recommendation of her Tariff Board. There has therefore been considerable dissatisfaction at the way Australia has interpreted the Ottawa Agreements. Although the new cotton duties applied only to about 3 per cent of Australia's purchases of cotton goods from Lancashire, they were so high as to be prohibitive, being at the rate of 100 per cent or more on some products, and a storm of protest resulted. In several Lancashire towns boycotts of Australian produce were organised, and, although such action was regarded by British cotton manufacturers and by members of the British Government as ill-advised, likely to aggravate the situation and cause reprisals, objection was raised to the duties on the ground that they violated the principles of the Ottawa Agreement by not permitting reasonable competition on the basis of relative cost. In Australia the duties were described by Dr. Page, leader of the Federal Country Party, as being "like a body-line attack on Ottawa."[1]

[1] The duties were intended not merely to protect cotton manufacturers in Australia, but also cotton growers in Queensland. They seem to have been designed to secure the support of the cotton growers in the then pending elections. In return for favourable terms for Lancashire manufactures exported to Australia certain Lancashire firms stated their willingness to consider buying Australian-grown cotton, with a view to meeting the demands of Australian cotton growers.

Industries which required such high protection could not be regarded as having reasonable prospects of success, and, if duties of 100 per cent or more could be imposed, the Ottawa principles would be of little value to British industry. Therefore, although the scope of the new duties was restricted and although Australia had long maintained valuable preferences for British cotton goods, the question at issue was the observance of the Agreement, and the British protests were fully justified. If prohibitive duties were imposed on some commodities they could be extended to others.

Later in 1934, as a result mainly of the Country Party's influence, which feared that high Australian import duties would reduce Australian exports to Britain and increase the prices of manufactured goods to Australian consumers, the Australian Government made substantial reductions in the duties on cotton goods imported from Great Britain, thus removing Lancashire's grievance.[1] Lower rates were fixed on a considerable number of other commodities, although a few increases were introduced. Reductions were also made upon goods from other countries, but the British preferential margin was generally maintained, or even increased on some commodities. Although this was a move in the right direction, British and also foreign traders still experience difficulty in selling to Australia because of the combined effect of the tariffs and depreciation of the Australian currency. From the point of view of Australian industries, the tariffs on British goods are considered by the Australian Tariff Board to give adequate protection to Australian interests at existing rates of exchange, and if British currency depreciates the tariff rates are automatically increased.

Although it is yet too early to estimate the full effects of the Ottawa Agreements, certain preliminary indications can be given. In general the Agreements have operated

---

[1] On shirtings, undyed sheetings and drills, for example, the rates were reduced to 5 per cent *ad valorem* from 20 per cent *ad valorem*, plus 6d. per square yard. In the spring of 1935 reductions on other goods were arranged.

more favourably for the Dominions than for Great Britain. This is not surprising, as Great Britain was introducing for the first time preferences on a wide range of commodities, whereas the Dominions were making little departure from their traditional policy. They were continuing an established system, somewhat modified by widening the margin of preferences and reducing certain duties so as to increase the opportunities of British exporters. The smallness of the reductions has been a disappointment to British manufacturers. In amount, the reductions have been greatest in New Zealand and least in Canada and Australia. One important development is the recognition by India in an Agreement in January 1935, supplementary to the Ottawa Agreement, of the principle of Imperial Preference and the arranging of preferences to Great Britain covering more than one-quarter of her exports to India.

Trade statistics show that since the Ottawa Agreements came into operation there has been an increase in Inter-Imperial trade mainly by expansion of exports from the Dominions to Great Britain, with a considerably smaller improvement in British exports to Empire countries. The new British preferences gave Empire countries an opportunity to expand their markets in Britain at the expense of foreign countries. Also, with the shrinkage of world trade, Britain's imports and exports within the Empire form an increased proportion of her total trade. This is illustrated by the statistics[1] shown opposite.

The table shows a substantial increase since the Ottawa Conference in the value of Empire products marketed in Britain, and also in the proportion which these products represent of total British imports. The gain in British exports, including re-exports, was much smaller, and was more than offset by a decline in British exports to foreign countries. Whereas the trade of the Dominions and India

[1] They are based upon data taken from *Empire Trade Before and After Ottawa: A Preliminary Reconnaissance*, by Sir George Schuster, published as a special Supplement to the *Economist*, November 3, 1934. Some of the conclusions which follow are based on this Paper.

with foreign countries was proportionately greater during
the years 1924 to 1929 than before the war, there was a
marked increase during the depression in the relative
importance of their trade with Britain, this increase, as
already indicated, being greater in their exports to than in
their imports from Britain.

Although the growth in the relative importance of Empire
to foreign trade has been influenced by the Ottawa preferences other factors have also contributed to the change.

UNITED KINGDOM TRADE WITH EMPIRE COUNTRIES*

Year	Imports		Exports (Including Re-exports)	
	Values in £ millions	Percentage of Total Imports	Values in £ millions	Percentage of Total Exports
1913	192	24·9	209	32·9
1924–29†	335	26·8	303	35·2
1931	209	23·2	148	32·6
1933	231	34·3	150	36·0
1934	254	34·7	172	38·4
1935	266	35·1	190	39·5

* Excluding trade with the Irish Free State.
† Average.

The linking together of the Empire countries by sterling as
a common monetary standard has facilitated trade between
them. Another factor has been the continuation of lending
by Great Britain to Empire countries and the almost
complete cessation of loans to foreign countries during the
depression; this must have tended to increase the proportion
of Inter-Imperial trade, since loans usually result in export
of goods from the lending to the borrowing country. During
the depression also Britain has proved to be a much more
stable market than foreign countries for Empire produce,
many foreign countries having gone farther than Great
Britain in restricting imports of food and other primary
products. When more normal conditions of world trade are
restored foreign countries will be likely to increase con-

siderably their demand for these commodities, and so to some extent reverse the recent trend. In addition to the policy of trade and financial preferences, the lifting of the boycott in India against British goods accounts for part of the rise in the relative importance of her imports of British goods.[1] Economic uncertainties in the United States explain some of the diversion during recent years of Canadian trade from that country to Britain.[2]

In considering the general implications of the new Imperial economic policy it was certain that preferential treatment of Empire countries would follow the conversion of Britain to protection. The method of reciprocal tariff bargains between the Dominions and the Mother Country was a less inevitable corollary. Only a few years before the Ottawa Conference the Balfour Committee had considered the idea of such bargains as quite alien to the spirit and practice of Imperial relations, which should be conducted on a higher plane. In the development of Britain's new tariff and preferential policy consultation with the Governments of the Dominions is of mutual advantage, but there is danger of frequent friction especially in the application of general principles and the fixing of quotas.

These difficulties arise both when the interests of British and Dominion producers are in conflict and when the Dominions urge against foreign countries claims which Britain may find it inconvenient or inadvisable to grant. For example, Australia and New Zealand demand increases in their share of the British market at the expense of Denmark and the Argentine, while Canada presses for further restrictions upon timber and other commodities imported by Britain from the U.S.S.R. Since the demands of sectional and vested interests are unlimited it will be desirable, when

[1] This rose from 36·7 per cent of India's total imports in 1931 to 41·2 per cent in 1933. During the same period Indian exports to Britain rose from 22·8 per cent to 31·8 per cent of her total exports, the gain being largely the result of the British preferences.

[2] These two countries—India and Canada—showed greater changes between 1931 and 1933 than other Empire countries in the proportions of their British to total trade.

the Ottawa Agreements are revised, to avoid methods involving frequent adjustments which give occasion for conflict. Thus in the operation of the quota system frequent changes are necessary, and each change may give rise to bitter controversy, whereas preferential tariffs can be fixed for longer periods and impose less strain upon Imperial and international relations.

CHAPTER VI

AGRICULTURAL POLICY

British agriculture has experienced changes of policy during recent years comparable in magnitude with those in monetary and commercial policy. For eighty-five years from the repeal of the Corn Laws in 1846 a long-range policy of *laissez-faire* scarcely distinguishable from neglect had been applied. It suited the predominant industrial interests that food and raw materials should be purchased in the cheapest markets, thus ensuring low manufacturing costs and low selling prices in world markets. Investment overseas was also facilitated and demands for shipping and shipbuilding were stimulated, but British agriculture, in competition with the developing overseas areas, suffered almost continuous decline. The policy was consistent on the assumption that agriculture could be sacrificed without injury to the national interests.

There is, however, widespread agreement that a prosperous rural community is an essential element in the economic and social structure of any country, however developed may be its industry and trade. The war years indicated the risk incurred by producing only a small proportion of the nation's food supplies at home and depending upon supplies from abroad, which would be cut off if control of trade routes were lost. But, although British agricultural production was considerably increased during the war to compensate for the curtailment of overseas supplies and to provide, so far as possible, against the danger of still greater restrictions upon trade as a result of the German submarine campaign, the recovery was not maintained and in post-war years the declining trend was resumed. The industrial electorate resolutely opposed food taxes, being convinced that the standard of living and competitive efficiency of the country would be thereby impaired, to such an extent that to

propose protection for agriculture was virtually an act of
political suicide.

Already experiencing difficulties in the first post-war
decade, British agriculture seemed in danger of being
overwhelmed by the depression. Reduced consumers' incomes
caused a heavy fall in demand, and the consequent catas-
trophic collapse of world agricultural prices threatened chaos
to British farmers, as to those of other countries. The extent
of the fall in British agricultural prices is shown by the
following index numbers of average prices:[1]

Commodity Group	Index Numbers (1911–13 = 100)	
	1925–9	1931
Cereals	142	86
Live stock products	152	127
Fruits and vegetables	172	134

In these circumstances the British National Government
began to evolve a new policy with the two objects of helping
the British farmer to survive the temporary difficulties of
the depression, and of ensuring the rehabilitation of British
agriculture on a more permanent basis. Certain tentative
measures had been taken by earlier Governments, but it
was not until after the Ottawa Conference that the
new policy began to take shape and become something
more than a succession of uncoordinated emergency
measures.

Before reviewing the main features of the new policy
a brief indication may be given of the position of agriculture
in the economic life of the country, and the relation of its
food production to the total food consumption of the population. Despite long neglect and decline, agriculture, together
with horticulture, is still Britain's largest single industry,
with a capital value of over £1,000 million, an estimated
annual output in England and Wales of £202,660,000 in

---

[1] Price indexes compiled by the Ministry of Agriculture.

1930–1[1], and employing over a million persons. Although predominantly industrial, Great Britain produces more food than any of the Dominions. Production is highly specialised; thus more than 70 per cent of the annual value of output in 1930–31 consisted of live stock and live stock products. The following figures for England and Wales are the values of output and the percentages of total annual value in 1930–1 represented by the various products:

LIVE STOCK AND LIVE STOCK PRODUCTS

	Value in £ million	Percentage of total value
Milk	47·5	23·4
Milk products	7·5	3·7
Beef and veal	29·9	14·8
Pig products	19·5	9·6
Mutton and lamb	15·6	7·7
Wool	1·3	0·6
Poultry and eggs	21·0	10·4
Total	142·3	70·2

OTHER PRODUCTS

	Value in £ million	Percentage of total value
Wheat	3·6	1·8
Other corn crops	6·2	3·0
Potatoes	11·7	5·8
Sugar-beet	6·8	3·3
Hops	0·9	0·5
Hay and straw	4·0	2·0
Fruit, vegetables, etc.*	27·2	13·4
Total	60·4	29·8

* Including flowers and glasshouse produce.

The general tendency for some years was a growth in importance of live stock in British farming, accompanied by a steady changeover from arable to pasture land. The cultivation of sugar-beet, under the stimulus of the subsidy,

[1] This figure represents the value of output sold off the farms, the value of crops which were fed to live stock or retained as seed being excluded; it includes, however, the value of certain feeding stuffs, etc., and live stock for fattening bought from abroad, and also the value of farmers' food.

made rapid progress during the years 1925 to 1931, while the importance of poultry farming also considerably increased.

British agriculture during the period from 1925 to 1931 supplied only about 40 per cent of the total value of the food consumption of the country, which was dependent for the remaining 60 per cent upon imports from abroad, the degree of dependence being greater in this period than before the war. Home production, however, rose from 38 per cent of total supplies in 1925 to 42 per cent in 1930–1. If account be taken of the low prices of imported meat (chilled and frozen) which enters largely into the consumption of the poorer sections of the community, the dependence in terms of quantities was even greater than that in terms of money. Of the total value of the chief agricultural commodities imported into the country in 1931—the last year before the introduction of the new policy—just under three-fifths (58 per cent) came from foreign countries and just over two-fifths from Empire countries. In very approximate round figures about 40 per cent of Britain's food requirements were supplied by home production, a little more than 35 per cent by foreign countries, and under 25 per cent by Empire countries.

The figures on page 160 show the values in 1931 of some of the chief food commodities imported into Great Britain from foreign countries and Empire countries.[1] Competition in some of the commodities was keen between foreign and Empire producers, as well as with home producers, while in others, for example fresh vegetables, distance excluded Empire countries, competition being, however, considerable between home and neighbouring foreign producers.

In the following sections the chief features and effects of the new agricultural policy are outlined only in so far as they involve economic relations with foreign countries,

---

[1] In addition to food products the figures of raw wool imports may be given:—from foreign countries £5·7 million, from Empire countries £27·0 million.

VALUE OF CERTAIN BRITISH FOOD IMPORTS IN 1931

(in £ million)

	From Foreign Countries	From Empire Countries
Bacon and hams	34·6	1·7
Chilled beef	20·1	—
Frozen beef	0·9	1·9
Frozen mutton and lamb	5·0	13·2
Butter and cheese	25·9	29·4
Wheat and wheaten flour	18·0	16·4
Barley, oats, and maize	14·6	1·4
Eggs	13·3	3·3
Apples	4·3	3·6
Other fresh fruit*	5·5	2·2
Potatoes	5·9	1·0
Fresh vegetables	1·6	—

* Including tomatoes.

whether by preferential treatment of home or of Empire producers. No attempt is made systematically to review matters mainly of domestic interest, and reference is made to forms of marketing organisation and methods of administration only where this is necessary for an understanding of international aspects.

OBJECTS OF POLICY

The primary objects of the new policy are to protect British agriculture by emergency measures from being overwhelmed by the threatened flood of imports at ruinously low prices during the depression, and to stimulate a revival of British farming under conditions which will ensure its permanent welfare. Subject to these objects being achieved, Empire countries are to be given preferences over foreign countries in the British market; in other words the Ottawa principle is to be applied, the interests of the home producer coming first, Empire producers second, and foreign countries last. This implies abandoning the former policy of buying food and raw materials all over the world in the cheapest markets, and, in applying emergency measures, attempts have been made to raise prices in the interests of the British farmer.

The long-range policy represents in part a reaction from over-industrialisation and from the high degree of dependence upon imported supplies of food and raw materials purchased by exports of manufactured goods. Increased difficulties of the export trade and the tendency for the balance of trade to become less favourable lent support to the policy of producing more food at home. In certain branches of agriculture there seemed no reason why, with encouragement of more efficient methods and cooperative marketing, British farmers should not be able to produce at costs which would compare favourably with those of other countries. Economic reasons have been reinforced by non-economic considerations, such as the social advantages to a country of a stable and prosperous agricultural population, and diminution of the risk of food shortage in time of war.

The short-period or emergency policy involves restriction of food imports from abroad in the interests of the British farmer, while, although the long-range objective could largely be gained by improving the efficiency of British agricultural production, there are indications that protective measures will be established on a permanent basis. These measures will be likely to react unfavourably upon British consumers, industrial and shipping interests, and overseas investors, who will resist a policy of high protection for agriculture, although they may acquiesce in the application of moderate measures to ensure greater stability in the rural community.

Externally, the British Government is faced with uneasiness on the part of the Dominions and of those foreign countries which have been large suppliers of agricultural produce for the British market. It is an example of dramatic irony that Britain should decide upon the revival of her own agriculture at the very moment when it became politically possible for her to grant substantial preferences to Dominion farmers. Dominions and foreign countries alike are anxious to know how far Britain intends to develop her agriculture and produce her own food. Alike they point out that restriction of their sales of food and raw materials to Great Britain must inevitably reduce their ability to purchase British manufactures and must add to their difficulties in meeting payments due on their borrowings from Britain. Reduced opportunities in the British market would compel them to seek markets elsewhere, which in turn would involve their purchasing more manufactured goods from Britain's industrial competitors. But although the same factors affect both Empire and foreign farmers, they do so in differing proportion owing to the preferential treatment of Empire countries.

Some of the preferences are definitely specified, but others are merely general principles capable of being applied with greater or less advantage for the Dominions. Thus, as mentioned in the previous chapter, the British Government undertook at the Ottawa Conference to give the Dominions an expanding share of meat imports into Great Britain. This agreement, though of value as a safeguard against a diminishing share, gives no guidance as to the extent or rate of expansion. The application of these general principles has therefore given occasion for political manœuvres between the British, Dominion, and foreign Governments, with three main variables involved—the extent and direction of British agricultural expansion, the volume of agricultural products to be admitted to the British market, and the proportion in which this volume of imports would be divided between Empire and foreign countries.

METHODS APPLIED

The new agricultural policy has been applied by a wide variety of methods to suit different objects, to meet the needs of particular branches of production, and to satisfy the demands of political expediency. The situation called for many experiments rather than for a single stereotyped method, and changes have been made in the light of experience. In some branches of agriculture intense competition from abroad was the chief problem, sometimes aggravated by depreciating rates of exchange; in others, decline in home demand was more important than the volume of imports. Some commodities are produced mainly at home with only a small importation, while others are in the reverse situation with home production forming only a small proportion of total supplies. Remedies appropriate in the emergency of the world depression were not always easily related to the needs of a more permanent programme. Inconsistencies and compromises were inevitable, the claims of British agriculture being modified for the benefit of Dominion farmers, while concessions were made to foreign farmers in the interests of British coal, manufactures, and investments.

The methods applied include the tariff, quantitative regulation, subsidy, levy, and organised marketing of home production, or some combination of these methods. The first two methods involve restriction of imports in the interests of the home producer. During 1930 and 1931 British consumers had enjoyed the benefits of exceptionally low food prices resulting from the collapse of world demand and to the maintenance of free entry into the British market. But prices were unremunerative and British farmers were threatened with ruin. It seemed reasonable that they should be given first claim upon the great market represented by the British industrial population, and that those branches of British agriculture which could hold their own in normal times should be sheltered during the emergency. A policy of restriction might result in higher prices, but the increase would be from an unduly low level below costs of production. A higher price level would also be consistent with the Government's general desire for an upward price movement as one of the ways of ending the depression.

Tariff Protection

The first important measure was tariff protection against foreign countries, and the tariff method has been retained and has increased in favour in comparison with quantitative regulation.

The Import Duties Act, 1932, imposed a 10 per cent *ad valorem* tariff on all foreign imports, with certain specified exceptions, the chief agricultural products on the free list being wheat in grain, maize in grain, meat, live stock, wool, hides, and skins.[1] Additional duties were later imposed on a number of agricultural commodities by orders issued by the Import Duties Advisory Committee.[2] In November 1932, in accordance with the Ottawa Agreements, additional duties were placed on various imports from foreign countries, the commodities including dairy produce, eggs, raw and dried fruits, and rice, and a duty of two shillings a quarter was placed upon foreign wheat, subject to the provision that the Dominions could supply adequate quantities at the world price. Agricultural and also other produce from the Dominions continued to enjoy free entry, being entirely exempt from these duties.

Under the exceptional conditions of the world depression, however, low tariffs upon foreign supplies afforded little protection to the British farmer, who was still exposed to the full force of competition from within the Empire. More comprehensive measures were therefore necessary. Instead of general remedies applied to a wide range of products the method was adopted of dealing separately with particular products by schemes appropriate to the special circumstances of each. As indicated in the previous chapter,

---

[1] In November 1931 the Horticultural Products (Emergency Duties) Act had been passed, giving temporary tariff protection for fruit and vegetables, the prices of which had fallen heavily in 1931, but subsequently its duties were, with some variations, brought within the scope of the Import Duties Act.

[2] The commodities included fresh fruit, vegetables and flowers, potatoes, oats in grain, barley, condensed milk, various preserved fruits, canned vegetables, and poultry. By 1934 the duty on oats had been raised to 3s. a cwt., or about 50 per cent *ad valorem* at current prices. Special duties at high rates were imposed in July 1932 upon live stock, meat, dairy produce, eggs, and poultry imports from the Irish Free State. These duties were a weapon in the political controversy between the Governments, but were of value to the British farmer; in 1936 they were lowered.

the British Government's policy at Ottawa foreshadowed protection in the interests of certain branches of British agriculture by duties or quantitative regulation against both foreign and Empire products, with preferences instead of unrestricted entry for imports from Empire countries. The commodities concerned were meat, dairy products, eggs, and poultry, and measures were soon taken to regulate the quantities of these products imported, first from foreign countries and later from the Dominions.[1] With the imposition of a tariff on foreign wheat, and the quantitative regulation of meat imports, two of the chief food commodities which, under the Import Duties Act, 1932, remained free, were soon subjected to restrictions.

Marketing Organisation and Quantitative Regulation

The method of quantitative regulation in combination with other methods, including tariffs and subsidies, has been applied in various schemes under the Agricultural Marketing Act, 1933, and in the regulation of the markets for beef, mutton, and lamb. These schemes will now be outlined to illustrate the problems which arise; then an account will be given of schemes in which the levy or the subsidy is the chief feature. Marketing schemes were first established under the Labour Government's Agricultural Marketing Act, 1931, which enabled a substantial majority of producers in any branch of agriculture to adopt a system for organising the marketing of their product, subject to approval by the Minister of Agriculture and by Parliament.[2] The scheme then became obligatory upon all producers. Regulations could be adopted for the grading and packing of products, for establishing terms of contracts for producers, and for fixing minimum and maximum prices, but no means were

---

[1] By the terms of the Ottawa Agreements, measures might be applied to Dominion meat after June 1934, and to Dominion dairy products, eggs and poultry after three years.

[2] The expression "marketing" in these schemes is understood to mean the first stage of distribution from the producer, the retail end of distribution being unregulated.

available for regulating the volume of imports. Yet, with the deepening of the depression, it was soon recognised that schemes for regulating the marketing of home production would be seriously handicapped, even if not rendered unworkable, because of increasing imports and falling prices.

This difficulty the National Government undertook to remove, and in 1933 the second Agricultural Marketing Act was passed, which retained the chief features of the earlier measure but provided that if a satisfactory marketing scheme is evolved for any product the Government would regulate the quantity and/or the quality of imports of the product concerned.[1] The scheme itself may regulate the quantity to be sold by any registered producer. Prospects of import regulations served as a bait, and soon marketing plans were operating or in preparation for bacon, potatoes, milk, hops, eggs, and poultry, and special arrangements were made for meat. In the marketing of home produce the chief features are elimination of competition between producers, methods designed to reduce costs by more efficient marketing arrangements, and improvement of quality and grading of products. In this study these features are of only indirect interest, and attention is directed chiefly to regulation of imports and other measures which give advantages to home producers.[2]

The volume of imports may be regulated by unilateral decision of the British Government, by formal trade agreements with other countries, or by other countries voluntarily restricting their imports into Britain in view of the condition of the market, with the probability that a flood of imports

[1] Where importation is regulated the Minister of Agriculture may control the sales of domestic produce if necessary in the interest of the efficient reorganisation or organised development of the branch of agriculture concerned. By a third Act, also passed in 1933, some minor modifications of the second Act were introduced.

[2] In making any order for the quantitative regulation of imports the responsible Ministry (the Board of Trade) must take account of the interests of consumers, of the probable effect on commercial relations with other countries, and of existing international agreements. A Consumers' Committee is empowered to make an investigation if a complaint is made, and to report to the Minister of Agriculture.

would cause a collapse of prices, and of their fear that the British Government would impose restrictions in the absence of voluntary arrangements. All these methods have been tried. The British Government, however, has not always been free to impose restrictions, being bound by existing agreements, and this has led to the adoption of temporary expedients until these agreements expired.

1. *Bacon.* The marketing scheme for pigs and bacon, which began operations in September 1933, is of interest in illustrating a developed system for regulating imports and giving home producers first claim on the British market. The scheme deals only with bacon and ham, and difficulties have arisen from the alternative use of pigs as pork.[1] During the years 1927-8 to 1931-2, about 85 per cent of the bacon consumed in Britain was imported, and of this more than 90 per cent was supplied by foreign countries, particularly Denmark. There seemed here to be big possibilities of expanding home production if protection could be given, marketing made more efficient, and qualities raised so as to satisfy the consumer. Also, an increased share of imports might be accorded to Empire countries, especially Canada. Such a policy would be likely to react unfavourably, especially on Denmark, which had organised her production with great efficiency to supply suitable qualities to the British customer.

At the basis of the scheme is the decision for the present to stabilise the supplies of bacon and ham on the British market at a total of 10,670,000 cwts. annually, this being the estimated average supply during the period from 1925 to 1930, when the quantities imported were over 20 per cent less than in 1932. This restriction would be likely to raise prices and stimulate home production. Home producers

[1] Two marketing boards have been set up to operate the scheme, the Pigs Marketing Board, representing the farmers, and the Bacon Marketing Board, representing the curers. Although a marketing scheme has not been established for pork an increase in imports in 1933 resulted in quantitative regulation of imports from foreign countries in 1934 and 1935.

undertake to supply specified quantities to the curing factories in any year, and the quantity of imports permitted is the difference between home production and the total of 10,670,000 cwts. By this method the home producer has a right to such part of the total quantity on the market as he cares to supply; indeed, apart from the terms of trade agreements with foreign and Empire countries, there is nothing to prevent his expanding production so as to secure the whole market, to the complete exclusion of imports. In the report upon which the scheme is based it was recommended that any increase in Dominion or Colonial quotas should be made at the expense of foreign quotas.[1]

Minimum prices are fixed from time to time, with a premium for the higher grades, and the home-produced supply of pigs for bacon depends largely on the relative attractiveness of the price of pigs for bacon or in the alternative market for pork.[2] The first price fixed under the scheme was so attractive that contracts for delivery of bacon pigs were 50 per cent greater than had been expected, and although actual deliveries were less than contract quantities they represented a big increase in supply.

During 1933 Danish producers had already agreed voluntarily to restrict their exports to Britain by 20 per cent of their former volume, but in November the British Government, faced with the unexpected increase in home supplies, endeavoured to secure a further reduction of Danish exports and, when negotiations with this object failed, imposed a cut of 16 per cent.[3] This was a violation

---

[1] The British Government has undertaken that Canadian bacon and hams shall be allowed free entry up to a maximum of 2¼ million cwt. per annum, and that New Zealand shall gain a reasonable share in the expansion made possible by the reduction of foreign imports. As a result of this arrangement Canada made substantial increases in her bacon exports to Great Britain and now ranks after Denmark as the second largest supplier from abroad of the British market.

[2] The minimum prices are based upon the prices of feeding stuffs and of bacon and offals.

[3] British bacon curers were also in difficulties in paying for the large deliveries of pigs at the prices fixed, and the British Government made a loan of £160,000 to them, this amount to be repaid during the next

of the quota principle enunciated by the British Government at the World Economic Conference, 1933, that a very definite distinction should be drawn between import quotas arbitrarily fixed for protectionist purposes, which are undesirable, and the very proper use of production or marketing quotas established by international agreement with a view to raising prices; the British Government was, however, in no way bound to observe this principle, which was not embodied in any binding agreement at the Conference. The smaller Danish supplies did not result in a rise in the price of English bacon, larger quantities being marketed at about the same price, but demand for Danish bacon remained keen, prices rose, and in consequence more money has been paid for a smaller quantity of Danish bacon.

Later figures show considerable fluctuation in home supplies,[1] but the general trend has been an expansion of the share of total supplies represented by home production. In the spring of 1935 home production was estimated to be about 25 per cent of total supplies, compared with only 15 per cent a few years earlier. Empire bacon forms a growing proportion of imports, being 17 per cent of imports in 1934 compared with only 8 per cent in 1933.

2. *Potatoes.* The Potato Marketing Scheme, which began operations in March 1934, differs from the bacon scheme, as it deals with a commodity the imports of which are small in comparison with home production. Prices are determined very largely by home production and not by the quantities imported. The main task of the scheme is, therefore, to organise the marketing of the home crop. Nevertheless, restrictions are imposed upon foreign supplies. Imports of early potatoes have formed a considerable proportion, about

contract period. It may here be noted that in the Danish Trade Agreement Denmark was guaranteed a minimum quota of 62 per cent of total imports of foreign bacon and ham.

[1] Thus, in the spring of 1934, the price of pork being high, there was difficulty in securing an adequate supply of pigs for bacon. In 1935 also there were deficiencies in the number of pigs which farmers contracted to deliver to the bacon factories.

one-third to one-half, of total supplies of early potatoes each year, being imported mainly in May, June, and July, but main crop potato imports are now almost negligible, being often less than 1 per cent of total supplies, except in years when the home-grown crop is small.[1] Importation of early potatoes is restricted by relatively high tariffs at rates which vary from month to month, as well as by voluntary limitation by the exporting countries. Main crop potatoes are subject to a duty of £1 a ton, and since November 1934 may be imported only by license, the quantities to be imported being announced periodically.[2] The object of this quantitative restriction is to prevent increased imports from nullifying the effect upon prices of decisions by the Marketing Board limiting the amount of home production marketed when the crop is substantially in excess of estimated requirements for human consumption. Experience is not yet sufficient to show whether a liberal licensing policy will be applied to imports in years when the home-grown crop is small. The following figures showing British imports and home production of potatoes during recent years are of interest:

Year	Imports (million cwt.)	Home Production (million cwt.)
1929–30	5·4	117·3
1930–31	10·3	89·2
1931–32	22·2	77·0
1932–33	4·4	111·5
1933–34	3·2	110·1

3. *Milk*. A marketing scheme for milk was introduced at the end of 1933. This commodity is important in British agricultural production, and is, owing to its nature, almost free from direct competition from abroad. Indirect competition both from the Dominions and from foreign countries is, however, considerable in the form of manufactured milk products, including milk-powder and condensed milk, butter,

---

[1] Average importation during the period from 1922–3 to 1932–3 was about 4 per cent of total supplies.

[2] Before that date the exporting countries had voluntarily agreed to limit their exports to Britain.

and cheese. Many consumers turn to condensed milk if its price is relatively low, while home producers of milk sold for manufacturing receive a low price if imported butter and cheese are cheap, and this reacts unfavourably upon the price of fresh milk unless a method of regulation is adopted.

The Milk Marketing Scheme is based on the compulsory sale of milk through the machinery of the Scheme and on a rigid separation of the marketing of fresh milk from milk for manufacture, the prices of both being fixed periodically, that of milk for manufacture being determined largely by the prices of imported dairy products and the supply of home-produced milk. About 70 per cent of the total supply is sold as fresh milk at wholesale prices more than three times that of milk for manufacture, the price of which is below 5d. a gallon, and, in order to avoid direct competition, part of the revenue from the sale of fresh milk is used to compensate farmers whose milk is sold for manufacture.[1] British manufactured milk products are therefore being subsidised by the consumer of fresh milk against the interests alike of foreign and Dominion manufacturers of dairy products. The price policy of the Scheme has been criticised on the ground that fresh milk is too dear, that production is being increased but that consumption shows little gain and is even declining among the poor, and that the best way to help the farmers would be to stimulate consumption by lowering the price.[2]

An attempt is being made to sustain the market by tariffs and by voluntary agreements restricting the volume of imports of manufactured milk products from foreign countries. In 1935 such imports were restricted to about 30 to 40 per cent of imports in the base year (June 1932

[1] In the year 1934–5 the average price for liquid milk was 1s. $3\frac{1}{12}$d. per gallon, while milk for manufacture realised 4·92d. per gallon, to which 1d. was added from the Government grant mentioned later.

[2] One method of increasing consumption has been adopted, milk being distributed at low price or free to school children, the Government bearing part of the cost. In 1935 the number of children receiving milk under this scheme was 2,750,000.

to May 1933). As, however, about 60 per cent of British imports of butter, cheese, and other dairy products come from the Dominions, the raising of the price of manufactured milk in Britain considerably above its present unremunerative level depends upon restriction of imports from the Dominions as well as from foreign countries. In 1934 New Zealand for the first time supplanted Denmark as the principal source of imported butter, and Empire supplies comprised 54 per cent of total imports, which is the largest proportion recorded.[1] In the same year Empire countries accounted for 92 per cent of British imports of cheese, New Zealand being the principal supplier. The Ottawa Agreements precluded restriction by Great Britain of imports of butter and cheese from the Dominions until November 1935, and the Dominions rejected a proposal that they should agree to reduce their exports of butter and cheese to Great Britain by 10 per cent provided that foreign exports of these commodities to Great Britain were cut by 20 per cent.[2] The Dominions have consistently urged expansion of their trade and have resisted restrictions, even where their share of British imports would be increased.

In these circumstances the British Government resorted to a subsidy as a stop-gap measure. This took the form of a Treasury guarantee of a minimum price for milk sold for manufacture of 5d. a gallon in summer and 6d. in winter for a period of two years to March 1936. These advances are repayable during the two following years if the price of milk for manufacture is higher than 6d. a gallon in summer and 7d. in winter. As, however, the high price of fresh milk is stimulating production and discouraging consumption there is a tendency for the quantity of milk for manufacture to increase and little likelihood of substantially higher prices. The advances during the two years

[1] Data from *Dairy Produce Supplies in 1934,* a survey published by the Imperial Economic Committee.

[2] By some of the trade agreements with foreign countries, minimum quotas of butter were guaranteed, e.g. 2,300,000 cwt. annually from Denmark.

amounted to more than £3 million, there seems no prospect of this sum being repaid, and in 1936 the subsidy was extended until September 1937.[1] As already indicated the direct subsidising of milk for manufacture helps home dairy products equally against Dominion and foreign products.

4. *Hops.* A marketing scheme for hops, which was the first of these schemes to be adopted, was put into operation in September 1932. This crop is only a small branch of agriculture, though during the war the acreage under hop cultivation considerably increased. From 1917 to 1925 home production was controlled and imports prohibited except under license. Since 1925, imports have been subject to a duty of £4 per cwt., while since 1934 imports have been restricted to 15 per cent of total demand, compared with nearly one-quarter of total supplies formerly imported. Internally the effect of the scheme has been to increase prices considerably, and the consequent tendency for production to expand has resulted in the necessity for regulating the output of each producer by a quota system.

5. *Eggs and Poultry.* For several other branches of British agriculture reports and proposals on marketing schemes have been prepared, without, however, the schemes having yet been put into operation. The chief of these is the poultry industry, which comes next after live stock and dairying in British agricultural economy. Its annual production is valued at about £25 million, two-thirds being represented by eggs and one-third by table poultry. A marketing scheme is under consideration for eggs on the recommendation of the Reorganisation Commission for Eggs and Poultry, which advised that only by gradual development could a satisfactory scheme be prepared for poultry.[2] The Commission also recommended an increase in the duty on eggs

[1] The Government is also granting considerable sums for the encouragement of milk consumption.

[2] Report of the Commission, Ministry of Agriculture and Fisheries, Economic Series, No. 42. See also Report No. 43.

from foreign countries and the imposition of a preferential duty on eggs imported from Empire countries, which now enjoy free entry.[1]

The production of eggs and poultry in Great Britain shows very rapid growth during recent years. During the decade from 1924 to 1934 the output of the industry almost doubled in England and Wales, but expansion was less rapid in Scotland and Northern Ireland. Before the war only 32 per cent of the total supply of eggs on the British market were produced at home. By 1924 the percentage was 52; in 1934 it had risen to 68, and imports from foreign countries had fallen to 22 per cent, the chief supplying countries being Denmark, the Netherlands, Poland, and Belgium; the remaining 10 per cent came from Empire countries, including the Irish Free State, Australia, and South Africa.[2] The increase in British production was achieved without restriction of imports until 1932, when a tariff was imposed on eggs from foreign countries. Quantitative methods of regulation have not been yet applied, except in the form of a guaranteed minimum importation included in some of the trade agreements with foreign countries, and of voluntary restrictions made by the chief foreign supplying countries in accordance with a request made by the British Minister of Agriculture. Importation has only a small effect upon price.

6. *Beef*. The greatest difficulties have arisen in the meat industry, especially beef, which, with associated milk and dairy products, is Britain's chief agricultural asset and is well suited to British conditions. No marketing scheme has yet been approved for beef or mutton, but quantitative regulation of imports has been in force for several years. Supplies of

[1] The Commission proposed that 25 per cent of the proceeds of the higher tariff should be used for the further development of the home industry.

[2] British production of poultry in 1934 was 78 per cent of total supplies, while 14 per cent were imported from foreign countries and 8 per cent from Empire countries; only 12 per cent of fowls, but 70 per cent of turkeys were imported.

beef in the British market consist of home produce, chilled beef, and frozen beef. Until a few years ago chilled beef came solely from South American countries, chiefly the Argentine, but it is now being exported in small but increasing quantities by Australia and other Dominions; frozen beef is imported chiefly from Australia and New Zealand, but substantial quantities also come from South America.[1] The following figures show the exports of chilled and frozen beef from the chief exporting countries in 1933:[2]

EXPORTS

(In thousand tons)

	Chilled Beef	Frozen Beef
Argentine	344·4	30·9
Uruguay and Brazil	54·7	39·5
Australia .. .. ·.	0·1	70·7
New Zealand	0·1	46·5

Among beef importing countries Britain is of predominant importance, representing about 70 per cent of world trade in 1928, about 80 per cent in 1933, and 83 per cent in 1934. With South America taking four-fifths of the total volume of trade in 1933 and a still higher proportion of the value, with declining demand for frozen beef of which Australia and New Zealand supplied a greater part of the market than South America, and with the British Government pledged to a policy of Imperial Preferences, it is not surprising that Australia and New Zealand have resisted proposals made during the depression to adopt a policy of restriction with a view to raising prices. Instead, they have persistently demanded an expanding share of the British market at the expense of South America.

For a number of years beef prices have tended to fall, due in part, it is thought, to a growing preference

---

[1] Chilled beef sells at higher prices than frozen beef. Formerly it could not be transported over the long distance from Australia and New Zealand, but recent developments have made this possible, thus permitting competition with South American supplies.

[2] *Cattle and Beef Survey*, published in 1934 by the Intelligence Branch of the Imperial Economic Committee.

among consumers for mutton, lamb, and pig products. Demand has also been transferred from frozen to chilled beef. Further, though British home production of beef has tended to fall, production in the chief exporting countries has greatly increased. Aggravated by the world depression the industry has been involved in a crisis, which increased in severity during the years 1932 to 1934 in spite of certain restrictions upon imports.[1] In these circumstances the British Government in the spring of 1935 declared its firm intention to safeguard the position of the British live stock industry, its primary object being to assure a reasonable return to home producers, without stimulating artificial expansion. It also indicated that, as the Dominions cannot absorb the whole of British exports of coal and manufactured goods, restriction of meat imports from foreign countries must be considered both in their relation to conditions in the meat market and to their effects upon the British export trade.[2] The problem is, therefore, how to arrange the best compromise between the interests of the British cattle industry, of Dominion cattle farmers, and of British exporters to meat-producing countries outside the Empire.

The British Government's freedom to regulate the beef market has been restricted by the terms of the Ottawa and Argentine Agreements. At Ottawa the British Government had agreed not to reduce the supplies of meat from Australia and New Zealand before the end of June 1934, after which it was free to introduce quantitative regulation, though it

---

[1] Restrictions upon the Argentine were greatest on frozen meat, but as her exports of frozen meat to Britain were small the effect of the restrictions could reduce British imports of frozen beef by only about 6 per cent. On the other hand, imports of frozen beef from the Empire increased in 1933 and 1934 so that, with declining demand, prices remained unremunerative.

The restrictions applied to mutton and lamb need not be discussed in detail. Supplies from the Argentine were subject to the same reductions as those applied to beef. Australia and New Zealand, however, dominate the market and, with restriction of their exports to Britain and increased demand, prices improved in 1933, so that conditions were favourable by contrast with the fall in beef prices.

[2] Statement of the Views of His Majesty's Government (Cmd. 4828), March 1935.

desired to secure an agreement by negotiation rather than to impose a scheme unilaterally.[1] It also undertook at Ottawa not to impose an import duty on meat from the Dominions before August 1937, without their consent. In the Argentine Agreement, as already indicated in the chapter on Commercial Policy, British imports of chilled beef from the Argentine were to be reduced below the quantities imported during the year ended June 1932 only if necessary to secure remunerative prices in the British market.[2] Any such reduction was to be limited to 10 per cent, and was not to be maintained if meat from the Argentine was merely being replaced by meat from other sources.[3] Reductions of more than 10 per cent were to be made only if proportionate reductions were imposed upon all the chief meat-exporting countries, including the Dominions. Also until November 1936, when the Argentine Agreement expires, the imposition of a tariff on meat from the Argentine is possible only if its Government agrees.

In consequence of these agreements the British Government was free from the middle of 1934 to restrict imports by the method of quantitative regulation but not by tariffs. It recognised that, if prices were to be raised, some reduction of Dominion as well as of foreign supplies would be necessary. The Governments of Australia and New Zealand strongly opposed this policy and refused to agree to reductions, even though an increase in prices might have resulted, enabling their exporters to receive a larger payment for

[1] In return, the Australian Government undertook to limit the export of mutton and lamb to the British market to the level of the 1931-2 shipments, and to use its best endeavours to ensure that exports of frozen beef in 1933 should not increase by more than 10 per cent over those in the base years.

[2] Imports of frozen beef and also of frozen mutton and lamb from the Argentine into Great Britain were to be progressively reduced during 1933 and the first half of 1934 until they reached a level of 65 per cent of imports during the year ended June 1932.

[3] This reduction was made in the first quarter of 1935, and imports from Empire countries were restricted to the level of the average quantities imported during the corresponding quarter in 1932, 1933, and 1934. The Argentine had previously made a voluntary reduction of 10 per cent.

M

a smaller quantity of beef. To the Dominions reduction of their exports seemed to be a violation of the Ottawa principle of more and freer Empire trade.

In these circumstances, in order to gain time for further negotiations, the British Government in the summer of 1934 decided as a stop-gap measure to grant a subsidy from the national revenues during the next seven months for British home-produced beef.[1] Pending the adoption of a long-range policy the British Government hoped to obtain the consent of the Dominions and the Argentine to variations of their agreements so as to enable it to impose a levy on imports of meat with or without moderate quantitative regulation.[2] Negotiations with this object proved abortive, and the subsidy, which was at the rate of over £4¼ million a year, was successively renewed throughout 1935 and continued into 1936. Also a succession of short-term agreements regulating the quantities of beef and mutton exports to Britain were reached with the Governments of Australia and New Zealand.

The Government's long-range policy, which it intends to apply on the termination of the Argentine Agreement, is to impose a levy on imports at rates giving preferences to the Empire, and to distribute the proceeds to home producers. The rates of levy will depend upon the quantity of meat imported and the sum required to make up the market price of home-produced meat to a remunerative level. It is hoped that agreements regulating the quantities of meat shipped to Britain will be reached with the meat-exporting countries. The levy suggested is 1d. a lb. on meat imported from foreign countries, and ½d. a lb. on supplies from the Dominions. The criticism has been made that such a levy would be a particularly unsatisfactory form of

---

[1] Payments were to be at a rate not exceeding 5s. a live cwt. (9s. 4d. a cwt. dead weight) on various classes of cattle sold for slaughter; sums advanced are recoverable from the proceeds of any levy which may be imposed on imported meat as part of a permanent scheme.

[2] The British Government regarded this as the only satisfactory alternative to a drastic reduction of imports from all sources, which it is free to adopt.

food tax; imported meat is largely consumed by persons with small incomes, while the proceeds of the levy would be distributed to subsidise home-produced beef, which is mainly consumed by persons with more ample means.[1]

The Dominions raise no serious objection to the proposed levy for the benefit of the British farmer, but they desire maintenance of existing quantitative restrictions on foreign meat. They fear Argentine competition and desire the continuation of regulations ensuring to them an expanding share of the British meat trade, as promised at Ottawa. The following figures show that since 1932 Empire countries have gained both an increased volume and an increased share of British imports of meat:[2]

BRITISH IMPORTS OF MEAT, 1930–4

(In thousand tons)

Year	BEEF AND VEAL			MUTTON AND LAMB		
	Imports		Home Production	Imports		Home Production
	From Empire Countries	From Foreign Countries		From Empire Countries*	From Foreign Countries†	
1930	63	583	622	205	112	228
1932	84	531	573	253	92	271
1933	115	496	560	252	79	275
1934	149	451	—	287	64	—

* Australia and New Zealand.

† The Argentine, Uruguay, and Chile.

Levies and Subsidies

Reference has already been made to the use of direct and indirect subsidies for the benefit of home producers, direct subsidies from the Exchequer usually being used as tem-

[1] Objection may be raised if the levy is applied to imports of mutton and lamb as well as of beef and the proceeds distributed to home producers of beef only.

[2] Figures from an article on "Meat Supplies and Prices," published in the *Economist*, December 29, 1934.

porary expedients to gain time for the elaboration of long-term solutions. The levy and subsidy methods are best illustrated by the schemes applied to wheat and sugar-beet. The levy for wheat growers is obtained indirectly from consumers of bread, while the sugar-beet subsidy comes from the taxpayer out of the ordinary revenues of the State. The wheat scheme will be described first. This is regarded with growing favour by British agriculturalists, who prefer it to the method of a direct subsidy for application to other products. The wider application of this method is foreshadowed in recent declarations of Government policy. Thus the Minister of Agriculture stated in a speech in June 1935: "The Wheat Act policy is the policy which has worked best so far, and the policy which the Government desires to develop and extend."

1. *Wheat.* Wheat growing is a small branch of British agriculture, supplying less than one-sixth of the country's total requirements. Only certain districts are suited to its cultivation, but these areas have produced wheat from Roman times. During the war, measures were taken to increase production as a safeguard to food supplies, and these measures were continued until 1921, taking the form chiefly of a guaranteed price. By 1920 the area under wheat was about 1,900,000 acres. Subsequently it declined steadily until in 1931 it was only 1,200,000 acres, and there was then danger that the collapse of world wheat prices, high world production, and growing stocks would make still greater inroads into British production. At the time a high tariff would have been politically inexpedient. The Wheat Act, 1932, was, therefore, passed to provide British wheat growers with a secure market and an enhanced price for their crops, without a subsidy from the Exchequer and without encouraging the extension of wheat cultivation to unsuitable land. It was also claimed that the measure would help to safeguard British food supplies, afford relief to British farmers in certain areas during the depression, and prevent the impact of the depression from forcing out

of wheat cultivation land suited for this crop under normal market conditions.

The Act was passed for an unlimited period, and the war-time method of ensuring to home growers of millable wheat a guaranteed average price was again adopted, the price being fixed until 1935 at 10s. a cwt. To make up the difference between the average price realised by all registered growers and the guaranteed price, the farmers receive deficiency payments. In order to discourage undue expansion of production, the deficiency payments are made in full only if actual deliveries of millable wheat do not exceed the "anticipated supply" fixed each year by the Minister of Agriculture, and are not more than 27 million cwt.; the deficiency payments are proportionately reduced if more wheat is delivered.[1]

The money required for the deficiency payments is obtained by a levy on each sack of flour consumed in the country, whether made from wheat grown at home, in Empire countries, or in foreign countries, the levy being paid by the British miller or importer of flour. The amount of the levy is fixed each year, and varies according to the price of wheat and the volume of home and imported supplies. As wheat prices rise the amounts of the levy and of the deficiency payments fall, and at a market price of 10s. a cwt. they would entirely cease. This method of a guaranteed price and a levy to make deficiency payments was adopted largely to avoid a high protective tariff.[2] A relatively small levy on the large flour consumption yields a substantial amount and enables a handsome subsidy to be paid on the small wheat production of the country. The effect on the price of flour is small, but on the other hand the State receives no revenue.

[1] The Minister of Agriculture has certain powers to require millers to purchase home-grown wheat in order that surplus stocks will not accumulate. The statutory limit of 27 million cwt. applies during the initial five years.
[2] By the Ottawa Agreements foreign wheat imports are subject to a duty of 2s. a quarter.

During the years 1932–5 the selling price of wheat was only about one-half the guaranteed price; thus the average price realised was about 5s. 4½d. a cwt. in 1932–3 and 4s. 7½d. a cwt. in 1933–4, while the estimated price for the 1934–5 crop was 5s. a cwt. The levy on flour rose by stages from 2s. 3d. a sack of 280 lb. in June 1932 to 4s. 6d. in November 1933, but was reduced to 4s. in August 1934. The attraction of the subsidy resulted in a considerable increase in acreage and production, and in consequence the deficiency payments were reduced some-what below the amount necessary to make up the guaranteed price of 10s. a cwt.; they were, however, so substantial that in the second year the farmers received more in subsidy than they obtained from the sale of their wheat. The total amount distributed in deficiency payments was nearly £4¾ millions in 1932–3, and about £7 millions in 1933–4, the average rates being respectively 4s. 5d. a cwt. and 4s. 10¼d. a cwt. The area under wheat cultivation rose from 1,288,000 acres in 1932 to 1,759,000 acres in 1934, and was 5 per cent higher still in 1935. The quantity of home-grown wheat sold was 20·3 million cwt. in 1932–3, 29·4 million cwt. in 1933–4, and about 35 million in 1934–5—an increase of 75 per cent in two years and an amount considerably in excess of the limit of 27 million cwt. contemplated by the Act.[1] Production is the highest on record, both in total amount and yield per acre, the farmers not only extending their acreage but also culti-vating more intensively, some of them even at the risk of exhausting the soil in order to benefit as much as possible from the subsidy "while the going is good."

The subsidy has undoubtedly helped the wheat grower during a time of difficulty, but it has been costly. The burden falls as an indirect tax upon the bread consumer, and, being borne largely by the poor, is an example of regressive taxation. The substantial benefits are reserved for a small

[1] For the 1934 crop the average total price received was about 8s. 9¼d. per cwt., as a result of production in excess of the statutory limits.

section of agriculture largely localised in a few counties.[1] An expansion of production beyond the limit which Parliament contemplated has resulted, and cultivation seems to have extended to unsuitable areas; thus a large increase has taken place in the area under wheat cultivation in Scotland. The levy system with guaranteed price is subject to less frequent Parliamentary supervision than a subsidy voted from the national revenues.

The Act properly provides for the periodical adjustment of the guaranteed price, and if the levy system under the Act is continued on a long-term basis, it is desirable that a proper relation should be maintained between the guaranteed price and the world price. If, for non-economic reasons, wheat cultivation is to be fostered artificially a small margin in favour of the home producer could be maintained under normal conditions, and the margin increased during periods of depression when world prices are exceptionally low. Maintenance of the standard price of 10s. a cwt. for a further period of three years was, however, recommended in the report of a Committee set up in 1935 under the Wheat Act to consider the future of the guaranteed price.[2]

2. *Sugar-beet*. Before the war Britain was entirely dependent upon supplies of sugar from abroad, especially beet sugar from the Continent of Europe and to a much smaller extent cane sugar from Colonial areas; thus, in 1913, about 66 per cent of British supplies were imported from Germany, Austria-Hungary, France, Holland, and Belgium. Shortage of sugar during the war, owing to interruption of supplies from the Continent, caused much discontent and feeling of hardship. Since the war the cultivation of sugar-beet has been heavily subsidised by the State, largely on the ground that it is desirable to reduce dependence on sugar supplies

[1] Other cereal crops have, however, received favours; oats are protected by a high tariff on foreign supplies, while in return for remission of taxation, the brewers undertook, in a gentleman's agreement with the Chancellor of the Exchequer in 1933, to buy as much home-grown barley as possible.

[2] Report of the Standard Price Committee.

from the Continent. It was also argued that the cultivation of sugar-beet would provide employment and that the crop would be valuable in the rotation system in preparing the soil for cereals. Little attention was given to West Indian supplies of cane sugar as an alternative to development of production at home.

With a view to stimulating sugar-beet cultivation the excise duty on sugar produced from home-grown beet was abolished in 1922, and about three years later a subsidy system was adopted for a period of ten years to assist the industry during the early stages of its development.[1] The subsidies, which have been paid from the Exchequer revenues, were fixed at a diminishing rate and it was generally assumed that at the end of the ten year period the industry would have established itself and would no longer require artificial support. The subsidy was paid direct to the factories according to their sugar production, and the growers benefited indirectly through the price received for beet deliveries; there was no limit to the amount of sugar on which the subsidy was paid.

The subsidy and excise relief resulted in a rapid expansion of production, chiefly in eastern counties. The acreage under sugar-beet cultivation rose from about 22,500 in June 1924 to 396,500 ten years later, while the amount of home-produced sugar rose from 24,000 tons in 1924-5 to over 600,000 tons in 1934-5.[2] This represents between one-quarter and one-third of the country's requirements, a little less than one-half of the remainder being supplied by Empire countries and a little more than one-half by foreign countries; during recent years the proportions of home-produced and Empire sugar have greatly increased at the expense of foreign countries. Although the rate of subsidy per cwt. was greatly reduced during the ten years, the cost to the taxpayer rapidly increased as production expanded.

[1] With the granting of the subsidy, the excise duty was reimposed, but only at the lower rate equivalent to the preferential duty on imports from within the Empire.

[2] In 1919 the acreage was only 386.

The following figures show the various rates of subsidy and of subsidy and preferential excise combined, the former representing the advantage to home producers over Empire producers and the latter the advantage of home producers over foreign producers:[1]

Year	Rate of Subsidy Per cwt.		Subsidy and Preferential Excise Per cwt.	
	s.	d.	s.	d.
1925	19	6	22	5
1926–28	19	6	23	9
1928–30	13	0	17	3
1931–34	6	6	10	9

The cost to the Treasury in subsidy alone rose from under £500,000 in the first year to about £3¾ million in the last year, while if the value of the preferential excise be added the total subsidy in the last year was £6¼ million. During the ten years of the subsidy period the total amount of subsidy and remission of excise was over £40 million; this was about 60 per cent of the total receipts of the sugar factories, many of which were enabled to make remarkably high profits. Over the whole period the amount of State assistance almost exactly equalled the amounts paid for beet at the factories, the farmer actually receiving less, as these amounts include cost of transport from farm to factory. Thus the value of the crop was almost entirely created by the State's assistance.[2] It is true that the cost of production of the sugar fell greatly, from 28s. a cwt. in 1928 to 12s. a cwt. in 1934, owing to improved efficiency and increased sugar yield per ton of beet, but the fall was not nearly enough to enable home-produced beet sugar, if unsubsidised,

[1] The Report of the United Kingdom Sugar Industry Inquiry Committee stated that in 1934 the rates of assistance enjoyed in the United Kingdom were: Home produced sugar, 11s. 2d. per cwt. (including molasses subsidy); Colonial sugar, 5s. 9d. per cwt.; Dominion sugar, 3s. 9d. per cwt., and in addition Dominion sugar receives assistance in the country of origin. Also the operation of refining in the United Kingdom is protected to the extent of 2s. 4d. per cwt. of refined sugar, while, since 1928, the system of drawbacks provides a direct export premium of 7½d. per cwt., which is of benefit to British refiners.

[2] See *Majority Report* of the United Kingdom Sugar Industry Inquiry Committee, published April 1935 (Cmd. 4871).

to compete with imported sugar. Cane sugar can be produced at between one-half and two-thirds the cost of beet sugar.[1]

In view of the original intention that the subsidy should be only temporary, and of the disquiet caused to the Treasury and the country by the growing cost, the question of future policy demanded consideration, the vital questions being whether the industry had any reasonable prospect of becoming self-supporting, and, if not, whether the Government should continue its support and, if so, to what extent and by what methods. In order to obtain recommendations on these and allied questions a Sugar Industry Inquiry Committee was set up in April 1934, and, pending its report and the Government's decision on policy, the subsidy was continued for a further year at a reduced rate per cwt. and with a maximum of 375,000 acres, but involving a direct cost of more than £4 million.

The Majority of the Committee were of the opinion that the evidence submitted was not strong enough to support the continuation of assistance. They considered that the chief value of assistance had been as a measure of relief to farmers, and that as such it was haphazard, inequitable, and extravagant. The advantages obtained, including direct and indirect employment, were quite inadequate for the expenditure involved. They recognised that the withdrawal of assistance would result in a big decline in production, and proposed compensation to existing beet growers at a diminishing rate during a transitional period of three years. In the event of the Government deciding to continue long-term assistance the Majority preferred the method of Exchequer subsidies to the proposal, supported by the growers and refiners, that assistance should be based upon a special levy on all sugar consumed in the country. They

[1] This was partly due to improved methods applied in the cane-sugar industry, which had not been anticipated when the development of beet sugar in Great Britain was initiated, and partly to the world depression. Beet sugar prices have also been exceptionally low during recent years. Thus in February 1935 foreign raw beet sugar was sold in London at 4s. 5¼d. a cwt., which, being much below the cost of production in any country growing beet, was a "dumped" price.

recommended that continued assistance should be combined with drastic reorganisation and control in the interests of the community, and rejected as inadequate the schemes for sugar-beet and sugar put forward in 1934 by the growers and refiners under the Marketing Acts.[1] On the other hand, Mr. Cyril Lloyd, in a Minority Report, supported the continuation of State assistance for a further period and favoured the method of a special levy on sugar consumption.

From the standpoint of the community as a whole the Majority view was largely unanswerable and its recommendations well founded. There is general agreement that the industry has no prospect of becoming self-supporting and of competing with cane-sugar on anything like equal terms. The industry is small and restricted to a small part of the country. On economic grounds the charge on public funds during recent years was indefensible, while non-economic reasons, such as safeguarding sugar supplies in time of war, were inadequate to justify the cost. If other industries had been subsidised according to their size at a similar rate, shipbuilding would have received about £30 million annually, general engineering £80 million, and coal mining around £150 million. The subsidy was without relation to the price of sugar, with no limit upon the volume of production, and without restriction upon the profits of the producers. If, for non-economic reasons, an industry needs to be so heavily subsidised it should be operated on public utility lines and not for private profit. Account must, however, be taken of the dumping of sugar, especially beet-sugar, in the British market at prices below costs of production, and protection against such dumping is fully justified.

The Government, faced with demands for revision of the system but unwilling to withdraw the whole subsidy, decided upon a compromise, which, though removing some

[1] These schemes would give private monopoly power to the existing refiners and replace the subsidy by an import levy, the proceeds of which would be handed over to the industry and would cost the country more than the subsidy.

of the worst features of the original scheme, involves a heavy charge upon the community.[1] Under the new arrangement the subsidy is to be continued indefinitely, but a limit is to be set to the volume of production receiving direct subsidy, this being the equivalent of 560 tons of white sugar annually. Partly in consequence of the outcry against the high profits earned by many factories, the factories are to be amalgamated into a single corporation owned by the companies and conducted by their directors, but subject to the general supervision of an independent Sugar Commission acting in the interests of the public. The rate of subsidy will be varied periodically in accordance with changes in the world price of sugar, the price of beet, and other factors; during a transitional period of five years, assistance will be given at a diminishing rate. In 1936 the estimated rate is 5s. 3d. per cwt., involving a total charge to the Exchequer of about £2,940,000. The preferential excise rate will also be maintained. The scheme is intended to permit the industry to continue permanently on a substantial scale.

CONCLUSIONS

The conclusions of this chapter fall into three groups, dealing respectively with the relative merits of the methods adopted for the protection of British agriculture, the results already obtained, and the appropriate lines for future developments. As already indicated, the methods include quantitative regulation, subsidies, levies, guaranteed prices, tariffs, and marketing schemes, or some combination of these methods. Some of them are more suitable as emergency measures or for short-term than for long-term application. Indeed, some of the defects of method and lack of coordination in the new agricultural policy are attributable to its origin under conditions of emergency.

At first quantitative methods of regulation were favoured,

[1] Details of the new arrangement are given in a White Paper on *Sugar Policy* (Cmd. 4964).

and the 1933 Marketing Act associated internal marketing arrangements with the regulation of imports by quotas. The quantitative control of imports is of value when prices are fluctuating widely, when producers abroad are dumping large supplies at unremunerative prices, or when exchange depreciation abroad results in unfair competition. Thus, depreciated exchanges gave producers in Australia, New Zealand, the Argentine and Denmark a competitive advantage over the British farmer.[1] In these circumstances tariffs cannot be adjusted rapidly enough to prevent abnormally large imports, but quotas are effective. In 1933, however, quotas were favoured not only for emergency purposes but as a long-term method of planning, designed to introduce order and stability into agricultural production and trade.

Experience and changed conditions have reduced the prestige of the quota system. As currencies and prices became more stable in 1934 and 1935 the special value of quotas declined. The British Government, being directly responsible for the fixing and continuous manipulation and readjustment of quotas, has been embarrassed by interminable pressure and clamour by Dominions and foreign countries as well as by the home producer urging their rival claims upon the lucrative British market. It could not give general satisfaction to all the claims made upon it, and the danger arose of strained Imperial and foreign relations. In the absence of agreement the Government is compelled to fix quotas unilaterally—a policy which it had condemned at the World Economic Conference.

Although not necessarily restrictive, the quota system tends by its rigidity to reduce trade. It involves the organisation of export control for each branch of trade in each exporting country even though this might be unwelcome to the traders. Under a tariff system, each producer abroad is free to decide, according to his costs, how much he will

---

[1] The depreciation of Argentine currency in terms of sterling was nearly 40 per cent, and that of the other three countries around 20 per cent; all these currencies except the peso have been stable since 1933.

export, whereas with quotas he is allowed little or no elasticity. The quota system was also associated with marketing schemes in Great Britain which British farmers in some branches of production began to dislike. British farmers' organisations soon started to advocate tariffs or levies, combined sometimes with a limited amount of quantitative regulation, in place of schemes mainly dependent upon quotas. The Government also began to indicate its preference for tariffs or levies rather than quotas as being more flexible and more appropriate for long-term application. This change of outlook was indicated in speeches by Government spokesmen towards the end of 1934 and during 1935.

Payments from import levies, which are borne by consumers, and subsidies from the national revenues may be considered together, as they are similar in providing financial assistance for home producers. From the economic point of view both methods should be reserved mainly for emergencies, as a stop-gap, or for short-term developments, for example, to foster a new branch of agriculture. Where, for non-economic reasons, a product needs long-term assistance some other method should be adopted. Thus, the subsidy was a suitable method, though excessive in amount, for sugar-beet during the experimental period, but it is not satisfactory for long-continued application. For short periods the subsidy has the advantage that it is brought under regular review by Parliament, and also that, being paid out of the ordinary revenues of the State, its cost is distributed in accordance with principles of equity and progressive taxation applied by the State. Interested producers, however, desiring to avoid the regular scrutiny of Parliament and recognising the difficulty of securing the continuation of a subsidy for more than a short period, have increasingly preferred levies to subsidies.

The levy is raised on all consumption of the commodity or on all imports, and part or the whole of the proceeds is distributed to home producers. It may be combined with Imperial Preference. If the levy is upon imports alone the home producer enjoys the double benefit of a tariff on imports and a subsidy on home production. Where the home production of a commodity represents a small part of total supplies a low rate of levy, which does not add much to the price nor greatly restrict the supplies available to consumers, yields a sum large enough to provide a substantial subsidy to the home producer; this is true of the wheat levy. If instead of the levy similar assistance were to be accorded by a tariff a high rate would be necessary which would restrict imports and raise prices considerably, though the State would gain in revenue. Where a levy is operated so as to give a guaranteed price to producers the price should be adjusted periodically to the long-term trends of world prices.

The levy method is open to such objections that it should be used only exceptionally and for short periods, and even then a tariff combined with a subsidy from national revenues is preferable. The burden falls directly upon the consumer, usually involving regressive taxation with the heaviest load as a food tax upon the poor, and there is danger that a proper balance between direct and indirect taxation will not be preserved. The State obtains no revenue, while large sums are diverted to producers without regular Parliamentary control; the risk is, therefore, incurred that the system will be continued longer than is necessary. The British Government has indicated that it does not intend to maintain for any long period its direct subsidies to agriculture, but it would do little more than alter the name if it were to convert subsidies into levies.

Subsidies and levies for agriculture have become much more costly than is generally realised, and, as has been indicated, some of the most expensive schemes are for the benefit of small branches mainly located in a few counties. The total subsidies for wheat, sugar, milk and beef were at the rate of about £18 million in 1934–5, and to this should be added £10 to £12 million annually as the cost to the consumer of quota policies designed to raise prices by restricting supply.[1] Account must also be taken of the value of relief from central and local taxation and from tithe, estimated to benefit British agriculture to an amount of £18 million a year, and of grants for education and research amounting to £4 million a year.[2] Apart from the need to prevent subsidies and levies from becoming a permanent burden on the community, whether as taxpayer or as consumer, some of the existing costly schemes, particularly those for wheat and sugar-beet, are unfair to the farmers as a whole. If financial assistance is to be given to agriculture it should be distributed equitably instead of being concentrated upon small branches of production. Also where substantial financial assistance is extended beyond a short term it should be accompanied by effective public control in the interests of the community.

Of the various methods of assisting British agriculture the tariff is the least objectionable and should be made the basis of any long-term protection afforded. At the most, a low tariff not exceeding 20 per cent is the maximum protection which for non-economic reasons should be afforded under normal conditions against imports from foreign countries, and this gives an ample margin for Imperial preferences. A branch of agriculture which, with the advantage of nearness to its market and opportunities for personal contact with consumers to consult their needs, cannot maintain itself with such protection is too costly for the community to retain. A moderate tariff would give shelter from all ordinary disturbances in world production and trade, and would ensure reasonable stability for efficient British producers. It would give the home producer some priority in the home market, and would be preferable to taking special measures whenever a change in conditions abroad threatened to dislocate home production. Some protection may also be accorded to facilitate the develop-

---

[1] See article in the *Round Table*, September 1934, p. 757.
[2] Figures given by J. A. Venn in his Presidential Address to the Agricultural Economics Society, July 1933.

ment of greater efficiency after the long neglect from which British agriculture has suffered, but this protection may reasonably carry with it obligations upon the farmer to adopt higher standards both of production and marketing.

With such a tariff, British market prices would move with world prices, and consumers would benefit from reductions in costs abroad or at home. Subsidies should be reserved for exceptional circumstances and should be granted only for a specified short period at a diminishing rate and usually at diminishing cost to the State. Other methods affecting imports should be reserved for abnormal conditions. Marketing schemes as such do not involve external trade relations, although in practice under the 1933 Act they have been associated with regulation of imports. They may make a useful contribution to internal marketing efficiency and to improvements in quality, and for these purposes they are suitable for inclusion in a long-term agricultural policy.

To summarise, agricultural policy should be based upon a low tariff to afford some shelter from disturbances in the international market, together with marketing schemes to improve efficiency in distribution, and subsidies from national revenues for limited periods in special circumstances. Even where it is desirable for political or social reasons to foster agriculture, seriously uneconomic production should be avoided. Levies borne by the consumer should be reserved for emergency conditions only, and quantitative methods are also chiefly of value during emergencies, when care should be taken not to restrict supplies so that prices are forced up to levels which considerably curtail consumption.

Turning now to the results of British policy during the emergency conditions of the world depression, the British farmer has suffered less severely than farmers in the chief countries which export agricultural products. He has benefited both from nearness to a great market, from protective measures, and from substantial subsidies. The new policy has not, however, resulted in growth in employment on the land. The number of agricultural labourers continuously declined between 1926 and 1932, about 100,000 leaving the land during this period. In 1933 the numbers employed increased by 18,000, but fell again by about 28,000 in 1934.

British consumers have not suffered from the rise in prices of foodstuffs which was sometimes predicted to be the inevitable result of protection, although prices would have fallen lower if this policy had not been applied. Producers abroad adjusted their prices in order to retain a large share of the British market, so that, notwithstanding the introduction of protection, the general level of agricultural wholesale prices in Great Britain fell from an average of 120 in 1931 (pre-war = 100) to 107 in 1933; an upward movement then began, and by the end of 1935 agricultural prices had almost reached the 1931 level. The retail prices of foodstuffs entering into the cost of living showed a similar trend, the Ministry of Labour's index falling from 130 in 1931 (pre-war = 100) to 120 in 1933, after which it rose to about 126 towards the end of 1935. Wholesale and retail prices of foodstuffs throughout the years 1931 to 1935 were considerably below the levels during the period from 1927 to 1930. This was of great benefit to consumers, and there was considerable justification for their being called upon to assist the farmer during the emergency.

The upward movement of prices which began in 1934 is likely to continue as the depression lifts, and some further increase is desirable. However, a considerably smaller increase is now needed to restore remunerative conditions than would have been appropriate if international action could have been taken in 1932 or 1933 to achieve a rapid rise in prices. The intervening years have enabled adjustments of costs to be made which now permit of a lower level of prices than was needed a few years earlier. As prices rise with the passing of the depression, measures should be taken to remove the emergency restrictions; otherwise unduly high prices based upon restriction of supplies will injure the consumer and check the expansion of his demand.

The export trades and shipping have no doubt suffered somewhat as a result of the agricultural policy, though there is no reliable means of measuring their losses. Under the conditions of the depression the losses of the export trades as a result of British agricultural policy must have been small, since markets for British manufactures were difficult to secure and there was no immediate close relation between the volume of imports and the volume of exports. As the depression passes, however, this relation will be restored and British exporting interests as well as those of British consumers will require a relaxation of restrictions upon food imports. British shipping, which has suffered most from agricultural policy, would benefit from a diminution of import restrictions.

Exact information is not yet available to show what change has taken place in the proportion which the farmers of Great Britain produce of the total food requirements of the British people, but there are general indications of an increase in the proportion since 1933. Trade returns, however, show the effects of restrictions upon imports from foreign countries and the results of Imperial preferences. The index numbers on page 196 illustrate the changes in the sources and quantities of imports during recent years of the chief foodstuffs which compete directly with British farm products.[1] They show a decline in total imports of about 11 per cent from the high level of 1931 and a big expansion in imports from Empire countries of 17 per cent, this being more than offset by a reduction of 27 per cent from foreign countries. Fruit from foreign countries shows the biggest decline, while the group of dairy products was the only one in which foreign countries increased the volume of their sales. Empire countries gained their greatest expansion in fruit and dairy products. The figures show that Empire countries have gained considerably

[1] The figures are taken from the *Farm Economist*.

in the British market from the Ottawa policy of Imperial Preference.

Whereas shortly before the policy of Imperial Preference was applied Britain imported about 38 per cent of her food

INDEX NUMBERS OF BRITISH IMPORTS OF FOODSTUFFS

(1927–9 = 100)

Year	Meat	Dairy Products	Wheat and Flour	Eggs	Vegetables	Fruit	Total
From Foreign Countries							
1931	117	112	114	104	172	115	116
1932	114	109	56	80	154	99	99
1933	95	110	63	68	75	49	86
1934	81	114	76	77	70	44	84
From Empire Countries							
1931	117	135	106	106	102	133	117
1932	109	147	142	104	106	164	123
1933	114	157	150	104	134	244	141
1934	123	172	116	100	122	195	137
From All Countries							
1931	117	123	110	104	156	120	117
1932	112	127	96	84	142	118	111
1933	101	133	103	76	87	107	107
1934	94	142	95	81	81	88	104

supplies from Empire countries, the proportion has increased to 50 per cent or more since 1933. These figures show that the Government has honoured its Ottawa Agreement to give Empire countries an expanding share in the British market.

There remains to be considered the question which has caused much concern abroad, both within the Empire and outside: How far will Britain proceed with the expansion of her own agricultural production? Also, how far will she reduce her dependence upon foreign supplies? These questions cannot be answered, as the course of events will be determined not only by British policy but by the policies of

Empire and foreign Governments, and measures may be forced upon Great Britain which she would not wish to adopt. She is unlikely to proceed far in the direction of national self-sufficiency, since this would involve injury to standards of living and to the exporting industries.[1] A moderate trend towards reduced dependence upon imported foodstuffs is, however, probable.

Empire self-sufficiency in most foodstuffs would be practicable, but would deprive British manufacturing industries of large markets in foreign countries, and would prevent foreign countries from meeting their obligations on British investments, as well as involve the additional costs of transporting goods from long distances instead of obtaining them from neighbouring countries.[2] Politically, agriculture in Great Britain is dependent upon the goodwill of the urban industrial population. In practice the predominantly industrial interests of Great Britain will support a fair deal for the British farmer and increased opportunities for Empire countries, but only so long as this involves little increase in prices and little restriction upon British exports. Only exceptionally will they agree to any wide margin of difference in costs between home and imported supplies. In other words, though they are willing to support some revival of British agriculture for political and social reasons they are likely to oppose long-term policies for sheltering or subsidising production which is seriously uneconomic in comparison with that of farmers abroad. The volume of British agricultural production is not likely to increase by more than 10 or 15 per cent during the next few decades, nor is it probable that under the most favourable conditions additional employment on the land will be

[1] It has been said with reasonable foundation that if Britain were agriculturally dependent only on her own resources she would suffer from semi-famine every five years and from severe famine every ten years.

[2] In a speech at the annual dinner of the Association of British Chambers of Commerce, 1935, Mr. Runciman said: "With such varied industries as ours and with a population dependent so much on what is bought abroad of our products we cannot risk our fortunes and the employment of our people only on home trade or only on Empire trade."

found for more than 100,000 workpeople. British food imports supplied by Empire countries are not likely to increase much beyond the present proportion of 50 per cent, although the quantity purchased will increase as standards of living rise. To a greater extent than is often realised British imports of foodstuffs from Empire and foreign countries, especially those outside Europe, are complementary to rather than competitive with one another and with home production.

Britain will concentrate her farming upon those foodstuffs which she is best fitted to produce, and she is not likely to subsidise heavily more than a very few obviously uneconomic crops. Already wheat production has been extended quite far enough, while sugar-beet cultivation is near the limit of its expansion and may even decline somewhat under the new conditions of subsidy. On the other hand, the products which have proved their suitability include beef, mutton and lamb, bacon, milk, cheese, butter, eggs and poultry, vegetables and certain fruits. These products have a special claim to be protected from disaster during periods of chaos and unremunerative prices in world markets, and to long-term conditions which will permit of improved efficiency and quality, and expansion of production so as to supply a somewhat greater share than at present of British needs. Account should also be taken of the increased demand which will result from rising standards of living.

CHAPTER VII

LABOUR POLICY

British foreign policy in the field of labour conditions is almost entirely associated with its membership of the International Labour Organisation of the League of Nations. In the monetary, financial, and commercial affairs reviewed in previous chapters the chief features of policy have been applied unilaterally by the British Government alone, but the negotiation of bilateral agreements and also participation in international conferences with a view to multilateral agreements have also been included. In labour policy the predominant method has been that of multilateral agreements, in the form of draft conventions adopted by the International Labour Conference.[1]

INTERNATIONAL CONVENTIONS

Britain has been a member of the International Labour Organisation from the time of its inauguration in 1919 in accordance with the provisions of the Peace Treaties, and British Government representatives have consistently expressed their support of the objects for which the Organisation was established. Its essential purpose is to improve conditions of labour by international agreement,

[1] This method had been adopted before the war, conventions respecting the prohibition of night work of women in industrial employment, the employment of young persons during the night, and the prohibition of the use of white phosphorus in the manufacture of matches having been concluded at International Conferences held at Berne in 1906 and 1913. It has been much more extensively and systematically applied since the establishment of the International Labour Organisation in 1919. In addition to this method, bilateral treaties dealing with certain labour conditions have been concluded with several foreign countries. Thus treaties of reciprocity in workmen's compensation have been reached between Great Britain and France (1909) and between Great Britain and Denmark (1927) providing that each country will accord to workmen of the other country injured in accidents arising out of their employment in its territory the same protection as is enjoyed by its own workpeople.

particularly by securing the removal of injustice, hardship, and privation. It is recognised that the existence of such conditions is a cause of unrest by which "the peace and harmony of the world are imperilled," and that universal peace can be established only if it is based upon social justice. "Also the failure of any nation to adopt humane conditions of labour is an obstacle in the way of other nations which desire to improve the conditions in their own countries."[1] Thus the task of the International Labour Organisation is associated with that of the League of Nations and attention is directed to the intimate relation between standards of working conditions in different countries.

Two distinct problems are involved in the establishment of international agreements upon working conditions: the raising of unduly low standards in backward countries mainly for humanitarian reasons, and the restraining of the severity of international competition as it affects working conditions in the more advanced countries, so that deterioration of standards may be avoided and that progress in the improvement of conditions in different countries may be facilitated by cooperation. The low standards in certain backward countries frequently do not involve severe competition as their efficiency is generally poor, and the purpose of improving conditions is primarily humanitarian. Britain is concerned with both the humanitarian and the "restraint of unfair competition" aspects of international labour regulation. She has a traditional interest, from the days of the suppression of the slave trade, in the prevention of abuses and exploitation of backward peoples, while her high standard of working conditions and her dependence upon international trade make desirable the regulation of competitive conditions.

The adoption of an international draft convention or recommendation by the International Labour Conference

[1] See the Preamble of the Constitution of the International Labour Organisation.

requires a majority of two-thirds of the votes cast by the delegates present.[1] The terms of such an agreement do not constitute a binding obligation upon a member country unless it ratifies the agreement. Each country retains full sovereignty, being free to adopt or reject the agreement, and, in the event of rejection, it is under no further obligation. Each member country is, however, required to bring any draft convention or recommendation before its Parliament or other competent constitutional authority generally within one year but at the latest within eighteen months from the closing of the session of the Conference. Ratification of a draft convention is usually based upon the passing of national legislation bringing the regulation of labour conditions within the country into conformity with the provisions of the international agreement. When ratified, a convention becomes a binding obligation between the countries which have ratified, and must be observed during the period of years specified in the convention. Failure to observe the provisions of a convention may result in the appointment of a Commission of Enquiry, and even in the last resort in the adoption of economic sanctions against a defaulting Government, although it is unlikely that such drastic action will ever be taken.

During nineteen sessions of the International Labour Conference from the Washington Conference, 1919, to the 1935 Session, forty-five draft conventions have been adopted.[2] In reviewing British policy, attention is first directed to the conventions which the British Government has ratified, distinguishing those involving little or no change in British standards of labour conditions from those necessitating

[1] Each member country is entitled to send four delegates to the Conference, two of whom are Government delegates and the other two represent respectively the employers and the workpeople of the country; in practice, however, delegations are not always complete. Of the two kinds of agreement by the Conference (draft conventions and recommendations) the present chapter deals only with draft conventions which when ratified constitute binding obligations upon the countries, whereas recommendations serve only as a general guide to labour policy.

[2] In addition four conventions have been revised.

important changes. Then an account is given of draft conventions which the British Government has not yet ratified, together with the chief reasons for non-ratification.

Before proceeding to this review it is relevant to note the methods by which labour conditions are regulated in Great Britain. During the nineteenth century, with few exceptions, working conditions were determined by individual relations between employers and their workpeople or by collective agreements. In the latter part of that century collective agreements increased greatly in importance, and in the present century they had become, by the end of the war, the predominant method for regulating wages and hours, the agreements covering directly or indirectly the great majority of British workers and undertakings. The Government's policy was generally to avoid intervention in the regulation of wages and hours except in certain trades in which organisation for fixing wages and hours was inadequate and in which conditions were consequently unsatisfactory.[1] In other fields, particularly health, safety, and other factory conditions and also social insurance, conditions are largely determined by legislation.

This distinction between conditions regulated mainly by legislation and those regulated mainly by collective agreement is important in considering the ratification of international draft conventions. Where the subject of a draft convention falls mainly in the field covered by legislation the Government's chief preoccupation is whether ratification calls for considerable changes in legislation and administrative practice, whether the political situation is favourable for making any necessary changes, and whether additional expenditure of public money will be involved. If, however, a draft convention deals with some question mainly regulated by collective agreement, the Government must

---

[1] For such trades, machinery for regulation was set up under the Trade Boards Acts of 1909 and 1918. The State also influences wages and hours in private industry by the conditions fixed for persons employed in central and local government undertakings, and by the use of the fair wages clause in contracts for public authorities.

consider not only the Parliamentary situation but even more the attitudes of the employers' organisations and of the trade unions. If these bodies are opposed to a draft convention, either because it would increase costs of production and reduce competitive power in international markets or because it would require the abandonment of a long-established practice, the Government is unlikely to ratify. It will wish to avoid a controversy which might tend towards a deterioration of industrial relations. Thus the difficulties in ratifying draft conventions are in some ways increased in a country in which employers' organisations and trade unions are strong; on the other hand working conditions will have been raised and standardised by collective agreements, so that they are more likely to equal or even exceed the provisions of the draft convention than in countries where organisations are weak.[1]

It may be noted that where, as in Great Britain, those labour conditions (wages and hours) which are of chief importance in international competition are mainly determined by collective agreements the Government can do little by manipulation of wages and hours to increase the country's competitive power in international markets. During the depression certain foreign Governments with greater powers of control over wages undertook deflationary adjustments of prices and money wages which would have been impracticable in Great Britain. The independent regulation of wages in Great Britain by collective agreements was one of the factors which, by making difficult the alternative policy of deflation, contributed to the British abandonment of the gold standard in 1931.

[1] The question was raised by Mr. F. W. Leggett, one of the British Government's representatives, at the 1934 Conference, whether a method could not be found by which the Organisation could take account of high standards adopted by voluntary collective agreements without legislation instead of judging countries on the arithmetical number of the conventions which they have ratified.

BRITISH RATIFICATIONS

A Government's decision about the ratification or non-ratification of a draft convention depends mainly upon the standard established by the national legislation being already at least equal to that of the convention, or alternatively upon its willingness to pass new legislation where the national standard is lower than that of the convention. If in the discussion of a draft convention at the International Labour Conference the representatives of a Government can secure the adoption of a text in conformity with or not superior to their national legislation, their Government can ratify the convention without passing new legislation [1] All Governments have this interest, and the British Government is no exception in generally directing its efforts at the Conference towards ensuring that draft conventions do not conflict with British practice. If all Governments succeeded in this policy draft conventions would merely represent the practice of the country with the lowest standard, or the least common denominator of the practice of all the member States. The British Government is, however, often, though not always, justified in adopting this policy as its standards of labour conditions are relatively high.

Representatives of the British Government refer to the high standards of working conditions in Great Britain and seem to suggest that the essential need is for other countries to bring their standards up to the British level.[2] This raises

---

[1] Even before a draft convention reaches the stage of discussion at the Conference its provisions are influenced both by the existing national legislation of the various countries and by the answers which Governments give to questions asked by the International Labour Office to guide it in preparing the draft. There still remains the problem whether, in the light of these data, the Office will submit provisions corresponding closely with the practice of many countries or alternatively provisions in advance of the standards of most countries, which will involve substantial reforms if the convention is ratified.

[2] At the 1932 Conference, Sir Henry Betterton, Minister of Labour, stated that "No country stands to gain more [than Great Britain] from a general raising of the standard of life among the working classes all over the world."

the general question whether conventions should be equal or even superior to the best practice of the most advanced countries, being an ideal towards which progress would be made, though the number of immediate ratifications would be few, or whether they should correspond closely with the existing law and practice of most of the chief industrial countries, while being in advance of conditions in backward countries. The latter course, which is the one favoured by the British Government and adopted on most subjects by the International Labour Organisation, enables many of the industrially developed countries to ratify without making any change, or only slight changes, in their existing conditions. For other countries, however, ratification often means a distinct advance. As circumstances permit, conventions may then be progressively revised to provide for higher standards than those originally adopted.

Of the 45 conventions adopted by the International Labour Conference during its first 19 sessions, the British Government up to the beginning of 1936 had ratified 19. As, however, some time is necessary to complete ratification it is fairer to omit recently adopted conventions, and if only those conventions are considered which were adopted by the Conference up to 1932 the comparison is 19 ratifications out of 32. The British record corresponds closely with that of other important industrial countries, the numbers of whose ratifications up to January 1936 were as follows:

Belgium ..	..	.. 23	Poland ..	..	..	17
Italy	..	.. 21[1]	Sweden ..	..	..	17[3]
France	..	.. 18[2]	Netherlands	..	..	17
Germany	..	.. 17	Czechoslovakia		..	13

[1] The ratification of one convention (Hours of work in industry) is conditional upon ratification by certain other countries. In other words, a convention ratified conditionally is not applied until other specified countries have also ratified. This method is adopted to ensure that a country is not placed at a disadvantage in relation to countries with which it is in competition.

[2] Two conditional ratifications—hours of work in industry, and inspection of emigrants.

[3] Ratification of the Convention on Inspection of Emigrants is conditional.

The conventions ratified by Great Britain are as follows:

Unemployment, which includes the establishment of employment exchanges by the public authorities.

Night work of women.

Night work of young persons.

Minimum age for industrial employment.

Minimum age for employment on board ship.

Minimum age for employment as trimmers and stokers on board ship.

Medical examination of young persons on entering employment on board ship.

Unemployment indemnity for shipwrecked seamen.

Seamen's articles of agreement.

Inspection of emigrants.[1]

Right of association of agricultural workers.

Workmen's compensation for accidents to agricultural workers.

Equality of treatment of foreign workers in accident compensation.

Workmen's compensation for occupational diseases.

Protection of dockers against accidents (revised convention).

Sickness insurance for workers in industry.

Sickness insurance for workers in agriculture.

Minimum wage-fixing machinery.

Forced labour.

The British Government was able to ratify twelve of these conventions without making any legislative changes, existing law and practice being at least equal to the standards of the conventions. For the remaining seven ratifications new legislation was necessary, but several of them required only minor modifications of existing legislation. Ratification of the Convention fixing fourteen years as the minimum age for admission to industrial employment involved abandoning

[1] This ratification is conditional, but legislation in conformity with the terms of the Convention has been passed.

the practice of granting special permits at thirteen years of age to children who had reached the required school standard. The Convention prohibiting, with certain exceptions, the night work of young persons under eighteen years of age required legislation extending prohibition, which already applied to factories and workshops, to a few new industries, particularly construction. It also involved raising from fourteen to sixteen years the exceptional age limit permitted for certain continuous processes, including iron and steel, glass, and paper manufacture. The obligation to pay wages to shipwrecked seamen for a period up to two months as indemnity for unemployment actually resulting from the loss or foundering of their ship was new not only in Great Britain but in all the other important maritime countries which have ratified the Convention on this subject. British legislation was brought into conformity with the Convention by the passing of the Merchant Shipping (International Labour Conventions) Act, 1925. This Act also included the requirement of a compulsory medical examination of children and young persons entering upon employment at sea, and fixed the minimum age for admission as trimmers and stokers at eighteen years; these requirements for ratification were also new in British practice, but no opposition was encountered.

Only slight changes were necessary to permit ratification of the Convention on the minimum age of admission to employment at sea. Ratification of the Conventions providing sickness insurance for industrial and agricultural workers involved certain legislative changes, the chief being extension to Northern Ireland of the provision of medical benefits under the National Health Insurance Scheme. There can be little doubt that the desire of the British Government to ratify the Convention promoted and hastened this change. The Convention on night work of women is of interest, because, though ratified by Great Britain in 1920, it was revised by the 1934 Session of the International Labour Conference at the request of the British Government to overcome the objection that it placed women at a disadvantage in obtaining posts as managers and technicians.[1] In the revised convention it is explicitly provided that the prohibition of night work does not apply to women holding responsible positions of management, who are not ordinarily engaged in manual work. The Convention for the protection of dockers against accidents adopted by the 1929 Conference is one which the British Government refused to ratify in its original form. Objections by the British and German Governments led to its partial revision in 1931, and it was then ratified by the British Government.

The changes made represent definite, though not great, improvements in British legislation and practice. The unratified conventions, to which attention is now directed, require more important changes, and these changes would generally have greater effect upon costs of production and international competitive relations.

UNRATIFIED CONVENTIONS

The chief reasons for a Government's failure to ratify a convention are unwillingness to change its existing practice and fear that the country may be placed at a disadvantage in its competition with other countries. These reasons have affected the British Government's attitude towards certain conventions. Where changes affecting costs of production and therefore competitive power have been involved two different lines of policy have been pursued, (1) to propose revision of the convention so as to bring it into conformity with British practice, and (2) to delay action until simultaneous ratification by all the chief competing countries can be arranged. The second of these methods is evidently

[1] Before revision, the question of interpretation of the original convention was submitted to the Permanent Court of International Justice, as, while the British Government considered that the convention could not be interpreted to exclude persons in managerial positions, other Governments held that it admitted this interpretation. In an Advisory Opinion the Court upheld the British contention by six votes to five, and the procedure for revision was then initiated.

reasonable. The first may not always be so, and it has led to inconsistency in British policy. With a view to enabling certain British practices to be continued, the British Government has made proposals to increase the elasticity of some of the clauses in conventions. On the other hand, flexible clauses are criticised as giving opportunity to evade the intention of the agreement. British Government representatives have not infrequently expressed the opinion that in certain foreign countries the provisions of conventions are not applied so strictly as in Great Britain, where a well organised inspectorate and a strong and vigilant trade union movement ensure a high standard of observance of legislative obligations. They have, therefore, proposed defining with greater precision some of the provisions of conventions.

These features of policy may be illustrated by reviewing the British Government's attitude to various conventions which it has not ratified. Of the thirty-two draft conventions adopted by the Conference during the years 1919 to 1932, thirteen remain unratified by the British Government.[1] Five of them deal with hours of work or the related questions of night work (in bakeries) and weekly rest, three with seamen and dockers, two with the minimum age of entry into agriculture and non-industrial employment, and three with other questions (provisions for women workers before and after confinement, workmen's compensation for accidents, and prohibition of the use of white lead in internal painting). These unratified conventions as a whole are somewhat more specific than the ratified conventions, some of which establish general principles rather than particularised obligations.

Special attention is here given to the British Government's attitudes towards the conventions on hours of labour, partly because they illustrate different aspects of policy

---

[1] As already indicated, a convention on protection against accidents (dockers) passed by the 1929 Conference was revised in 1932 at the British Government's request, and Great Britain has ratified the revised convention.

and also because the question of hours is one of the two labour conditions of chief importance in international competition, the other being wages. At this point it may be noted that, although valuable results in establishing many desirable standards of working conditions and in mitigating the effects of international competition upon the workers may be obtained by the application of international conventions, the task is incomplete so long as wages are unregulated. High standards of working hours, social security and labour welfare may be adopted, and yet the costs involved may be covered at the expense of wages, which may remain unfair in certain countries. In consequence the impact of international competition may continue to involve hardship upon the workers and to retard the improvement of labour standards. Representatives of the British Government at the International Labour Conference have not neglected to lay stress upon the necessity for going much further with wages than the general principles on which the Minimum Wage Fixing Machinery Convention is based. During the discussions at the Conferences in 1933, 1934, and 1935 on the subject of a forty-hour week in industry the relation between hours and wages was seen to be fundamental.

The most famous of the conventions is the Washington Hours Convention which, with certain exceptions, provides for an eight-hour day and a forty-eight hour week in industrial undertakings. Overtime to deal with exceptional pressure of work may be allowed, but the rate of pay for overtime must not be less than one and a quarter times the regular rate. The British Government proposed the placing of the forty-eight hour week on the Agenda of the Conference in 1919, and the Convention was adopted by 82 votes to 2, all the British delegates (Government, employer, and worker) voting for it. It was then expected that the British Government would proceed to early ratification, but this hope has been continually disappointed. Meanwhile, the Convention has been ratified by more than twenty countries, but many of them are not industrially important, while others have ratified conditionally so that the terms of the Convention will not be applied until certain competing countries, including Great Britain, have also ratified. The only highly industrialised States which have yet ratified unconditionally are Czechoslovakia, Canada, Belgium, and Luxemburg. The ratifications of France, Italy, and Austria are conditional. It is also probable that the German Government would have ratified the Convention if Great Britain and other competing countries would have done so simultaneously.

To ratify the Convention, a new Act of Parliament would be necessary as British legislation on hours of work is scanty. By Acts of Parliament, the length of shift of underground coal miners is fixed at $7\frac{1}{2}$ hours, which, with one winding time, makes slightly more than eight hours below the surface. For other adult male workers in industry, except in a few dangerous and unhealthy trades, there is no statutory limitation of hours. The hours of work of women and young persons in industry are regulated by the Factory and Workshop Acts.[1] In practice, these Acts have had the effect of restricting to some extent the hours of adult male workers, in so far as their work is dependent upon that of women and young persons. They limit the total hours of work of women and young persons to twelve, including $1\frac{1}{2}$ hours—in textile factories 2 hours—for meals, on each working day, Saturdays excepted when, for example, in the textile industry, work must cease at midday. The effect is to fix a maximum legal limit of $55\frac{1}{2}$ hours in the textile industry and of 60 hours in other industries.[2] But poverty of legislation is made up by wealth of collective agreements. These generally fix weekly hours of work at 48 or less, and on several occasions before the depression British Govern-

[1] In commerce the Shops Act, 1934, fixes the normal maximum working hours of young persons employed about the business of a shop at forty-eight in any week, and regulates overtime.

[2] A strictly limited amount of overtime in excess of these hours is allowed in certain industries for female workers over eighteen years of age on weekdays other than Saturday.

ment representatives stated officially that about 90 per
cent of the wage earners of the country enjoyed an eight-
hour day or a forty-eight hour week as a result directly or
indirectly of collective agreements. During the depression,
however, there has been some tendency to revert to a longer
working week. According to the Annual Report of the
Chief Inspector of Factories and Workshops for the year
1934, the full legal limit of $55\frac{1}{2}$ hours was worked in certain
undertakings in the textile areas, while in other areas a
working week of 54 or 56 hours was frequently found, the
legal limit being worked on all days except Saturday.[1]

It might be thought that the British Government would
have little difficulty in passing legislation confirming and
somewhat extending the standards established by collective
agreements. Bills to permit ratification of the Washington
Convention were, indeed, introduced in the House of
Commons by the Labour Governments in 1924 and in 1930
but, being minority Governments, they were unable to pass
contentious measures, including these bills. At certain
times Conservative Governments have also declared their
intention to ratify the Convention. Thus in May 1927
Lord Balfour, Lord President of the Council, speaking in
the House of Lords stated: "It is the object and policy of
His Majesty's Government to proceed with the necessary
legislation to give effect to the terms of the Hours Convention," and he added that "The British Government still
maintain the view that ratification by the chief industrial
Powers of Europe ought to be simultaneous and ought to
involve at least an approximate equality of obligation."
He said that steps should be taken to ensure that each of
the parties to the Convention attached a precise and identical
meaning to its various provisions. Actually, British Governments, other than the Labour Governments, have vacillated
between simultaneous ratification by the chief industrial
countries of Europe, with an agreed interpretation of various
clauses, and revision before ratification. Since the 1921

---

[1] Cmd. 4931.

depression, however, when revision was first proposed, the latter policy has generally been preferred, although consultations in London in 1926 between the Ministers of Labour of Belgium, France, Germany, Italy, and Great Britain raised unrealised hopes of agreed interpretations and simultaneous ratification.[1]

The proposals for revision include:

(1) Greater precision in the definition of "hours of work." In Great Britain this means hours during which a man is at the disposal of the employer, but in some countries it is regarded as "hours of effective work" and, on some classes of work, men might be at the disposal of the employer for ten or twelve hours a day, part of the time being spent in attendance and only eight hours reckoned as effective work.

(2) Authorisation of a five-day week of 48 hours. The Convention provides that, apart from specified exceptions, the daily limit shall not exceed 9 hours when hours are distributed in other ways than 6 days of 8 hours each.

(3) Precision in the extent to which the time lost owing to holidays may be spread over future weeks in addition to the normal 48 hours.

(4) The definition of "continuous processes" for which a 56-hour week is permitted, so that the same types of work shall be covered in each country.

(5) Greater elasticity in the regulation of overtime so as to include conditions permitted by many British collective agreements. Of special difficulty is the British system established by agreement giving railwaymen a guaranteed week of 48 hours, with Sunday duty at regular intervals for which overtime rates are paid, whether or not the total hours are in excess of forty-eight. This system of regular Sunday duty, favoured by the railwaymen because of its higher rate of pay, would not be allowed by the recognised

[1] See Report of the Governing Body of the International Labour Office upon the working of the Convention, submitted to the International Labour Conference, 1931.

exemptions of the Convention, such as that in Article 6, which only permits temporary exceptions "so that establishments may deal with exceptional cases of pressure of work."[1]

In its attitude towards this Convention the Government has been influenced by the opposition of British employers to the Convention and by fear that discontent might result from interference with certain long-established practices approved by employers and workers and embodied in collective agreements. The employers resist extensions of Government intervention in industry and prefer the existing freedom to bargain with the trade unions rather than the limitations and rigidities which would be involved by ratification of the Washington Convention. Nor are the trade unions unanimous about the advantages of ratification. The British Government's refusal to ratify without revision has been met by equally determined refusal of the Governing Body of the International Labour Office to recommend revision, the workers' representatives and also Governments which have already ratified the Convention opposing the British Government's policy. While this dilemma remains, the adoption in 1935 of a general Draft Convention embodying the principle of a forty-hour week makes the Washington Hours Convention seem almost out of date, although a forty-eight hour week would still be of value as a basic legal standard.

The second of the unratified conventions on hours is that adopted by the 1931 Conference to regulate the working

---

[1] The question may be raised whether this difficulty and similar ones arising in connection with other conventions might be overcome by making use of the provision in Article 405 of Part XIII of the Treaty of Versailles which stipulates that "In no case shall any Member be asked or required, as a result of the adoption of any recommendation or draft convention by the Conference, to lessen the protection afforded by its existing legislation to the workers concerned." Where the Government of a country, in agreement with the employers' and workers' organisations concerned, is of the opinion that certain practices, which could be embodied in legislation, are more advantageous to the workers than those laid down in a convention it might ratify the convention on the basis of the stipulation just quoted. The question arises, how broadly this provision of Part XIII should be interpreted, and safeguards against its abuse would be necessary.

time of coal miners underground.[1] The British Government representatives voted in favour of this Convention at the time of its adoption. It limits the normal day of any worker in a coal mine to $7\frac{3}{4}$ hours, including the time spent in descending and ascending, but extension of the time is allowed in cases of emergency and for continuous services, and a maximum of 60 hours overtime in a year at time-and-a-quarter wage rates may also be worked. With certain exceptions, the Convention prohibits underground work on Sundays and legal public holidays. The standard of $7\frac{3}{4}$ hours is about 15 to 20 minutes less than the present British standard. However, in view of unemployment, of the satisfaction which the reduction of hours would give to the miners, and of the fact that for some years until 1926 the British shift was shorter than that of the Convention, the Government expressed its willingness to ratify, provided that certain revisions were made, and that simultaneous ratification could be arranged with the other six European countries concerned (Belgium, Czechoslovakia, France, Germany, the Netherlands, and Poland).

The chief points upon which amendments were desired by the British Government were:

(1) The length of day for continuous shift workers (including those operating underground drainage pumps and ventilation fans). The Convention allowed their shift to be

---

[1] The adoption of the Convention on Hours of Work in Coal Mines is part of an attempt, through the I.L.O., the Economic Organisation of the League of Nations and in other ways, to establish some form of international regulation of the European coal-mining industry. A Convention on Hours of Work in Commerce and Offices adopted by the 1930 Conference is not discussed here, as it is on somewhat similar lines to the Washington Hours Convention. It provides for an eight-hour day and a forty-eight hour week, but the week can be so arranged that the hours of work in any day do not exceed ten hours. The British Government gives among its reasons for not ratifying this Convention that it covers too wide a range of occupations to be included in any single instrument and permits such a variety of exceptions as to render it unsuitable as a basis for international regulation. Recent British legislation on hours of work in commerce and offices (the Children and Young Persons Act, 1933, and the Shops Act, 1934) deals only with young persons. The provisions of previous Acts covering adult workpeople fall far below the requirements of the Convention.

half an hour more than the normal shift, whereas British legislation allows an hour more. About 10,000 workers in Great Britain were affected.

(2) The regulation of Sunday work. The Convention's prohibition of Sunday work conflicted with the widespread British practice of keeping Saturday afternoon free and starting the Monday shift at ten o'clock on Sunday night. The Government considered that to start the Monday shift two hours later would involve working two hours more on Saturday afternoons and it held the view that neither the Government nor the trade unions could get the miners to agree to any tampering with their free Saturday afternoon. In view of these difficulties, together with others raised by several Continental countries, the Convention was revised by the 1935 Session of the Conference, and the British Government has since declared its willingness to ratify the revised Convention provided it is simultaneously ratified by the other European countries mentioned above. The prospect of simultaneous ratification has been greatly diminished by Germany's withdrawal from the International Labour Organisation, which took effect in October 1935.

The British Government's policy towards the forty-hour week proposal is of interest, especially in view of the adoption of a Convention on the principle of a forty-hour week, with maintenance of the standard of living, by the 1935 Session of the Conference, and the initiation of a procedure to apply this principle in particular industries. This standard is considerably in advance of existing legislation and practice even in the highly industrialised countries, except the United States in so far as the hours of work fixed by the ill-fated N.R.A. Codes are maintained, and it would, if applied, be a major factor in international competition. It also raises the fundamental wage issue by linking reduction of hours with maintenance of standards of living. In its original intention the proposal differed from the Washington Convention, its primary purpose being not to ensure the welfare of the employed by prohibiting

an unduly long working day, but to bring about a reduction
in unemployment resulting from the world depression and
from labour-saving machinery and methods. Its chief supporters laid special emphasis upon its value as a means of
mitigating the depression.

The British Government, while agreeing that the problem
should be thoroughly investigated, maintained from the
outset that all available information supported the conclusion that the adoption of a convention providing for
the general application of a forty-hour week or other substantial reduction of hours throughout industry was impracticable. It considered that limitation of hours could
only be dealt with, either nationally or internationally,
industry by industry in the light of the special circumstances
of each industry. Employers and workers are generally
organised and negotiate agreements separately industry by
industry, and the proper course would be to consider a
series of conventions for particular industries, along the
lines of that adopted for coal-mining.

The forty-hour week would not, in the opinion of the
British Government, provide a remedy for unemployment.
Also, the question of wages was closely bound up with
reduction of hours. The Government would not support a
convention which merely limited hours and afforded no
protection to wages. In Great Britain the proposal was
understood to be reduction of hours without reduction of
weekly earnings, and the British workers were strongly
opposed to any other scheme, but in some other countries
the demand seemed to be for a work-sharing scheme to
benefit the unemployed at the expense of the work and
earnings of persons fully employed.[1] In countries without

[1] The two proposed draft conventions submitted to the 1934 Session of
the Conference (one providing for the application of the forty-hour week
to all industrial undertakings except coal mines, and the second to commerce and offices) made no provision for maintaining wages, although a
proposed draft recommendation concerning the maintenance of the
standard of living was submitted to the same Session. The Conference
adopted none of the proposals, but decided to reconsider the whole question
at its 1935 Session.

adequate machinery for the protection of wages any additional cost from a reduction of hours would be offset by a reduction of wages. This, in the opinion of the British Government, would react through international competition upon other countries and a period of severe industrial conflict over wages would result. The Draft Convention on Minimum Wage-Fixing Machinery, though establishing a useful principle, only touched the fringe of the problem and, without further development, made no substantial contribution towards the regulation of international competition.

The British Government considered the problem of dealing with wages so as to prevent earnings from being reduced coincident with hours to be insuperable,[1] but even if the difficulties could be overcome a number of unsatisfactory dislocations would result. Thus the effect of the adoption of a forty-hour week would be much greater for industries now working forty-eight hours than for those working only forty-two or forty-four hours; in some industries the shorter week might result in an increased rate of production per hour, while in those where the machine sets the pace output would fall in proportion to the reduction of hours; unless more shifts were worked, industries with expensive plant would suffer more as a result of its longer idleness than industries in which plant is of less importance. Also countries such as Great Britain in which wages are comparatively high might be placed at a relative disadvantage in competition with low-wage countries. Some of these difficulties would remain, even with the method of adopting a series of conventions, industry by industry.[2]

When decisions on the forty-hour week were postponed

[1] An international agreement providing for the detailed regulation of wages would involve an obligation upon Governments which they are not, in most countries, in a position to undertake; in most countries employers and workers do not desire Governments to assume responsibility for the fixing of wages. Other difficulties include the disturbances due to frequent fluctuations in foreign exchange rates and the constant changes necessary to adjust wage rates to changes in the cost of living and in economic conditions within countries.

[2] Here it may be noted that the policy of the British workers was to secure a forty-hour week convention of general application, and this

by both the 1933 and 1934 Sessions of the Conference the delay largely changed the problem from one involving rapid action with a view to mitigating unemployment during the depression to one of long range. The 1935 Session, however, succeeded in reaching decisions which indicate the lines of future development. Its agenda included proposals for five draft conventions for applying the forty-hour week in the first instance to public works undertaken or subsidised by Governments, iron and steel, building and contracting, glass-bottle manufacture, and coal mines. It also considered two draft resolutions, one being a general declaration approving the principle of the forty-hour week, and the other inviting Governments to take appropriate measures to ensure that any adjustment of wages and salaries related to reduction of hours would not result in lowering the standard of living of the workers.

The Conference transformed the first of these resolutions into a draft convention, adding that in applying the principle of the forty-hour week the standard of living is not to be reduced.[1] Henceforth, as indicated by Mr. Harold Butler, Director of the International Labour Office, the principle of the forty-eight hour week laid down in the Constitution of the Organisation is no longer its goal. The principle of the forty-hour week has taken its place. The Conference also adopted a Draft Convention providing for a forty-two hour week, averaged over four weeks, in the glass-bottle industry —which in effect stabilises existing conditions. The question

involved opposition from time to time between the British workers' delegate and the Government's spokesman. The Government's policy has been mainly presented on this subject, as on others, by a permanent official. It would seem desirable that on highly controversial questions of policy the Government's position should be stated by the appropriate political authority and not by a permanent official, who, after finding himself in opposition to the employers' or workers' delegate, may, on returning to his country, be engaged in work of conciliation in industrial disputes for which a reputation for complete impartiality is essential. The present Minister of Labour, Mr. Ernest Brown, has indicated his intention to attend the 1936 Session of the Conference.

[1] With this Draft Convention the Conference associated a resolution on maintenance of the workers' income and standards of living, and indicating methods for ensuring such maintenance.

of draft conventions for the other four industries was referred to the 1936 Conference, the Agenda of which also includes reduction of hours in the printing and bookbinding, textile, and chemical industries. The British Government delegate, Mr. F. W. Leggett, welcomed the decision of the Conference to deal with the problem industry by industry. By adopting this method, and also by recognising in the general convention that hours of work and standards of living could not be separated, he considered that the 1935 Conference had come closer to realities than at any other time since the Organisation began to discuss the question of the forty-hour week.

Brief indications may be given about other unratified conventions. The British Government has not ratified the Convention providing for a weekly rest of at least twenty-four consecutive hours in every seven days for persons employed in industrial undertakings, largely because of difficulties of inspection and enforcement which are increased by the provision for compensatory periods of rest for persons working on Sunday. The practice of a weekly rest broadly on the lines laid down in the Convention is very widely established in Great Britain both by tradition arising out of Sunday observance and by collective agreements.[1] The Convention prohibiting night work in bakeries, between the hours of 11 p.m. and 5 a.m., is a good example of a convention dealing with conditions of no significance in international competition. Its purpose, therefore, is to prevent the habits of consumers from needlessly requiring regular work at inconvenient times. But habit has proved strong; many consumers want fresh bread for breakfast, and few countries have ratified the Convention. The British Government has stated that, if the supply of bread were to be continued as at present, an increase in the cost of the

---

[1] A Sunday Observance Act of 1677 is still in force, subject to certain exemptions under subsequent legislation, and, though not used for more than half a century, the Act provides the penalty of a fine or two hours in the stocks for persons convicted of working on Sunday at their ordinary business.

loaf would result, and the Government was not prepared to support a measure which would adversely affect the cost of living.

As the chief maritime country Great Britain is specially interested in the conditions of employment on board ship, and these are directly affected by conditions on foreign vessels. The Convention for establishing facilities for seamen to find employment, which was adopted by the Genoa Conference, 1920, is designed to secure the abolition of profit-making or fee-charging agencies. Public employment offices making no charge are to be set up either by the State or by representative associations of shipowners and seamen jointly, under the control of a central authority. In Great Britain a jointly regulated system on the lines laid down by the Convention is in operation, but the Government has not ratified the Convention, as it considers that the joint system is not yet so fully developed as to provide complete compliance with the Convention.[1] The Repatriation of Seamen Convention provides that any seamen, unless engaged on certain exempted classes of vessel, who is landed during or on the expiration of his terms of engagement, shall be entitled to be taken back to his own country, or to the port at which he was engaged, or to the port at which the voyage commenced, as determined by national law. Repatriation shall not be a charge upon him unless his leaving the ship is due to his own fault or to any cause for which he can be held responsible. At the Conference the British Government delegates described this Convention as very useful and voted for it, but it has not been ratified, and reasons do not seem to have been made public in explanation of this policy. British law establishes conditions which are somewhat similar to those stipulated by the Convention, but certain changes in British legislation would be necessary to enable Great Britain to ratify.

[1] Statement made by Dr. Macnamara, the Minister of Labour, in the House of Commons, November 1921. A similar statement was made by Dr. Burgin, Parliamentary Secretary of the Board of Trade, in the House of Commons, June 3, 1935.

With a view to reducing the number of accidents to dockers caused by overloading the machines hoisting goods, a Convention was adopted by the 1929 Conference providing that any package of a gross weight of one metric ton or more consigned for transport by sea or inland waterway shall have its weight plainly marked upon it before it is loaded. The value of such a practice grows cumulatively with increase in the number of maritime countries by which it is adopted, and actually this is one of the most widely ratified of all the conventions. About thirty States have ratified it, including many of the chief maritime Powers. The British Government has not raised any objection to the Convention, and it is understood that the policy is to ratify when a convenient opportunity is found.

Although Great Britain has ratified the Conventions fixing the minimum age of employment in industry and for children employed at sea, it has not ratified those for agriculture and for non-industrial employment. Both these Conventions, like the two already ratified, fix fourteen as the minimum working age, but permit employment outside school hours under certain conditions, provided this does not prejudice attendance at school. In non-industrial work such employment is restricted to children over twelve, the work must be light and not harmful to the children's health, it must not exceed two hours per day, and is prohibited on Sundays, public holidays and during the night;[1] also national regulations must fix a higher age than fourteen for street trading and for employment dangerous to life, health or morals.

Ratification of the agricultural minimum age Convention was withheld largely because, until 1932, although legislation in force in England set a standard which would have permitted ratification, powers of exemption possessed by local authorities in Scotland stood in the way. However, the passing in 1932 of the Children and Young Persons

[1] A few safeguarded exceptions are allowed, including children employed as actors.

Act (Scotland) seems to remove most, if not all of the obstacles to ratification. Even before 1932 the exemptions which were not in conformity with the terms of the Convention were few and unimportant. The minimum age in non-industrial employment in Great Britain is determined by the Children and Young Persons Act, 1933, and the Government stated in November 1934 that in certain material points the Convention goes beyond British legislation, and indicated that, as the new British legislation was so recent, it was too soon to form any opinion as to how it would work. The Government, therefore, would postpone a final decision upon ratification but would keep the matter under consideration.

Whereas British legislation and practice differ little from the provisions of many of the conventions reviewed above the White Lead, Child Birth, and Workmen's Compensation (Accidents) Conventions set standards distinctly higher than or differ considerably in methods from those in force in Great Britain. The Convention dealing with white lead prohibits the use of this substance, sulphate of lead and similar products, in the internal painting of buildings, except under certain conditions for railway stations and industrial establishments.[1] Its sole purpose is to safeguard the health of workers by protecting them from lead poisoning. British legislation, which was introduced subsequent to and in consequence of the Convention, does not prohibit the use of white lead for painting the interiors of buildings, but regulations are in force prohibiting, with exceptions, the employment of women and young persons on this work. Manufacturers of the paints have been particularly active in their opposition to this Convention. The Government recognises that the occupation is a dangerous one, but has, so far, preferred regulation to the more drastic method of prohibition. It has, however, indicated that it would be prepared to adopt the method of prohibition if experience should prove regulation to be inadequate.

---

[1] For such work the employment of women, and of males under eighteen years of age, unless apprenticed, is prohibited.

The Childbirth Convention provides that a woman worker shall have the right to leave her work six weeks before and shall not be permitted to work during the six weeks following her confinement. During such absence from work she shall be paid benefits sufficient for the full and healthy maintenance of herself and her child either out of public or insurance funds; she also has the right to free attendance by a doctor or certified midwife. British legislation for women in employment is less favourable; employers may not knowingly employ a woman in a factory or workshop sooner than four weeks after confinement. Certain money benefits are paid both to women employed in insured trades and also to the wives of insured workmen, this arrangement for wives not in employment going beyond the terms of the Convention. Medical benefits are also available both for women workers and for the wives of insured workmen, though these do not include free medical attendance.[1] Various legislative and administrative changes and increased expenditure would be involved in bringing the British system into line with the Convention.

The Workmen's Compensation Act is below the standard set by the Workmen's Compensation (Accidents) Convention. Increased participation by the State would be necessary in the supervision of the use of lump sum compensation payments and in ensuring the payment of compensation to workmen in the event of the insolvency of the employer or insurance organisation. Additional expense either to the employer or to the health insurance scheme, which is maintained by the joint contributions of employer, worker, and State, would be involved in providing, as the Convention requires, additional compensation where an injured workman is incapacitated in such a way as to require the constant help of another person, and the right to medical, surgical, and pharmaceutical aid and to the supply and normal

---

[1] It is optional for local authorities to apply the Maternity and Child Welfare Act, 1918, by which they may provide various medical benefits.

renewal of artificial limbs and surgical appliances.[1] The British Government has not been willing to make the necessary changes, indicating that ratification would involve a number of serious alterations in the existing law, which, both on grounds of principle and in view of the additional expense entailed on the State and on industry, they are not prepared to entertain.[2] In its refusal to increase the State's responsibility in the administration of workmen's compensation the Government has, no doubt, been influenced by the opposition of the insurance companies.

This section may be concluded with a statement showing the number of countries which have ratified conventions not adopted by Great Britain. The significance of the figures depends, of course, upon the importance of the countries, the efficiency with which the conventions are applied and enforced, and the extent to which British practice falls below the standards of the conventions.

RATIFICATIONS OF CERTAIN CONVENTIONS AT JANUARY 1936

Convention	Number of Ratifications
Hours of Work (Industry)	22*
Childbirth	16
Placing of Seamen	24
Minimum Age (Agriculture)	19
White Lead (Painting)	23†
Weekly Rest (Industry)	27
Workmen's Compensation (Accidents)	16
Night Work (Bakeries)	10
Repatriation of Seamen	16
Marking of Weight (on packages transported by vessels)	32†
Hours of Work (Commerce and Offices)	7†
Hours of Work (Coal Mines)	1‡
Minimum Age (Non-industrial employment)	4§

* Four of these are conditional upon ratification by other States.

† One conditional.

‡ This ratification is by Spain. Most other countries are likely to wait for simultaneous ratification.

§ This Convention was adopted by the 1932 Conference and there has yet been little time for countries to ratify it.

[1] For operations, an injured workman usually goes to a voluntary hospital, but he has no legislative right to treatment.

[2] I.L.O. *Official Bulletin*, 1926, p. 365.

Conclusions

Britain's international labour policy may be judged by its effects upon working conditions and upon the closely related prosperity of industry. The ratification of conventions requiring no change in British practice is of value in confirming existing standards, as ratification is usually effective for a period of ten years. It is unlikely, however, that even without ratification there would have been any fall in Great Britain below the standards laid down by these conventions. Working conditions have been improved by ratification of the conventions involving changes in British practice, although the necessary changes have not been great.

The effects upon the prosperity of British industry are difficult to assess, but would seem to have been not unfavourable. The changes made to comply with certain conventions cannot fail to have reacted beneficially upon the welfare and efficiency of the workers protected, so that on balance ratification must have been an advantage to rather than a burden upon British industry. Even if it be assumed that some of the ratifications have imposed upon industry additional charges not offset by increased efficiency, an examination of the ratifications by Britain's principal Continental competitors shows that Belgium, Czechoslovakia, France, Germany, Italy, and Poland have undertaken at least as heavy obligations, while in most of these countries the legislative changes have been more considerable than those of Great Britain. In other words there has been a slight tendency to reduce some of the international differences in labour standards. Also important conventions not ratified by Great Britain have been ratified by some of her competitors.

Little progress has been made in the application of international standards of hours and wages, which most closely affect international competition. The international regulation of wages is the most difficult of the questions with which the International Labour Organisation is called upon to deal; the problem is complicated by differences in cost of living and habits of consumption in various parts of the world, while at the present time the difficulties are increased by currency instability. Nor are Governments, workers' and employers' organisations in many countries, including Britain, favourable to a great extension of Government responsibility for the regulation of wages, which would be necessary for the application of internationally agreed wage standards. The Convention on Minimum Wage-Fixing Machinery involves no international regulation of wages, although it is of value in establishing the principle of State responsibility for the fixing of wages by specially constituted machinery in trades in which wage conditions are unsatisfactory and voluntary methods of regulation inadequate.

In the regulation of hours of labour it is unfortunate that the British Government has been unable to ratify the Washington Hours Convention. The more extensive application of this Convention, especially by simultaneous agreement between the chief industrial countries of Europe, would establish the 48-hour week more firmly, would constitute an important extension of international cooperation in the regulation of working conditions, and would serve as a general starting-point for the introduction of a shorter working week in industries in which technical progress make this possible and desirable. One of the underlying reasons for unwillingness to ratify this and certain other conventions seems to be hesitation by the Government to assume any considerable extension of its responsibility for those conditions, especially of adult male workers, which normally enter into the scope of collective agreements.

The difficulties in the way of ratifying conventions affecting international competition have been increased by the withdrawal of Germany from the International Labour Organisation, although in some ways this has been more than counterbalanced by the entry of the United States of America and the Soviet Union. From the early days of the Organisation it was recognised that, in view of her industrial

228 BRITISH ECONOMIC FOREIGN POLICY

importance, Germany's participation was highly desirable and she became a member of the Organisation years before she was admitted to full membership of the League of Nations. No doubt, however, methods can be devised for securing Germany's adhesion outside the framework of the Organisation to conventions of interest to a group of countries, for example, by assuming separate mutual treaty obligations, based upon the terms of a convention, with each of the countries concerned.

The charge that other countries are less effective than Great Britain in applying and enforcing conventions seems well founded for some, though by no means for all, countries. There is every reason to ensure that conventions are drafted and interpreted so as to represent identical obligations in all countries. Standards of enforcement inevitably vary according to the number and efficiency of the inspectorate, the tradition of respect for the law, and the power of the trade union movement to secure observance of legally established standards of working conditions. For certain conventions a low standard of enforcement by a competing country may be an obstacle to British ratification. The evidence available seems to support the conclusion that in most industrially developed countries the enforcement of labour standards established by law, though often less effective than that in Great Britain, still ensures adequate protection for a considerable majority of the workers concerned.

The Constitution of the International Labour Organisation provides for annual reports on measures taken by countries in applying conventions, these reports being systematically examined by a committee of experts and by the Conference and steps taken to ensure uniformity of interpretation by different countries. The committee of experts has expressed the opinion that in the vast majority of cases the conventions are being applied loyally and satisfactorily. The British Government representative has said about this committee that no individual action taken by the Conference has been more fruitful of results in the present or is more likely to be fruitful of results in the future than the setting up of this committee. The Constitution also enables a country to file a complaint if it is not satisfied that any other country is effectively observing a convention which both have ratified.[1] Employers' or workers' associations also have the right to raise the question of non-observance. As already indicated, an international Commission of Enquiry may be set up to consider and report upon complaints, and in the last resort economic sanctions may be applied against a defaulting Government. It seems fairly certain, however, that the drastic course of applying economic sanctions for failure to observe the terms of an international labour convention will never be adopted.

[1] Article 411 of Part XIII of the Treaty of Versailles.

CHAPTER VIII

OTHER ASPECTS OF POLICY

In a complete study of British economic foreign policy
many questions would be subjected to detailed examination
in addition to those discussed in earlier chapters. The
policies already reviewed establish the conditions in which
British investors, producers, and traders may operate. But
in addition to determining the conditions of economic
activity for private business, the Government of a country
has direct interests of its own in which political and economic
factors are often closely related. The Government of a great
country is a powerful economic organisation, with wider
interests than any business corporation. Without going into
detail, a few illustrative examples of such interests may
be given.

Among general subjects not treated in detail in this
volume is the Government's policy towards shipbuilding
and shipping. Tariffs and other trade restrictions and the
great decline in international trade as a result of the depression have caused serious difficulties in the shipbuilding and
shipping industries. While the Government's policy has
been designed to help many other industries, the resulting
restrictions upon international trade have conflicted with
shipbuilding and shipping interests. Until recently the
Government was strongly opposed to subsidies for these
industries, and at the World Economic Conference, 1933,
condemned the policy of subsidies applied by other countries.

The difficulties of these industries and the continuation
of subsidies by foreign Governments has led to a modification of the British attitude. This is indicated by the
grant of financial assistance for the completion of the
Cunarder, *Queen Mary*, although the money advanced by
the Government is sometimes regarded as an investment
rather than a subsidy. A special arrangement has also been

made to help tramp shipping, the method being determined by agreement between the Government and the shipowners. The Government agreed to give a "defensive" subsidy of two million pounds for one year, but subsequently renewed, to ensure greater employment of British shipping and to encourage the abolition of foreign shipping subsidies. The scheme was made conditional upon shipowners formulating a satisfactory scheme, which would prevent the dissipation of the subsidy in domestic competition between British companies and ensure greater employment of British tramp shipping at the expense of foreign subsidised vessels. In certain sections of the tramp shipping trade schemes were devised and are in operation. In addition the Government is giving financial facilities to shipowners for a scrapping and rebuilding or modernising scheme for cargo vessels. Under this scrapping and building programme the Government is willing to make loans on favourable terms up to ten million pounds.[1]

Somewhat similar to the Government's interest in shipping is its concern for the development of commercial air transportation services. Apart from their use as auxiliaries to the air force in time of war these services are of great and growing value as a means of communication with the Dominions and in the administration of the Colonial Empire. As with shipping, the method of subsidies has been adopted. Imperial Airways Limited has been subsidised since its formation, and in a recent speech the Chairman indicated that when the Company started more than ten years ago it was hoped that a decade of development would see them free, or practically free of subsidies. They were not able to foresee at that time the increasing importance that would be attached to air services as an indication of national prestige and the comparative disregard of cost in other countries where that factor was concerned. He also referred to the confusion between commercial and military aviation,

[1] In order to become entitled to the favourable rates of interest for Treasury guaranteed loans, the owners are required to scrap two tons of shipping for every ton of new construction, and to scrap one ton for every ton of shipping modernised.

mainly on the Continent, which in a race for air supremacy had introduced almost unlimited political and commercial complications to the business.

Other politico-economic interests are also related to means of communication, or arise out of the Government's interest in supplies of raw materials, particularly minerals and oil, essential for war purposes. In certain circumstances the Government also intervenes to protect the interests of its nationals where they have been injured by the action of another State. Outstanding in means of communication is the British holding of shares in the Suez Canal Company involving political and economic relations especially with Egypt, Palestine, and with European Powers in the Mediterranean, while a more recent development is the British Government's interest in Cables and Wireless Limited.

Control of oil supplies has loomed large in international politics during recent years.[1] The British Government's direct interest in oil became important in 1914 when it obtained a large block of shares and also some of the stock of the Anglo-Persian Oil Company with the object of ensuring the oil supplies of the British navy. Disputes between the Company and certain foreign Governments have indirectly involved the British Government. Thus in 1920 the Albanian Government granted a concession to the Anglo-Persian Oil Company covering the whole country. The United States Government protested that this was an infringement of the open-door principle, and later the concession was restricted to a part of the country.[2] The Italian Government protested that the concession gave

[1] In addition to interest in oil produced abroad, mention may be made of the preference guaranteed by the British Government to petrol produced from British coal. This takes the form of a rebate of 4d. a gallon for nine years from April 1935 on all oil produced from British coal, whether by the hydrogenation process or by low temperature carbonisation. The cost of this guarantee to the Exchequer is uncertain, being dependent on the amount of petrol produced.

[2] The protest of the United States seems to have been made chiefly in the interests of the Standard Oil Company, and it is said that an agent of this Company arrived at Durazzo in an American destroyer at the time of the dispute.

monopoly power to the Anglo-Persian Oil Company, which was in violation of an Italian agreement with Albania that no monopoly would be granted without the consent of the other. This protest was made to the British Ambassador, and in settlement of the dispute the concession was maintained, but Italy was granted first claim upon oil exported from Albania.

In 1932 a dispute between the Persian Government and the Anglo-Persian Oil Company arose out of an alleged breach by the Company of the terms of its oil concession in Persia.[1] The Persian Government being dissatisfied with the operation of the concession announced its cancellation, although it was not due to expire for almost thirty years, and proposed the negotiation of a new agreement. The British Government considered cancellation to be a breach of the concession, and communicated to the Persian Government its intention of taking all legitimate measures to protect the Company's just and indisputable interests. It also stated that it would not tolerate any damage to the Company's interests or interference with their premises and activities. Failing to obtain satisfaction by direct negotiation the dispute was referred to the Council of the League by the British Government, acting not in its capacity as a shareholder of the Company but in the interests of one of its nationals which, in its opinion, had been injured by acts contrary to international law committed by another State. At this stage direct negotiations between the interested parties resulted in agreement upon the terms of a new concession and the dispute was settled on this basis.

A different kind of dispute arose in 1934 out of the setting up of a monopoly for the sale of oil in Manchukuo, which by eliminating or severely restricting foreign traders is a violation of the open-door principle of equal opportunity. The Japanese Government, which had undertaken that this principle would continue to be observed under the new

---

[1] This concession was made in 1901 by the Persian Government to a British subject and it was taken over by the Anglo-Persian Oil Company in 1909.

régime in Manchukuo, was involved, and the British and other Governments protested against the breach of obligations under the Nine-Power Treaty and of pledges by the Japanese and Manchukuo Governments.[1] The Japanese Government insisted upon Manchukuo's independence to deal with such matters, although indirectly the Japanese Government has a substantial financial interest in the Company set up to operate the monopoly. The protests were followed by certain concessions, including a moderation of the terms of the monopoly, in the interests of foreign companies which had established capital and developed organisations for the distribution of oil in Manchukuo.[2]

Another example of intervention by the British Government to protect the economic interests of its nationals is in the dispute between the Government of the U.S.S.R. and the British investors in Lena Goldfields Company Limited. After long and bitter controversy the Soviet Government agreed to pay £3 million over a period of twenty years. This was less than one-quarter of the amount fixed by an arbitral award not recognised by the Soviet Government, but when reference was made in the House of Commons to this award the Government spokesman said that "the prospects of any settlement at all without the assistance of His Majesty's Government would have been slight."

Protection of the interests of British investors in foreign Government bonds is undertaken by the Council of Foreign Bondholders, which operates with Government approval and maintains relations with the responsible ministries. Other financial activities of the Government include its participation whether by guarantee or otherwise in League

[1] The Japanese policy of abandoning the open-door principle in Manchukuo may be part of a manœuvre related to the non-recognition of Manchukuo by foreign Governments, the statement being made that the principle of the open door is considered binding only for countries which recognise Manchukuo.

[2] The British Government has been criticised for its policy, in association with the Governments of Australia and New Zealand, in controlling the production of phosphates in the Mandated Area of Nauru in the interests of these three countries but in opposition to the open-door policy.

of Nations loans. The Government also operates a system of export credit insurance; this was originally introduced to facilitate British trade with certain countries where the risks were exceptionally high, but it has been extended to cover any export trade.

Reference has already been made to the British Government's action in 1935 in substantially raising the duties on various categories of imported iron and steel to 50 or 60 per cent *ad valorem* with the object of helping the British iron and steel industry to reach a favourable agreement with the European Steel Cartel. When the terms were satisfactorily settled the additional duties, having served their purpose, were withdrawn. The Government has supported international agreements regulating trade in rubber, tin, and sugar. It also approves of and has given financial assistance to the British Cotton Growers' Association, the object of which is to develop the production of cotton in suitable areas within the Empire, thus reducing dependence upon foreign supplies, particularly from the United States, and increasing the variety and certainty of the supplies available. Since the beginning of this century the production of Empire cotton has greatly increased. Within the country British manufacturers are favoured by the policy adopted in public works schemes of requiring that, as far as practicable, all plant, machinery, and materials required for the works shall be of British origin.[1]

The above examples illustrate additional methods by which the British Government has protected and furthered its interests and those of its nationals. Similar methods are commonly adopted by other countries, and the British Government is merely conforming with practices extensively applied in international relations.

[1] This policy was adopted, for example, in the development announced in 1935 of London passenger transport facilities with the aid of a loan of £40 millions, the capital of which is guaranteed by the Government. Other things being equal, preference is to be given to firms in the depressed areas. The use of the "National Mark" and "Buy British" campaigns have the same object of assisting British producers.

CHAPTER IX

GENERAL CONCLUSIONS

A COUNTRY's economic foreign policy is an integral part
of a larger policy, the object of which is to ensure the
country's greatest security and welfare. Governments often
make errors of judgment in deciding upon the elements
which make up a nation's welfare and their methods of
achieving welfare may be wrong, but their intention is
usually to serve their country's best interests. According
to circumstances they will decide upon isolated independent
action, or upon international cooperation if this seems the
more effective method of serving the national interest. In
previous chapters general features of British economic
foreign policy have been reviewed. In estimating the value
of the measures adopted, it is not sufficient to consider
economic welfare alone; account must also be taken of
broader political issues, especially that of national security.

During the *laissez-faire* period the British Government
paid little attention to the political implications of the vast
trading and investment activities of its citizens throughout
the world, although it often came to their aid if they found
themselves in difficulties with a foreign Government. British
capital and commerce spread over the world to secure
economic gain, and political motives were rare. Diplomacy
did not neglect to use circumstances resulting from economic
penetration to extend British political influences and control
of raw materials, but there was no systematic attempt to
direct economic expansion for political purposes.

The present century has seen a growing tendency in
many countries towards the establishment of a closer
relationship between political and economic foreign policy.
This developed later in Great Britain than in various other
countries. For example, French foreign investments in
Russia and other parts of Europe before the war were

undertaken more for political than for economic reasons, while in the early years of this century the Government of the United States, by "dollar diplomacy," consciously extended its political influence and control especially in Central America. Britain has only recently adopted an active economic foreign policy. This new policy having been introduced during the world depression, economic objectives have predominated, but political and economic motives are now more closely related than in earlier years.

The most important change has been diminution of dependence upon imports from foreign countries by increasing the relative importance of home production and of imports from the Empire. Particularly significant have been the measures taken to safeguard the future of the British iron and steel industry, which is essential for national defence. Political and economic motives are associated in the establishment of Imperial Preference, with the object of strengthening relations between the Member States of the British Commonwealth.

National protectionist policy, Imperial Preference, and abandonment of the open-door policy have involved discrimination against foreign countries. Their purpose has been to increase the economic and political strength of Great Britain and the Commonwealth. Outside the Commonwealth the economic foreign policy of Great Britain shows little coordination with political policy. Only rarely has a policy of economic discrimination been directed against particular foreign countries, and then such a policy has usually been applied for economic reasons; for example, when retaliatory measures were taken against French trade in 1934.

Capital investment provides the easiest means of coordinating political and economic policy. During recent years, however, loans to foreign countries have been so restricted that British policy has taken the form of a virtual embargo on foreign lending. When foreign lending is resumed it will be of interest to see how far political and economic policies are associated. Monetary policy does not lend itself to manipulation for international political purposes, and British policy has been dictated solely by economic considerations. The negotiation of trade agreements with foreign countries has been determined by economic opportunity and not by political interests. Thus Britain has yet made little attempt to mould her economic relations with foreign countries into conformity with her political policy.

Reference may here be made to the obligation upon Great Britain, as upon other States Members of the League of Nations, to take economic measures, particularly the immediate severance of all trade or financial relations, against any Member of the League which resorts to war in disregard of its covenants.[1] This course was first adopted when economic sanctions were applied against Italy in consequence of her unprovoked attack upon Abyssinia in 1935. Such an obligation involves the use of economic measures for political purposes, and demands a much closer coordination of political and economic foreign policy, in certain circumstances, than has hitherto been contemplated.

Turning now to other aspects, the recent reorientation of British economic foreign policy is the result of political, economic, and social insecurity, and, of these, political insecurity is the most potent factor. The war gave a shock to security, and the situation has been aggravated by an accelerated rate of economic change. Also, progressively improved transport facilities have increased the impact of differing national standards of living through the channels of international trade. For political reasons countries are afraid to rely upon one another, while the severity of trade competition during recent years has threatened the disorganisation of important national industries. The price of greater political security resulting from reduced dependence on supplies from abroad is the economic loss involved in restriction of international specialisation.

[1] See Article 16 of the Covenant of the League of Nations.

The practicability of greater self-sufficiency must be determined by two criteria, first, the extent to which a commodity is essential for national defence or maintenance, and second, the cost of producing it at home compared with that of importing supplies from abroad. Among the commodities protected by British tariffs, some could be dispensed with in time of war without serious inconvenience, and others can be produced in Great Britain only at costs considerably above those of imported supplies. Thus political insecurity may justify measures for conserving the iron and steel industry, but it cannot be used to support the imposition of tariffs to reduce the importation of fresh flowers, new potatoes, and horticultural products generally.

Economic and social insecurity may require action to be taken to protect efficient and established British industries for a time against dumping and against the exceptionally rapid progress of certain industries in countries with low standards of living and working conditions.[1] However, neither political nor economic and social insecurity require Britain to proceed far in the direction of self-sufficiency, and she is not likely to move much farther along this road. Various manufactured articles can be produced in this country at costs which differ little from those in the countries from which they have been imported, and it seems likely that, with the shelter of a low tariff, these commodities will henceforth be produced here and the former degree of dependence upon foreign trade be reduced. But the limit of readjustment with little economic cost is soon reached and additional protection should be reserved strictly for the particular commodities essential for political security or temporarily where the economic cost to the community in higher prices is offset by the advantages of economic and social stability.

Even from the standpoint of political security it would

---

[1] Tariffs may also be useful on occasion for bargaining purposes, but there is no need to maintain a general tariff on all commodities in order that a bargaining instrument may be available.

be a misguided policy to attempt a large measure of self-sufficiency. Political security cannot be established upon the strength of this country alone but needs the support of other countries, and in times of danger countries are more likely to cooperate if they are mutually dependent upon one another for their prosperity and welfare. Also, a high degree of self-sufficiency would involve so great an economic cost in time of peace that the country's wealth and, therefore, its means of providing for national defence would be seriously diminished. There is danger of pressure by powerful and unscrupulous business interests to obtain high rates of protection for their own profit, regardless of the injury inflicted upon the community. Up to the present there is no ground for believing that the establishment of protection in Britain has been accompanied by political corruption and "log-rolling," but the experience of other countries serves as a warning and indicates the need for public opinion to insist upon the safeguarding of the general welfare against sectional interests.

The economic policy adopted during recent years has contributed to the partial recovery of British industry and trade from the depths of the depression. But the existence of a volume of unemployment of around two millions and especially the condition of the depressed areas, in which the exporting industries are mainly concentrated, are warnings against a too optimistic view of the economic success of the new policies. The point now seems to have been reached beyond which no further considerable advance in recovery is possible without improvement in exports, especially to foreign countries.

Among the various policies, that in the monetary field has been the most successful. In view of currency fluctuations abroad, the stability of sterling within the country and in the sterling area has been a remarkable achievement. During the years 1931–3 desire was expressed for a rise in the wholesale price level, and this would have been an advantage if world conditions had been favourable.

Now, however, that the present price level has been maintained for several years and many measures have been taken to bring economic relations into equilibrium at this level, the need is rather for continued stability or for a small further upward movement than for a big rise in the price level.[1] The sterling area has become a stabilising element in the world's monetary relations, and whatever agreement may be reached to set up once again a unified international monetary system, the maintenance of internal stability of sterling, which has facilitated the restoration of confidence among business men in this country, is essential. The best road towards a *de facto* restoration of a stable international monetary system is for other countries also to maintain the internal stability of their currencies, preceded by devaluation in the gold *bloc*, while progressively removing the worst restrictions upon international trade and investment.[2]

It may be agreed that strict control of British foreign investment was necessary during the years of crisis, but now that sterling is free from pressure, and in the absence of a developed system for the regulation of all new capital investment, the argument is strong for removal of the Government's discrimination against loans to foreign countries. Financial interests should generally be left free to decide on economic grounds about the desirability of making loans to foreign countries, but the Government might usefully retain powers in reserve to prevent any loan the granting of which would be in conflict with public policy.

Protectionist policy was introduced in Great Britain at a fortunate moment for its supporters. Under the conditions of the world depression, markets were glutted with food

[1] Professor Pigou recently said on the subject of reflation, "If 'twere done, 'twere well 'twere done quickly," and he indicated that, if the process is long delayed, reflation is no longer required.

[2] The international maladjustments caused during recent years by the general movement towards greater self-sufficiency in many countries has been one of the principal causes of the breakdown in the world's monetary system.

and raw materials, and producers abroad were often willing to cut their prices by the amount of the tariffs in order to maintain their sales in the British market. Therefore, in spite of the tariffs, there was little rise in prices. Also, increased revenue was obtained at a time of budgetary difficulty when other forms of taxation would have been less convenient. In the circumstances of the emergency in 1931 and 1932 the tariff policy as a temporary measure must be regarded as a success. The conclusions drawn from British experience of Imperial Preference are less favourable. The Dominions have derived more advantage than Great Britain from this policy, and the spokesmen of the British Government seemed to be more satisfied than British business men with the economic results of the Ottawa Agreements. Politically the Agreements have been more successful, as they have satisfied in part the desire of the Dominions for preferential treatment in the British market. Against this advantage must be set the political danger that if relations within the Empire are made unduly exclusive, other nations, especially those without colonies, will suffer injury and will resent discrimination.

Trade agreements with certain foreign countries have led to some improvement in British exports. The policy of subsidies, especially for agriculture, needs to be strictly circumscribed if considerable loss is to be avoided, while the recently favoured method of the levy is open to objection as a long-term system, being merely a combination of tariffs and subsidies. Embarrassment to the Government has been caused by the quota system, which involves fixing the amounts of particular commodities to be imported from each of the chief producing countries. The Government now prefers other forms of intervention in which its responsibility for the control of trade is less clearly defined.

In free-trade days the Government had no responsibility for adjusting the development of the different industries and other economic activities. It must now have a plan. The present arrangements are yet so confused that they can scarcely be recognised as a plan. They are more consistent in their political than in their economic aspects. For political reasons the Government has determined upon somewhat reduced dependence upon foreign countries, some increase in the relative importance of home production, and increased trade with Empire countries. But while it is easy to say "Britain first, the Empire second, and other countries 'also ran,' " the further questions must be decided: How far ahead is Britain to be, and how far are foreign countries to fall behind Empire countries? The problem is still further complicated when particular industries are considered, and, up to the present, the Government's plan is full of economic inconsistencies. Thus attempts are made at the same time to stimulate home production, secure increased exports, avoid distress in shipping and shipbuilding, and maintain the value of British investments abroad. In some quarters an almost physiocratic regard is shown for agriculture after decades of neglect.

Despite protests to the contrary, the policies of the Ministry of Agriculture, the Board of Trade, the Dominions Office, the Colonial Office, the Treasury, the Ministry of Labour, and the Foreign Office are not always harmonious. In the short period, excuse for inconsistencies could be found in the exceptional circumstances of the world depression, but, now that conditions are becoming more stable, there is need for a clearer definition of long-range policy and methods in the interests of the economic welfare of this country and of its relations with the Dominions and with foreign countries.

In pure economic theory *laissez-faire* can be shown to have long-run advantages over intervention and regulation. However, even under the most favourable conditions which Britain enjoyed in the nineteenth century, with small-scale producing and trading units, with expanding foreign markets and freedom from serious foreign competition, the system was not altogether satisfactory. British industrial workers operating the new machines frequently had reason to complain about their conditions; those who struggled on with the old processes suffered serious distress, while little was heard in Great Britain about the misery endured by the handicraft workers of foreign countries whose old-established crafts were destroyed by the onrush of British manufactures. Now the boomerang has returned and British industry is faced with competition from highly efficient foreign industries operated by workpeople with lower standards of living.

The weakness of *laissez-faire* is insecurity and that of protection and regulation is stagnation. The problem, therefore, is how to maintain efficiency and progress while protecting the capital and labour already specialised in an industry from being overwhelmed by competition from abroad. With perfect mobility of capital and labour no difficulty would arise. But mobility is far from perfect, and, although protection is required only for the period of reorganisation and adaptation, this period may sometimes extend over ten or even twenty years. Also the conditions of mobility favourable to *laissez-faire* have been destroyed by the growth of large-scale undertakings, combines, and cartels which adopt methods of self-protection in the interests of stability. The size, high capitalisation, and the magnitude of their interests have forced large-scale undertakings to adopt these methods, extending their agreements to restrict competition into the international field, and it is not surprising that great national industries seek to enlist the support of their Governments. Indeed, the foundations upon which a workable *laissez-faire* system could be built no longer exist.

Recognising that the economic problem is mainly to ensure reasonable stability and security for established industries while encouraging orderly adaptation to changes in methods of production and in consumers' demand, it is evident that protection is required only for the short period, although this may extend for a decade or more, and that it should be adjusted to the needs of particular industries. This argument gives no support to the British policy of a general tariff, but it can be used in favour of the system of special tariffs based upon the recommendations of the Import Duties Advisory Committee. Protection against dumping and the fostering of infant industries also involve special tariffs for limited periods, but not a permanent general tariff. The British general tariff can be justified by the non-economic arguments of political expediency, and of reducing dependence on foreign supplies, and also, in the short period, by its value in producing revenue and in assisting in the correction of an adverse balance of payments.

The issue is no longer between *laissez-faire* and intervention but between different degrees, methods, and purposes of intervention. The two great political parties are both interventionist, though with different objectives. The country is groping towards a policy, suited to present-day conditions of production and trade, which will permit of an orderly and coordinated economic development. Some of the recent experimental methods will be abandoned or substantially changed. The period during which Britain based her economic policy upon freedom from regulation was short, but the new system must not represent a reversion to the stagnation of pre-Industrial Revolution days. The conditions and outlook have fundamentally changed. Capital and labour stand in a new relation, opportunities of education now extend to all classes, the urge for greater security with higher standards of living is strong, and technical progress offers the promise of rising standards, though at the same time threatening security.

In seeking to establish greater economic security it is necessary to avoid the adoption of a neo-mercantilist policy of long-term restriction, of blind insistence upon a substantial favourable balance of trade or of payments, and of forcing foreign trade into bilateral frameworks. While recognising that certain industries may suffer from overproduction and that, for them, a policy of restriction may be temporarily desirable, such restriction should be limited to periods of crisis and transition. They should be used, like the Exchange Equalisation Fund, to smooth out short-period maladjustments and to compensate for the effects of temporary artificial factors, but should not run counter to long-period trends.

These trends cannot be resisted without economic loss. If, for example, the long-term movement of the world's price of wheat is downward it is unsound policy to maintain a much higher guaranteed price based upon market conditions that will never return. Though each country will make every effort to prevent its economic organisation from being overwhelmed by tidal waves of depression, no scheme can permanently dam the flow of world progress without lowering the national standard of living. British prosperity essentially depends not upon restrictions but upon progressive efficiency. In the long run the only safeguard is to adapt the economic structure to changing conditions, with rising standards of productive efficiency combined with rising standards of living.

This is the only reliable basis for long-term national economic security, and short-term policies must be adjusted to this requirement. Also, attempts to achieve economic stability, security, and prosperity within national frameworks can win only limited success. At the present time the state of international political and economic insecurity has compelled the adoption of restrictive policies for national economic conservation, but every opportunity should be taken to increase international security and cooperation which provide the essential foundation for the highest material and also cultural welfare of mankind.

INDEX

For Product Safety Concerns and Information please contact our EU
representative GPSR@taylorandfrancis.com
Taylor & Francis Verlag GmbH, Kaufingerstraße 24, 80331 München, Germany

www.ingramcontent.com/pod-product-compliance
Lightning Source LLC
Chambersburg PA
CBHW070400270326
41926CB00014B/2639

9 7 8 1 1 3 8 2 9 7 2 2 7